Direct Participation and Organisational Change
Fashionable but Misunderstood?

An Analysis of Recent Research in Europe, Japan and the USA

EF/96/38/EN

European Foundation
for the Improvement of
Living and Working Conditions

Direct Participation and Organisational Change
Fashionable but Misunderstood?

An Analysis of Recent Research in Europe, Japan and the USA

Dieter Fröhlich and Ulrich Pekruhl
ISO Institute, Cologne and
Institut Arbeit und Technik, Gelsenkirchen

Wyattville Road, Loughlinstown, Co. Dublin, Ireland
Tel.: (+353) 1 204 3100   Fax: (+353) 1 282 6456

Cataloguing data can be found at the end of this publication

Luxembourg: Office for Official Publications of the European Communities, 1996

ISBN 92-827-6673-X

Printed in Ireland

Content

Foreword

Preface

Summary   1

1 Direct Participation as an International Concern of
Organisations and of Social Science   17

1.1 What is New About Direct Participation?   17
1.2 Direct Participation as a Research Concern
     of the European Foundation   19
1.3 Different Social Science Approaches Towards
     Direct Participation   24
     'Classical' Industrial Sociology: The Impact of Automation   24
     Political Sciences and Industrial Sociology:
     Participation and Industrial Democracy   26
     Human Resource Management: Motivation by Participation   27
     Organisational Research: Structure, Functionality
     and Development of Organisations   28
     New Production Concepts: Direct Participation and Productivity   29
1.4 The Organisation of the Literature Study   30
1.5 The Potential and the Structure of the Report   33

2 Individual Participation   36

2.1 Upward Communication as Consultative Participation   36
     Suggestion Schemes   37
     Workforce Attitude Surveys   38
     Employee Appraisal and Development   39
2.2 Job Enrichment as Delegative Participation - the Older Approach   41
     Management and Job Enrichment in the QWL Phase   43
     Employees and Job Enrichment   45
     Summary   48
2.3 Job Enrichment and New Information Technology   49
     Effects on Employees   53
     Summary   56

3 Group Consultation: The Experience of Quality Circles   58

   3.1 Management's Motives for Quality Circle Introduction   58
   3.2 Quality Circle Implementation   60
   3.3 Training for Circle Work   62
   3.4 The Effects of Quality Circles   64
   3.5 Problems of Quality Circles   67
     The Management Perspective   67
     The Workforce Perspective   69
   3.6 The Role of Quality Circles in Integrated Management Strategies   73
     Summary   76

4 Group Work Between 'Volvoism' and 'Toyotoism'   79

   4.1 Two Contrasting Types of Group Work   81
     The Scandinavian Concept of Group Work   81
     Group Work in Lean Production   83
     The QWL and the Productivity Aspects of Both Types   86
     Japanese Inspired Production Systems   88
   4.2 Problems of Group Work   91
     Introducing Group Work   93
     Selection of Employees   96
     Personnel Training   97
     The Pay Issue   99
     Economic Effects of Group Work   102
     A Note on Labour Market Effects   107
   4.3 Workforce Reactions to Group Work   109
     The State of Research   110
     General Evaluation of Group Work   111
     Social Pressure and Social Control   112
     Skill Protection - the 'Inner Segmentation' of Work Groups   114
     What do Employees Expect From Group Work?   115
     Summary   118

5. The Debate Over the Role of Middle Managers   122

   5.1 Middle Management Problems With Various
       Types of Direct Participation   123
   5.2 Middle Managers as Supporters of Organisational Change   127
   5.3 Training for a New Role   129
   Summary   131

6 The Impact on Employee Representation   132

6.1 Direct Participation - a Union-Avoidance Strategy?   134
6.2 The Attitude of Employee Representatives
Towards Direct Participation at Establishment Level   141
6.3 Direct Participation as a Potential Source of
Conflict Between Workforce Representatives   147
6.4 Does Direct Participation Endanger Representative Participation?   150
6.5 The New Workplaces: Improved or Deteriorated?   155
General Assessment of Direct Participation   155
Assessments of Group Work   156
Additional Merits and Demerits   158
Summary   160

7 An Overview Of Direct Participation in Europe, Japan and the USA   163

7.1 The Separate Countries   164
Austria   164
Belgium   165
Denmark   166
Finland   168
France   169
Germany   171
Greece   173
Ireland   174
Italy   174
Netherlands   175
Portugal   177
Spain   178
Sweden   179
United Kingdom   181
USA   183
Japan   186
7.2 The Countries in Comparative Perspective   188

8 Conclusions   193

  Results and Problems from a Management Perspective   193
  Direct Participation: Between Profitabilty and Work Humanization   195
  Union Concerns   196
  Research Gaps   197

References   200

Table 1:   Types of Direct Participation   22
Table 2:   The Importance of Skills and Training for Implementing
            and Operating New Information Technology
            According to European Managers   52
Table 3:   Reasons for Introducing Quality Circles   59
Table 4:   Positive Effects of Quality Circles According
            to Circle Members and Circle Leaders   64
Table 5:   Quality Circle Effects in the Top-100-Companies
            in Germany   66
Table 6:   Contrasting Types of Group Work   86
Table 7:   Productivity Effects of Group Work at AAB   103
Table 8:   The Balance of Costs and Returns at ABB
            (in thousand SEK)   103
Table 9:   Evaluation of Teamwork by Union Representatives   157
Table 10:   Dimensions of Work Discretion of
            the Austrian Labour Force   164
Table 11:   Dimensions of Work Discretion of
            the Finnish Labour Force   168
Table 12:   Improvements of Workplace Facets of
            the Finnish Labour Force   169
Table 13:   Types of Group Work in the German
            Working Population   172
Table 14:   Work Consultation in the Netherlands:
            Employee Involvement in Decision-Making   177
Table 15:   Net Gains in Different Dimensions of Responsibility   181
Table 16:   Types of Flexible Work Organization
            in U.S. Establishments   185
Table 17:   Teamwork in Large Japanese Companies   187

Figure 1:   The Spread of Suggestion Schemes in European Companies
            in 1992   189
Figure 2:   The Spread of Workforce Surveys in European Companies
            in 1992   190
Figure 3:   The Spread of Quality Circles in European Companies
            in 1992   191

List of Abbreviations

Country codes: To enable easy identification of research regarding national origin, most cited sources are marked in the text with the following country codes:

A	Austria
B	Belgium
D	Germany
DK	Denmark
E	Spain
F	France
FIN	Finland
GR	Greece
I	Italy
IRL	Ireland
JP	Japan
NL	Netherlands
P	Portugal
S	Sweden
UK	United Kingdom
US	United States of America

Frequently used abbreviation in the text:

ABB	Asea, Brown & Boveri
CIM	Computer Integrated Manufacturing
CNC	Computer Numerically Controlled
GM	General Motors
HdA	Humanisierung der Arbeit (equals QWL)
IF	Integrated Factory
ILM	Internal Labour Market
JIT	Just In Time
JIPS	Japanese Inspired Production Systems
LP	Lean Production
NIT	New Information Technology
QWL	Quality of Working Life
TQM	Total Quality Management
UTE	Elementary Technical Units (at FIAT)

Foreword

European companies have been exploring a variety of programmes and activities designed to increase direct employee participation. Re-engineering, total quality management, group work and quality circles are fashionable labels for different company initiatives aimed at increasing the satisfaction, commitments, loyalty and performance of employees. As Paul Osterman from the MIT put it recently, direct participation in the organisation of work has become a kind of 'new conventional wisdom'. With high levels of unemployment, increased competitiveness and the growing expectations of an educated work force regarding the quality of their working life and the possibilities for individual participation, the social partners in Europe see in direct participation a way forward to improved working relations. Unions and employers in Europe are striving for a 'new deal' to redefine the interface between representative and direct participation and to establish the creation of value as joint responsibility.

However, many questions remain unanswered: what is the diffusion of the different forms of direct participation in Europe? How does the European experiments on direct participation e.g. in France (groupe d'expression), Sweden (Volvo experiments on group work) and Germany (Humanisierung des Arbeitslebens) compare with the Japanese approach? What are the inter-relations between increased competitiveness based on new forms of work organisation and the quality of working life? Do these new developments merely represent a new strategy of rationalisation with negative impact on employment? To what extent would direct participation diminish the influence of employee representatives and trade unions on the company level?

In order to answer these questions, the European Foundation initiated the EPOC project, (Employee direct Participation in Organisational Change). The objective is to provide information and to stimulate the debate between the social partners and the European Union institutions. Two major reports on the EPOC project have already been published. The first report by John Geary and Keith Sisson presents the conceptual framework of the EPOC project. The second report by Ida Regalia gives a description and an analysis on the positions of the social partners in the EU on direct participation in organisational change. It assesses the extent to which direct participation can humanise work while increasing profitability. The study is based on 195 personal interviews with senior officials of the social partners as representatives of national level peak organisations in all EU member states. As important industrial sectors, the metal industry and the banking sector were also included.

This third report presents a review of international empirical research on direct participation. It gives an overview on existing knowledge on the topic through world-wide research and tries to point out existing knowledge gaps. The report is based on more than 2500 pages of literature review in Europe, USA and Japan. It presents the most extensive literature abstracts on this topic published in Europe up to now.

With the publication of these research reports and with the organisation of European round tables and conferences the Foundation tries to provide information and to stimulate the exchange of experience between the social partners and the European Union institutions.

Dr. H. Krieger
Research Manager

European Foundation for the Improvement of Living and Working Conditions

Preface

This report is part of a major research exercise, initiated by the European Foundation for the Improvement of Living and Working Conditions on Employee Direct Participation in Organisational Change (EPOC). The project is an examination of direct participation and its role in organisational change. At present, there is a multiplicity of concepts and labels describing new managerial initiatives in the broad area of work re-organisation and employee participation. The current research initiative, known as the EPOC project, is an attempt to make sense of these practices and arrangements. In particular, it tries to identify the underlying principles of the different approaches to organisational change, so that they are rendered more accessible to the social partners, political actors and academics. Central to the EPOC project is an investigation of workplace practices in ten European countries. A representative survey has been designed to examine the nature and diffusion of direct participation; the means used to introduce it and regulate its operation and its consequent effects on organisational performance and quality of working life. The current exercise is an attempt to examine the broad research evidence in this area. Literature from member states of the EU is reviewed as well as available research from the US and Japan.

The orientating questions include: What do we already know about Direct Participation; what problems are associated with its implementation; how does it function, and what are its problematic aspects? Where do we have comparatively comprehensive knowledge? In this sense, the literature review was partly devised to inform the EPOC research of the gaps in our knowledge of Direct Participation practices.

By bringing together a diverse and scattered international literature, the report hopes to inform a wider public debate among social actors and social scientists, and as Direct Participation is seen as a critical element in economic competitiveness, the review scans literature in the US and Japan. In an attempt to circumvent the inevitable problems associated with language, a group of international experts were appointed to review the literature in the respective countries. A common template was provided to each country-expert so that the findings from each country would be compared. Further details on this are provided in the text. We thank those authors for their help and co-operation.

The report begins by clarifying the concepts associated with Direct Participation and their roots in the social science literature. Second, we describe the task of gathering out material. The presentation of the subject matter follows the main types of Direct Participation. We distinguish between consultative and delegative participation, which can either be geared towards individuals or groups. The main findings are presented in a thematic approach. Two widely discussed issues receive particular attention in separate chapters: the debate on the future role of middle management and the impact of Direct Participation on employee representation. A country-by-country overview on recent quantitative research is also included. For various reasons, our original intention to illustrate how far each country has moved in introducing Direct Participation could not be provided. If we found such material at all, it was too diverse to allow for comparisons. This disappointing experience underlines the necessity for further empirical research on this topic.

The overall EPOC project is carried out by an international Research Group and is supported by an Advisory Board, and members of both groups discussed and commented on the various drafts of this report. In particular, we want to thank Martin Blomsma, Wout Buitelaar, Neil Hoggar, Hubert Krieger, Keith Sisson, and Georges Spyropoulos, for their valuable comments on the final draft of the text. There was a rough division of labour between the two authors: Ulrich Pekruhl organised the research reviews and Dieter Fröhlich wrote the final text, with both assisting each other in their respective activities. In *Cologne*, Annette Schnabel not only contributed to summarising the German research on direct participation, she also served as a sounding-board in regard to the readability and clarity of the text. In addition, she took care of the report's lay-out. We want to thank everybody who helped us, knowing that the failings that still remain are our own.

Dieter Fröhlich and Ulrich Pekruhl

ISO Institute, Cologne, and Institut Arbeit und Technik, Gelsenkirchen

Summary

1 Reasons for the Study

During the 1980s and early 1990s terms such as 'quality circles', 'total quality management', 'lean production', 'flexible organisation', 'empowerment', 'employee involvement' and others have achieved a new currency and have become part of every-day language. They indicate the possibility of substantial change in the organisation of work as organisations face ever increasing competitive pressures. In many instances, these change processes rest on a re-discovery of the 'human factor' for organisational functioning and success. Management increasingly sees the need to involve employees, to grant them greater work discretion, and greater commitment to render organisations more flexible and productive. Under the concept of 'direct participation', the European Foundation's EPOC project focuses on these new developments. It is an attempt to provide a systematic and comprehensive overview of the existing forms of direct participation, the reasons for their application, the views of the actors involved, the preconditions for their success or failure and their merits and disadvantages.

The present review of international research has five key objectives: (1) It gives an overview on what we already know on the functioning and problems of various forms of direct participation. (2) It points to knowledge gaps which need to be filled if a proper understanding of the functioning and the effects of direct participation is to be achieved. (3) It describes the status of organisational change in the various European countries and their main competitors, the USA and Japan. (4) It informs and sensitises the EPOC research group to topics, knowledge gaps and methods. (5) Finally, it attempts to clarify concepts associated with direct participation and their implications and thus render them more accessible to public and scientific debate.

With these objectives, then, the literature review should be of interest to social actors, organisational practitioners and social scientists: social actors such as unions and employers' organisations might find the clarification of concepts and their implications helpful for their own internal debate. Governmental agencies might see the need or an opportunity to support the introduction of direct participation. Management might learn about the needs and constraints of Organisational change in regard to timing, financial input, training needs and the like. Unions and employee representatives are likely to gain a fresh insight into workplace change. For social scientists, the report might be helpful in clarifying a range of concepts and practices so that a common base for discussion would be provided to enable comparative research.

2

2 Research Methodology

The most obvious problem in reviewing research on direct participation in Europe, the US and Japan is that of language. As no scientist could ever master all languages involved, national correspondents had to be engaged to review the most important research in their countries and submit their reviews in English. This method also solved the additional problem associated with different cultural and national research traditions and peculiarities. Traditions which are likely to shape the selection and treatment of topics are unlikely to be known to a foreigner.

This approach poses an additional problem: given the diversity of languages and research traditions, how could a common understanding of the topic and its implications be arrived at by all national correspondents? As to this issue the conceptual preparation of the EPOC project (cf. Geary and Sisson 1994) proved very helpful. Here, 'direct participation' was defined as

> "opportunities which management provide, or initiatives to which they lend their support, at workplace level for consultation with and/or delegation of responsibilities and authority for decision-making to their subordinates either as individuals or as groups relating to the immediate work tasks, work organisation and/or working conditions."

This definition has a *nominal* character in that it enumerates certain indicators and attaches a verbal label to it in the end: 'direct participation'. As a verbal convention it enables the detection of organisational developments among the multitude of popular labels across cultures, traditions and languages. With regard to instructing national correspondents our brief simply said: "Whenever you encounter research which deals with the above topics, we are interested in it, regardless whether the writer used another label for it or not. "

Four forms of direct participation were identified:

Type 1:   employees are merely *consulted* with, on an *individual* basis, and are asked for their views, for example, through suggestion schemes and workforce surveys. Management, however, retain the right to act or not on these suggestions;

Type 2:   employees as *individuals* are given increased discretion to organise their own work, for example 'job enrichment' schemes;

Type 3:   this is the same as Type 1, except that employees are *consulted* with as a *group*, for example, 'quality circles';

Type 4:   like Type 2, employees are given increased discretion, but it is the *group* who *decides* who does what, with semi-autonomous work groups as an example.

These types could, of course, be extended further, by adding other dimensions: i.e. the permanency of groups, that is, to distinguish between temporary, 'project' groups and permanent groups. In addition, there is the issue of *coverage*: the proportion of certain kinds of employees to be drawn into and affected by various forms of direct participation (i.e. penetration among part-time and temporary workers, and variations across occupational categories). Another important dimension, that of the *regulation*, raises the question of whether direct participation is unilaterally imposed by management or are negotiated with employees and their representatives.

A scheme was developed to ensure that all reviews examined similar issues and that no relevant aspects were omitted. The number of important publications to be reviewed was set at 25 for the larger countries and at about 10 for the smaller ones. In all, the review generated more than 200 research abstracts. Reviewers were encouraged to review a broad literature including that which was relevant from industrial relations, human resource management, management studies, sociology and social psychology. This brought a rich and varied literature to bear on the subject of direct participation. Further, reviewers were encouraged to examine studies using different methodological approaches: quantitative studies to examine the diffusion of direct participation and qualitative studies to explore its impact on organisational life and economic performance. It was also thought important to review the views of the actors involved: employees, employee representatives, and management.

The national correspondents were academic experts in industrial relations and employment sociology in their countries. To further ensure a common understanding of the task and its implications, there were several meetings held in Germany, the first in spring 1994 to discuss the conceptual papers and the background material. The reviews were received between mid-1994 and winter 1994/1995. A second meeting took place in spring 1995 to discuss the first draft of the literature report.

Although we succeeded in ensuring a common frame of reference for the literature study, the report has some limitations. While each reviewer was to review the most important studies in each country, the requirement to confine this to at most 25 studies, has meant that the review cannot claim to be totally comprehensive. Nonetheless, we are satisfied that this review captures the state of the current debate in each of the countries reviewed and offers both the new and informed reader a detailed and informative account of the importance of direct participation.

The report is organised around a discussion of the four main types of direct participation. Each type of direct participation is explored, followed by an analysis of the background factors leading to its introduction and problems associated with its implementation. In general, the data are analysed cross-nationally, with national references used only when advisable or necessary. An overview of direct participation measures in each country is provided at the end of the report. Direct participation's effects on the role of middle management and on industrial relations issues are treated in separate chapters.

3 Individual Participation

'Direct participation', in many respects, is about the re-discovery of the 'human factor' in organisational success. It involves, among other things, 'open management', intensified communication and the creation of a new climate of trust in the organisation. Suggestions schemes, workforce attitudinal surveys and employee appraisal and development schemes - consultative forms of direct participation - have the potential to foster these outcomes. Some of these measures have a long pedigree and would seem to be well diffused throughout Europe. Suggestion schemes are applied on average in 28 per cent of companies in ten European countries. Workforce surveys are carried out more or less regularly in 24 per cent of those countries. Yet these forms of direct participation did not initially, at least, attract a great deal of attention; it has only been relatively recently that they have been rediscovered and discussed in the context of upward 'communication'.

While these individual forms of consultative participation have their own, specific features, all are 'united' by the feedback issue of upward communication: The evidence would suggest that where these measures do not elicit sufficient management interest and response, employees lose interest and develop a cynical attitude. Social science assessment of these schemes is ambivalent: they are regarded 'low impact' participation measures which elicit employees' ideas while retaining control over decision making.

With regard to delegative forms of participation, there would also seem to have been many instances of initiatives designed to enlarge the rights and responsibilities of individual employees through *job rotation, job enlargement* and *job enrichment*. This micro-approach to individual task participation, which we summarise as job enrichment, was popular with the Quality of

Working Life (QWL) movement in the 1970s and again, with the introduction of New Information Technology (NIT) in the 1980s. These experiments have not, however, attracted much attention in recent years.

The job enrichment concept is based on motivation theories stressing the importance of complex tasks and increased rights and responsibilities for employee work motivation, work satisfaction and productivity. The concept was developed in response to the alienating effects associated with mass-production. In the 1970s, the concept attracted much attention from employers who were faced with worker resistance demonstrated through high levels of absenteeism, turnover, sickness rates, strikes, and vandalism at the workplace. Investigation of the many job enrichment experiments of that period made this concept among the best researched topics in the direct participation field. Overwhelmingly the evidence would suggest that job enrichment increases job satisfaction which, in turn, leads to a reduction in absenteeism and labour turnover. But the effects of these initiatives on productivity, quality or customer service are less clear cut and are more ambiguous.

Perhaps because of this, 'job enrichment' lost some of its attractiveness and was largely forgotten. But it was applied nevertheless in the 1980s, albeit under different slogans and concepts. When New Information Technology made its inroads into European firms, the technology was often perceived as offering a 'technological option' to fully integrate and automate production processes, thereby making processes completely predictable and making management independent from an 'unreliable' workforce. But even companies trying to operate NIT with less grandiose ambitions soon learned that this technology could not be applied optimally without active workforce involvement. This insight was then 'codified' in concepts like New Production Concepts and Flexible Specialisation.

To support employees engaging in NIT implementation and operation, many employers invested in vocational training. As to its effects, NIT made work more complex, interesting and 'intellectually' more challenging; it reduced physical strain distinctly, yet increased stress and mental strain in like proportion; tasks took on a more abstract character, blurring distinctions between blue- and white-collar employees. But one expected outcome did not occur: NIT work did not increase employees' decision-making power and job autonomy. It seems that it increased responsibilities without granting more rights. But, on balance, employees distinctly preferred their new tasks to their traditional jobs.

4 Consultative Group Participation

One of the most identifiable forms of consultative participation is the quality circle. Quality circles attracted considerable attention through the 1980s and were often seen as a key ingredient in Japanese companies' success on international markets. Accordingly, competitive needs were often the primary reason for implementing quality circles outside Japan. But further motives were added quickly. First, they were seen as a suitable way to conform to formal quality norms and standard specifications. Second, they were extended to develop human resource capabilities and improve the quality of working life. The main problem, however, associated with circles' introduction was that management often considered them as an easy way out of problems without any need to alter established organisational structures. Of course, there was also the incentive to engage in a new employee involvement practice that was widely seen to be fashionable.

The evidence would suggest that to successfully introduce quality circles, implementation needs top management's commitment, a long time perspective and a significant financial input for training employees at all levels of the organisation. This training includes the imparting of problem solving skills and, in particular, training in 'social' skills enabling people to work in groups. The lack of attention paid to these social or 'soft' skills proved to be among the most significant obstacle to quality circles' introduction.

In many instances in Europe and the US, the emphasis was on fostering employee work motivation, communication, workplace improvements and commitment to the company. In this regard, quality circles clearly had their largest positive effects. 'Hard' economic effects were rarely measured, and the quality improvement of products and services were difficult to discern.

There is a widespread recognition in the literature that quality circles have faced a number of handicaps. Among the most important are: first, under pressure to meet production dead-lines, quality circles were likely to be ignored by management. Second, bottom-up approaches to employee participation were often not given adequate support from, or accepted by, management. Third, efforts to conform to textbook applications of quality circles, as laid down by Quality Circle Congresses and national Quality Circle Associations easily led to complicated procedures and bureaucracy. Fourth, and most significantly, quality circles did not directly affect existing organisational structures but created parallel structures and confused existing work roles, responsibilities and power arrangements. This created resistance from supervisors and middle management in particular.

Workforces had their grievances as well: circle participation was not always as voluntary as prescribed by theory. Informal management pressure to join was often widespread. Against that there was peer pressure *not* to join. Such pressure was most likely in the US, UK and in Mediterranean countries. When circle activities were not restricted to normal working hours, resistance and claims for extra pay were often common. When management did not take circle suggestions seriously, which would seem to have happened often, workforce disinterest in circle activities grew significantly.

Currently, quality circles do not generate the same level of enthusiasm among employers as they did in the early 1980s. Further, there is an increased awareness that where they are introduced as isolated experiments the chances of success are slim. In their original Japanese settings, such circles were just one approach in an array of management strategies, most commonly referred to as Total Quality Management. TQM is a set of integrated measures, often strongly relying on a group work approach, with groups having 'real', delegated rights and responsibilities. According to theory, quality circles can play a positive role here. In practice, there is considerable evidence in support of this view. Whereas most isolated circle applications 'died' after one to two years, their survival rate when introduced as part of a TQM strategy is far higher.

5 Group Work Between 'Volvoism' and 'Toyotism'

The present public and scientific debate on direct participation focuses, in the main, on team working or group work. Group work involves a significant departure from traditional divisions of labour and task fragmentation. Its main aims include: task integration, decentralisation of decision-making, greater flexibility of work processes, the provision of higher quality goods and services, a better use of human skills, enriched workplaces and an improved quality of working life.

The group work principle was originally developed in the 1950s and experimented with in the Quality of Working Life movement in the 1970s, particularly in Scandinavia. It gained its present prominence through the MIT study on the automotive industry that advocated group work as one of the main secrets behind Japan's economic success. The present public debate often lacks a clear understanding of the fundamental differences between the original European type group work and the Japanese practices. Both can be conceived of as two extremes: Membership in *Scandinavian groups* is voluntary; the groups select their own members; qualifications of group members are mixed to enable members to learn from, and help, one another. Their tasks are rather complex and are usually independent from machine pacing. The groups regulate their own internal proceedings and have large autonomy in regard to task design and task execution. They also elect their own leader. The group work associated with *Toyota* or the *lean production models* displays very different features. Group membership is mandatory, and members are carefully selected and 'socialised' into group work. Members hold company and workplace specific qualifications to complete short-cycled, machine-paced tasks. Group members are expected to constantly streamline their task execution through the *kaizen* principle and in quality control circles. They are expected to recommend further possibilities to eliminate any variability in their work and to streamline the execution of their tasks. In task execution they have to adhere to solutions that are put forward and agreed upon by the members. The organisation of work is prescribed by superiors who are nominated by management.

From a quality of working life point of view, the 'lean production groups' run against many of the European notions of 'good work'. While group members have discretion in task design, they are completely rule-bound in task execution. This form of work organisation is highly disliked in Japan, but acceptance rests on guarantees of life-long employment and a remuneration system which binds employees to their employer.

The Scandinavian form of group work developed at a time of over-heated labour markets, with workforces unwilling to accept boring mass-production jobs. It has had considerable success, in particular in increasing work motivation, reducing absenteeism and sickness leave. But unlike the Japanese group solution, its potential for increasing productivity levels are far from clear.

Under the label of 'Japanese Inspired Production Systems' (JIPS), European and US companies are experimenting and applying group work concepts which try to combine the strengths of both systems while avoiding their handicaps. A unitary concept has not yet evolved: we find various types of group work in the same countries, and, in some instances, in the same companies.

It is also worth noting that Japanese transplants in Europe and the US do not apply their home system in a pure form, but try to modify their approaches to cope with local peculiarities and national traditions. In an effort to avoid resistance to organisational change, such transplants are often established on 'greenfield' sites, usually in structurally weak regions which offer few employment alternatives. Introducing group work in existing organisations has often consumed a lot of time, in one case, eight years. Company traditions, vested interests and power structures have often shown themselves to be significant obstacles and particularly where relations between managers and employees have been poor. Such change processes are very often made easier by the involvement of external advisors and consultants and, in particular, by the active inclusion of the workforces.

In greenfield sites, many employers have taken great care to screen employees for their capacity to work in groups during the election process. This has helped the success of such initiatives in these settings. Unfortunately, we have very little knowledge about group work in 'brownfield' firms.

For group work to function properly and be productive, additional training of employees is considered a necessity. The evidence would suggest that companies apply different training schemes of various duration for their workers to become multiskilled. Rarely is the extent or form of vocational training left to the group members themselves to decide. Many commentators point to the 'social dimension' of group work and the need for 'social skills' to enable members to deal with 'group dynamics'. The lack of such skills is often regarded as a significant impediment to the smooth functioning of group working. The variety of training schemes and the time and money invested to foster social skills would seem to suggest that most companies are aware of the importance of training in this area and have tried to cope with this problem.

The remuneration system is one of the most serious issues relating to group work. It has the potential to give rise to serious conflicts and has, on occasions, led to the termination of group experiments. A priori, one might assume that the remuneration system should reflect the common group effort and responsibility and should not be based on individual performance. But this system of compensation is rarely applied. In Europe and in the US, there is a movement towards adopting skill-based pay schemes, enhanced through various individual and/or group performance elements.

In regard of the economic benefits to be derived from group working, the MIT study has set the key note, where significant reductions in labour costs were associated with its introduction. The present review has also found significant gains from group work's implementation. And while it is always going to be difficult to isolate discrete effects, one can with some confidence claim that group work has led to significant productivity improvements. In only two instances, traditional production schemes were found to have superior productivity performance than that associated with group work.

The labour market effects of group work do not receive extensive treatment in the literature. We were unable, for example, to find any information on how the 'flattening of hierarchies' (often associated with group working) and the introduction of 'lean' approaches affected companies' workforce size. Equally unsatisfying is our knowledge about intra-company labour market effects and workforce segmentation. From Japan we know that large companies often operate with a core workforce and rely heavily on additional, peripheral employees.

Our knowledge of workforce reactions to group work is also very patchy. In Japan, working in lean production groups does not seem to be associated with great enthusiasm from employees. There are some indications that working in JIPS type applications in Europe and in the US meets with similar 'sceptical' employee responses. This is not to deny that there are some very positive employee reports on group work, but the basis for such an assessment is largely unclear. Particular safety and health hazards associated with group work are unknown, but it has increased stress levels. Part of this increase can be attributed to informal social pressure and social controls which are exercised by group members on their co-workers.

In general, highly skilled employees are more sceptical about working in groups, fearing loss of qualified work, skills, status and income. Where they do enter groups they often succeed in retaining the better jobs for themselves. In general, however, unskilled employees can identify positive advantages with working in groups and are often among its staunchest supporters. Contrary to theory, the extrinsic aspects of group work, payment in particular, seem to play a more decisive role for work motivation than the nature of the task itself.

6 Problems of Middle Management

'Direct participation' is about increased workforce rights and responsibilities. Associated practices of total quality management and lean production intend, among others, to substitute hierarchies by introducing work groups. This has obvious implications for the number and roles performed by middle managers. There is a common understanding in manufacturing that foremen and front-line supervisors are the main losers of group work. Many of their functions are taken over by the groups. We know very little about middle management behaviour in regard to cross-functional reorganisation, although we have some indication that labour turnover of middle managers increases in such cases. Other forms of direct participation affect middle management in different ways. Workforce surveys, for example, are sometimes devised to evaluate managers. Quality circles have generated considerable resistance among middle management who feared the creation of parallel structures and 'shadow hierarchies' in their firms which were seen to confuse work roles and power relations.

But middle management reactions are not as clear-cut as they often seem to be. Senior executives who are the prime source of information on middle management, are much more critical about this group's resistance than middle managers themselves. If middle managers see a new role for themselves, if they are supported by senior management and can acquire new skills through adequate training, then, the evidence would suggest that middle managers, particularly the younger ones, can be active supporters of direct participation's introduction. Middle management is still needed in 'transformed' firms. In many cases, this group is likely to be 'leaner', and its role will change: top-down functions will decrease, and moderating, coaching and facilitating roles will increase in importance. It has also been found that where middle management has been given training to acquire these new skills their resistance to direct participation often quickly dissipates.

7 Employee Representatives' View of Direct Participation

Where management systematically promoted organisational change through various forms of direct participation, the evidence would suggest that many unions and works councils were alarmed and concerned about management's motives. Among the main worries were: is direct participation being introduced to improve the organisation's economic performance? Or does management intend to use direct participation as a means to weaken union or works council influence? How should unions and works councils react to direct participation? What are the dangers for their constituency, for their own organisations, and for established forms of representative participation? And how might workforce attitudes towards unions be affected by direct participation? Finally, in what ways are working conditions likely to be affected, and how can employees' interests be best protected?

Although we have gathered and analysed a considerable amount of empirical research from different countries, most answers to these questions are still tentative. It is plain, however, that in *Continental* Europe, direct participation was fostered by management, in the main, for competitive and productivity reasons. There is little or no evidence to suggest that management are using direct participation to deliberately weaken and marginalise trade union or works council influence. Indeed, in most European countries employers have involved trade union representatives or works councils in the introduction of direct participation. In the US, too, management's motives for introducing direct participation have been similar to employers in Europe, but the evidence of management's intentions in regard of unions is more ambiguous. Some research has shown that management are using direct participation to marginalise trade unions, but this has not been a common management strategy.

Since the introduction of quality circles in the early 1980s, unions at the outset, at least, have shown themselves to be concerned with management's motives for implementing direct participation. In some countries, like Ireland, Germany and Sweden, unions decided, following much debate and discussion, to actively engage with management's efforts to introduce direct participation measures, so long as their own interests could be guarded carefully. But despite some initial reservations and apprehensions, works councils and unions at a local level in most European countries have rarely sought to oppose the introduction of direct participation. In some instances, early suspicions quickly turned to disinterest, as unions realised that direct participation did not affect the vital interests of representative bodies and their constituency. In other instances unions have been far more active in their co-operation with, and support for, direct participation. This was particularly the case in countries that had a long history of experimenting with direct participation and, in same cases, unions had developed a sophisticated understanding of direct participation and had been proactive in its introduction. In general it would seem that where employee representation is supported by legal measures, unions and work councils have worked closely with management in introducing direct participation.

Whether direct participation has the capacity to create tensions between different elements of employee representation depends to a large degree on the particularities of national representative systems. In the case of dual structures, with unions and elected works councils at establishment level, rifts between both parties have appeared when works councillors gave precedence to the perceived benefits which direct participation may bring for employees and their employers, without regard for national union policy. Where such tensions have arisen, the evidence would suggest that employees have in the majority of cases favoured the strategy of the organisation's work council above that of the union. Similar tensions are also evident in the UK and Ireland between shop stewards within the workplace and union representatives outside the organisation. This has led to a significant re-appraisal among some trade union officials of their role and response to direct participation.

In summary, the review of the literature seems to show that direct participation and indirect representative participation are not competing concepts. There is considerable research evidence to suggest that employees have a clear preference for dealing with task related problems on their own. Here direct participation brings obvious benefits. There is also a clear recognition among employees that there are other issues which are best handled by other mechanisms and by representative bodies. As such, direct and indirect participation are not contradictory concepts, but may rather complement one another. This is not to suggest that direct participation poses no problems for trade unions and work councils on the ground, but the weakening of employee representative structures is not a likely outcome. Evidence from the EPOC Social Partner Study would also support this view.

Other union concerns with direct participation relate to the extra demands it may impose on employees. Notwithstanding the benefits it may bring in many instances, there was the view that direct participation led to increased effort and stress levels. It can also lead to increased competition between individuals and groups, to problems within groups, and may possibly disadvantage particular sections of the workforce, like unskilled female employees and older employees. These effects were particularly pronounced where group work is associated with lean production methods. Other problems associated with direct participation identified by employee representatives were: inadequate investment in vocational training and difficulties in adapting payment practices to the introduction of team working. But such apprehensions in regard to working conditions under various schemes of direct participation are far from being systematic: some unions and employee representatives see danger where others see hopes, and such inconsistencies cut through national cultures and industrial relation systems.

8 The Countries in Perspective

While the current review of the existing literature has brought together some very rich and interesting material in regard to many topics, there are significant variations in the scope and depth of information on the spread of direct participation in the individual countries. At the outset it was hoped to answer a number of questions, like: how diffuse is direct participation in Europe? Do businesses and organisations pursue similar practices in all countries or do we find regional or industrial variations? What proportion of the national workforces are affected by these new developments? But such information, which can only be gathered by representative surveys, is scarce in the European countries, and it often refers to very different 'research universes' such as companies, economic sectors, or employees and to single forms of direct participation.

In some countries like Austria, Denmark and Finland, for example, the evidence relates only employee interviews. In other countries like Greece, Italy and Spain, we mainly learned about the spread of quality circles, without much reference to other types of direct participation. For Germany, we have to rely mainly on management consultancy research of poor methodological value, plus a workforce survey on the spread of group work in the working population. For Belgium, France, the Netherlands, Portugal, Sweden, United Kingdom, the US and Japan there are more general surveys. But they, again, tap different dimensions of direct participation which makes comparison difficult. Thus, if we did not find quality circles or other forms of direct participation mentioned in one country, this does not mean that they do not or did not exist. They simply were not investigated.

The Price Waterhouse Cranfield project is the only European comparative study so far. In its study of ten EU countries it supplies comparative data on the spread of suggestion schemes, workforce surveys and quality circles in 1992. Suggestion schemes were a rather traditional and 'low-impact' type of individual direct participation (cf. chapter 2). Against a European average of 28 per cent it was found that companies in the Nordic countries made greater use of suggestion schemes, while organisations in Southern European made less use of them. Workforce surveys were applied in about 23 per cent of all European companies, although there were wide variations between individual countries. They were particularly popular in Finland and Sweden where 50 per cent and 43 per cent of all companies applied them. However, only 6 per cent of firms in the Netherlands used them, with all other countries somewhat in the middle.

Quality circles are the third rather 'low-impact' type of direct participation. The Cranfield study reveals that an average of 15 per cent of all European companies applied quality circles. The number of quality circles in Finland, France, Germany, Spain and the United Kingdom is above this average. In Danish, Irish, Portuguese and Swedish firms, only 9 to 11 per cent of firms have them.

We are unable to present comparable data on the spread of group work in the European countries. In most countries, representative company surveys are missing; there are a few branch specific surveys of limited scope. In a few countries employees were asked whether they worked in groups. But varying definitions and measurements do not permit us to make comparisons. It can be said, however, that group work is not highly diffused throughout Europe. Looking at the US and Japan some valuable insights can be gleaned. The best information we got through our literature search pertains to the US, both in regard to content and methodology. According to these results, US organisations seem to be in a process of dynamic organisational change, much more that even US observers expected. According to a recent representative survey, 55 per cent of all US establishments work with groups, 43 per cent apply job rotation schemes, 41 per cent quality circles, and 34 per cent have introduced a TQM programme. In Japan we learned that almost all large companies operate on group work basis, complemented by quality control circles. This applies to the production sector and the service sector alike, and such results seem to confirm 'conventional wisdom' that group work might be the secret behind Japan's economic success. But we have to remember that such information pertains to a relatively small share of employees. It neglects the large numbers of employees located in the so-called peripheral workforce.

It should also be emphasised that the Japanese conception of group work differs from that of many Europeans. In some instances it refers merely to departmental or line structures. It is thus difficult to draw clear, unambiguous conclusions from such data and we must be very careful about making claims for 'productivity secrets' or another 'one-best' type of work organisation.

9 Conclusions

This report is an attempt to inform the current debate on direct participation. It brings together, for the first time, research evidence on this subject from Europe, Japan and the US. A number of conclusions can be made: first, while consultative participation can be important in laying the ground for organisational change, it is not by itself sufficient to bring about significant improvements in organisational performance. For that, delegative participation is necessary. Second, there is the simple but important lesson that the introduction of direct participation is a demanding and time consuming exercise. Sufficient thought and resources have to be put into training employees and their superiors to adapt to this new way of working. The so-called softer social skills which enable and train people to work in teams would seem to be particularly important. Third, the introduction of direct participation, perhaps not surprisingly, is easier in greenfield sites than in older, well-established workplaces. Fourth, these initiatives must not be introduced as island solutions. Great care needs to be given to adapting other elements of human resource management practice and industrial relations policy to the introduction of direct participation. Fifth, the introduction of group work is more likely to be successful where employees and their representatives are intimately involved in its introduction. If union and work councils' fears are not quickly addressed by management any consequent resistance or apathy is unlikely to aid the implementation of direct participation. There is also compelling evidence that where management actively invite employees and their representatives to come forward with their own independent views on direct participation the path for its introduction can be considerably eased. Finally, great care needs to be given to the management of employee remuneration. This is particularly important with the introduction of group work. There is no simple answer here: some commentators argue that a group based payment system is necessary, while others disagree. The predominant view would be that some form of skill-based pay is called for and, if necessary, to supplement it with individual and/or team performance bonuses.

In summary, the great benefit of direct participation is its potential to resolve a perennial dilemma of employers: how can organisational effectiveness be improved without taking from, or giving inadequate consideration to, employees' quality of working life. Unions and work councils, too, are aware that the potential benefits to be derived from direct participation, but are concerned primarily that they should be involved in its introduction. The evidence from this review and from the EPOC social partner study suggests that there is considerable support among employers, trade unions and employees for direct participation. Certainly there is little basis for believing that any party is against the principle of its introduction, concerns usually focus on its regulation and what balance is to be achieved between responding to organisational issues of productivity, quality, customer service and demands by employees to give sufficient consideration to their interests. Indeed, the evidence would suggest that the primary reason for the limited diffusion of direct participation in Europe has more to do with a management inability or unwillingness to depart from traditional work structures and less from employee or trade union resistance. This is probably the primary reason why Europe is behind Japan and the US with the implementation of direct participation, particularly in its delegative form. This, then, is the crucial task for policy makers in Europe: to convince employers of the necessity and desirability of looking seriously at the potential benefits from direct participation.

1 Direct Participation as an International Concern of Organisations and of Social Science

1.1 What is New About Direct Participation?

Since the 1980s new organisational approaches have been discussed throughout the industrialised countries. Terms like 'lean production', 'lean administration', 'flexible organisation', 'Total Quality Management' (TQM) and concepts like 'group work' have become part of every-day language in management literature and in industrial relations. These topics have gained prominence even in the mass media. The conceptual ideas behind these catchwords differ in detail, but they are united by one common, basic idea: Employees should be involved in matters of their companies, particularly in their daily work and their immediate work environment more intensively than any time before. They are asked and expected to identify with their companies and their jobs, to engage themselves in their daily work to constantly improve work processes and products. 'Direct participation' is an appropriate general label for these expectations.

Popular as direct participation may be with management, in the social sciences and even in the mass media, the concept is not at all new. However, it is now notable for two new dimensions:

First, direct participation is promoted by management. Management is the driving force which restructures organisations along these lines. It is willing to grant larger discretion to employees to carry out their tasks and encourages employees to take on responsibility. It is ready to reduce direct control of the work process and promotes the idea of self-organisation of employees. Thus, direct participation is not wrought away from management by government legislation, by union power or by employee protest, but is freely granted. The novelty of direct participation being promoted by management needs to be qualified in two ways: in a narrow sense, most direct participation measures were promoted by management, even in the Quality of Working Life movement. But the motivation behind management policies differs today: in regard to the older practices, management reacted to workforce behaviour such as high rates of absenteeism or difficulties to recruit manpower for certain jobs. The present reasons for direct participation (DP) are essentially proactive, and sometimes workforces are even talked into accepting direct participation, particularly group work. Present management driven direct participation does not preclude outside support through government legislation and union policies. In some countries, union bodies and legislation inspired management do venture into direct workforce participation.

Another new aspect of direct participation today is its conceptualisation as a set of integrated measures. Whereas older approaches to direct participation regarded it as an isolated or restricted measure intended to solve single organisational problems which affected limited groups of employees, direct participation now has the potential as a general approach to affect the whole organisation. Originally devised for problem-solving in the production sphere, it soon became evident that the expected benefits would be sub-optimal if the concept was confined to the production sections of a company. Only when all organisational parts, the administrative and service personnel included, are drawn and integrated into this concept, might direct participation produce the expected benefits. Positive examples of the implementation of such an integrated concept in the production units of private companies promoted the idea that direct participation is applicable in the private service sector as well, even in non-profit organisations and public administration. The popular terms 'lean administration' and 'lean government' testify to this potential for all kinds of organisations in the developed countries. As will be shown, many practical applications of different direct participation measures lack the character of a systematic approach. But this fact does not contradict the novel idea of integrating measures to change the whole organisation.

Direct participation gained new prominence through different convergent technological and economic developments: the advent of new information technologies in the 1970s which enabled very flexible changes in production and require highly skilled and motivated workforces to operate new technologies effectively; the worldwide accessibility and spread of these technologies based on the unitary concept of micro-electronics; the growth of a true world market and international competition with similar products where product quality develops into a competitive edge. In the context of worldwide competition, Japan has set standards of productivity, quality, and flexibility, and Japanese economic success in the 1980s has induced the Western industrial states to analyse the secrets behind it. They identified new organisational principles in which employee motivation and group work played an outstanding role. These new principles of organisation became popular in an era of structural economic change, decreasing economic activity in the highly industrialised states, and increasing financial difficulties of the Welfare State in need of economising its procedures. Under such auspices, not only private business firms but public and governmental organisations, experimented with direct participation to increase the efficiency of their proceedings and to ease financial burdens.

Although popular catchwords like lean production, lean administration, lean government, Total Quality Management and the like proliferate in the mass media, in management literature and in the social sciences dealing with organisations, we have comparably little systematic knowledge about direct participation, of their diverse forms, of how they are applied and what their effects are. Equally, there is almost no reliable information about the actual diffusion of this concept in organisations, nor do we know very much about factors which hinder or foster the spread of direct participation. In addition, there is considerable disagreement about its wider implications for work circumstances and for the working population. Some commentators see the spread of direct participation as an opportunity for humanisation and democratisation of work, while others see it as an essentially ideological project masquerading as greater management control and work intensification.

1.2 Direct Participation as a Research Concern of the European Foundation

Given this lack of clarity and evidence, the European Foundation for the Living and Working Conditions has launched a major investigation into the nature and extent of 'Employee Participation in Organisational Change - EPOC'. The main focus of investigation, which began in 1993, was on the twelve member states of the European Union at that time. But it included the new EU member states Austria, Finland and Sweden from the very beginning. The main activities either terminated, under way or planned include:

* the literature review which is presented here and which encompasses publications in the European Union, as well as Japan and the US;

* a study on the 'Position of the Social Partners on Direct Participation in Europe' which presents the attitudes and approaches of the peak employers' organisations and the trade unions in Europe, with special reference to two main economic sectors, namely mechanical engineering and banking (Regalia 1995);

* a postal survey of establishments in all EU states on their experience with different forms of direct participation;

* a programme of case studies drawing on examples of different types and experience of direct participation identified in the establishment survey.

In this context, the literature study is meant to give an overview of important research results on direct participation in Europe, Japan and the

USA for various reasons: It should inform the interested public and experts about the state of international knowledge on different aspects of direct participation. It is further intended to identify well documented results as well as knowledge gaps about the concept. It should inform our own research about shortcomings in our conceptual ideas, about well documented and neglected topics. Finally, the results of the literature study should provide us with additional reference information to discuss our own future research results in an international perspective.

To give this literature study as well as the other planned sub-studies a common frame of reference, an international research group[1] developed its own theoretical approach to analyse direct participation. Central to this concept is the definition of direct participation as

> "opportunities which management provide, or initiatives to which they lend their support, at workplace level, for consultation with and/or delegation of responsibilities and authority for decision-making to their subordinates either as individuals or as groups relating to the immediate work tasks, work organisation and/or working conditions" (Geary and Sisson 1994:2).

The concentration on the paramount role of management stresses the novel character of this kind of direct participation as a management driven concept which was pointed out above. Like all definitions the chosen one is intended to exclude as well as include. Some aspects excluded are obvious, such as indirect or representative participation through shop stewards, trade unions, works councils, or collective bargaining (although these organisations may well be involved in the regulation of direct participation). Other forms excluded are one-way communication, e.g. briefing groups and financial participation. Neither will the investigation be examining workers' co-operatives because of their special circumstances.

When choosing the above definition of direct participation, the research group was aware of the restrictions it entailed: Participation is a term that carries different connotations, and different social actors and social scientists might feel uneasy with the chosen delimitation. Thus, the social partners interviewed in the EU member states in an EPOC sub-study often expressed misgivings with our definition and preferred the use of other terms, such as 'employee involvement' or 'direct co-operation' (cf. Regalia 1995). Other

---

The research group consists of Alain Chouraqui, *France*; Dieter Fröhlich, *Germany*; John Geary, *Ireland*; Hubert Krieger, *Ireland*; Ulrich Pekruhl, *Germany*; Ida Regalia, *Italy*; Keith Sisson, *United Kingdom*; Georges Spyropoulos, *Greece*.

actors find its meaning as a day-to-day practice confusing and often associate it with systems of workers' membership in management bodies or a variety of advisory bodies at industrial and national levels (cf. Spyropoulos 1995). At this point, we want to make it very clear that we use the term 'direct participation' as a nominal definition, in which the content of the definition, its single elements, is the only important information, while the overarching term is to be understood just as a verbal convention to denote these content elements and to allow easy and precise communication on the subject matter. Or put differently: whenever we use the term 'direct participation' we are aware that we are dealing with a management driven strategy that aims at the workplace level, that holds the idea of more consultative and/or delegative rights, for individuals or for work groups. Facts which are not covered by this enumeration fall outside our research interests. Such an understanding, concentrating as it does on the content elements, helps us to communicate the topic across diverse fields of social science, and to consider the different connotations the term 'direct participation' might have cross-culturally or among different actors. It permits us to look beneath popular labels that might or might not denote the same content.[2]

To enable us to break away from the manifold labels which prevail, we even had to refine our own term: having one of its origins in Japanese organisational procedures, direct participation is easily and popularly equalled with group work. As our definition shows, the concept extends to individual employees as well, thereby indicating that our own approach is wider than the ones popularly discussed at present, that direct participation aims at a new understanding of work in organisations: active employee engagement in the organisation at workplace level, as individuals or in groups. Further, we differentiate the forms of participation as consultative and delegative participation: In the case of consultative participation, employees are encouraged and enabled to make their views known. Management, however, retains the right to accept or reject employees' opinions as well as reserving the right to take action. In the case of delegative participation, responsibility for what has traditionally been an area of management decision-making is placed largely in employees' hands: participation is designed into peoples' jobs. In its most developed sense management may grant autonomy to

---

[2]   Such nominal definitions - conventions of what we are talking about - are indispensible research tools for any science, and they must be strictly separated from *essentialist definitions* which ask about the 'nature' of a phenomenon, in this case: the essence of direct participation. Essentialist definitions are apt to carry implicit theories and 'Weltanschauungen', and venturing into essentialist definitions leads to endless scholastic debates leading nowhere.

workers to design and prepare work schedules, to monitor and control their own work tasks and methods, i. e. to be more or less self-managing.

A further distinction is that of regulation. As direct participation is likely to affect the whole organisation, problems of formal or informal regulation might arise between the parties concerned. Here the major analytical distinction is between unilateral regulation by management and bi- or multilateral regulation in which trade unions, employee representatives and employees are involved. Focusing on regulation is of particular importance in cross-national and cross-cultural research: the divergent systems of industrial relations and legal traditions between countries create different conditions that might affect the type of direct participation, the implementation process, the functioning and the effects of direct participation.

The research concept further asks who practices direct participation and who is affected by it one way or the other; when, why and how was it introduced; what effects (both objective and perceived) did direct participation have, and, finally, how is direct participation evaluated by the actors involved in terms of success or failure.

From these aspects, the groups affected by direct participation can be singled out under the dimension of coverage: what proportion of an establishment's workforce is drawn into these various measures? Which sections of the work force in terms of gender, ethnicity, hierarchical positions and skill categories are affected? We can further ask whether types of direct participation are temporary or permanent, thereby introducing the time dimension. 'Project groups' would be an example of a temporary measure of direct participation, whereas 'group work' would denote a permanent measure.

In order to handle the very large amount of research, we did not explicitly concentrate on the dimensions of regulation, coverage and time; neither did we exclude it. But we explicitly focused on the two core dimensions of direct participation: consultative and delegative participation which can be directed toward individuals or to groups. This leads to four main types of direct participation:

Table 1: Types of Direct Participation

	individual	group
consultative	1	3
delegative	2	4

These types, which form the backbone of the most measures of direct participation in the scope of our definition, can be summarily described as follows:

Type 1:   Employees are consulted as individuals. Management, however, retains the right to act or not to act on the suggestions given by the individuals. Such activities are generally typical of everyday Organisational life. In discussing this type as a conscious management strategy, one might think of a systematic application of suggestion schemes. Workforce surveys by which management gain knowledge of employees' wishes, intentions and suggestions are another type of individual employee consultation.

Type 2:   Employees are given increased discretion and responsibility as individuals to organise and carry out their own work. In practice, this would mean a substantial enlargement of the individual work role definition. Measures of what is named 'work re-design' and 'work structuring' such as job rotation, job enlargement and job enrichment, find their place here.

Type 3:   A permanent group without decision rights, which makes suggestions only, with management free to accept or discard - the typical Quality Circle.

Type 4:   A permanent group with decision rights is a work group, the most likely type of new work organisation which is often associated with concepts like 'lean production' and 'total quality management'.

Type 4, the work group, is presently the most cited, most discussed basic Organisational tool, and it is regarded to be the cornerstone of new managerial approaches. Very often, it is equated to the semi-autonomous work group. Enjoying delegated power and responsibilities to carry out tasks independently as a group, this type of group work is regarded a positive development in work organisation from a Quality of Working Life point of view. It suggest chances for learning and qualification, independence from hierarchical control, and possibilities for own decisions. Accordingly, the concept of semi-autonomous work groups carries the notion of something desirable and unequivocally positive. However, group work does not have this positive character per se, but can take on different forms that range from extremely narrow group discretion to very wide group rights and responsibilities. The diverse forms will be analysed and discussed in detail later (cf. chapter 4).

1.3   Different Social Science Approaches Towards Direct Participation

For a variety of reasons the authors of the literature study had to rely on social scientists from various countries to inform them about empirical research on direct participation in their countries. To gather the information necessary, the foreign experts were given detailed instructions, among them the request to scan the various approaches and traditions of social research which deal with the topic of direct participation in the scope of our definition (cf. section 1. 4). This research is spread over several research disciplines, such as sociology, management research, psychology, political sciences, with widely varying or even contradictory political and ideological points of view and interests. And, of course, in each of these numerous fields of research, the problems and questions are different.

In the following, we briefly delineate the main approaches dealing with direct participation. As a descriptive overview, it should serve as background information and provide a short summary of schools of thought in research on direct participation, their basic assumptions and their specific ways of reasoning.

'Classical' Industrial Sociology: The Impact of Automation

From the 1950s and up to the early 80s, most research within the field of industrial sociology centred around the question of how production automation would affect work and working conditions in industry. Within this general approach three strands of discussion are particularly related (either implicitly or explicitly) to direct participation: the impact of automation on workers' skills and qualifications, the socio-technical approach, and the debate on worker autonomy and control.

In the older discussion about the impact of automation on skill development, the amount of human skills used in working was implicitly equated with the concept of direct participation. As direct participation was almost synonymous to applying high qualification in the work process, research concentrated on the question of how human skills were likely to develop under the impact of technology: early studies by Touraine (1955), Popitz et al. (1957) and Blauner (1964), for example, questioned whether new technologies in the production process would result in a need for higher skills and qualifications, or whether an ongoing process of de-skilling of manual work could be expected. According to one opinion, human skills would be gradually incorporated into machinery, and only very simple jobs which could not be automated or where automation would be more expensive than labour, would remain. As a result, the vast majority of the workforce would need only low qualifications in order to fulfil the needs of the production process. The opposite argument stated that very simple Taylorized work tasks could be best automated and substituted by technology. Only tasks which could not be easily mechanised like planning, maintenance, regulation etc. , would survive. The remaining workforce would be highly skilled, whereas unskilled labour would tend to vanish in industrial production.

The many studies to test both hypotheses led to inconclusive results, supporting both arguments. This apparent contradiction could, finally, be explained by taking the important role of work organisation into account: dependent on how the work was organised, the same technology would allow for the use of low skills as well as high skills. In cases where high skills were available in a company, technology was moulded in a way to allow for the use of these skills (e.g. Sorge and Warner 1986). Such results underlined the importance of training and educational systems (both in companies and at state level) to create high skills. The German government programme 'Humanisierung der Arbeit' was partly inspired by the idea of raising skill levels and, as a consequence, the scope of direct participation.

At about the same time, the socio-technical approach (Trist et al. 1963) was 'rediscovered' and became very prominent in Scandinavia and in the 'Quality of Working Life' (QWL) movement. It differs from the concept of skill development and use of technology in being dependent on work organisation, stating that all organisations in industry have to be seen as social and technical systems. Both systems have to follow their own logic, but, at the same time, have to be closely related to one another to achieve high organisational efficiency. It is important to note that within the socio-technical approach, the shaping of the social system of an organisation does not only mean humanisation. A well functioning social system is mainly a precondition for economic efficiency. According to this argument the social system has much to do with workers' motivation to work efficiently and reliably. Although the state-funded QWL programmes of that time failed because they did not regard the efficiency part of the equation, the experience and knowledge gathered in the process prove to be valuable for the present discussion about direct participation.

Braverman's study 'Labour and Monopoly Capital' (1974) marks the beginning of another strand of theory and research, known as the labour process debate. According to Braverman, the development of work under capitalist production regimes is a process of ongoing de-qualification of workers and an increasing division of work tasks. The spread of Tayloristic principles is not explained by technical developments or organisational needs but by management's intention to gain control over the work process. The control problem arises from the fact that a work contract does not guarantee a work output. Management faces the problem of how to turn contractually agreed work performance into actual work performance. Since workers by nature try to avoid exploitation and struggle for self-control, management has to find ways to compel workers to invest all their work potential and their capabilities into the work process. Tayloristic principles are such mechanisms: fragmented, narrow and simple jobs and the split between mental and manual tasks leave all knowledge about the work process in management's hand. Fragmented and precisely defined single tasks make jobs and people interchangeable and decrease workers chances to use their knowledge as a means of power.

The main (Marxist) critics of Braverman (e.g. Burawoy 1979, Hildebrandt and Seltz 1989) aim at his one-dimensional concept of control. They accept that management wants control over the labour process, but regard Taylorism as only one and probably not even the most successful way of achieving it. Other management strategies using 'indirect', soft forms of control through shared norms, values and symbols ('high-trust company culture') are said to be more efficient as they meet the flexibility needs of companies much better. Such workforce consent and loyalty is primarily achieved by providing workers with some autonomy, and autonomy mainly means chances for direct participation. Thus, studies which have been investigating such management strategies in the control perspective are an important source of information on direct participation as well.

Political Sciences and Industrial Sociology: Participation and Industrial Democracy

Industrial Democracy (ID) has been defined "as the exercise of power by workers or their representatives over decisions within their places of employment, coupled with a modification of the locus and distribution authority within the workforce itself" (Poole 1992:429). Poole distinguishes four possible sources of origin of ID: democratic theory, socialist theory, human growth and development theory, and a productivity and efficiency orientation. Only the latter directly refers to the work sphere and its necessities and restraints. All other schools of thought are based on a normative approach: democracy is taken as a social and cultural aim which has to be achieved in society as well as in the workplace. One major hypothesis in this concept postulates that workplace experiences mould human attitudes and behaviour in general. Accordingly, democracy in companies would be an important pre-condition for a democratic society.

Compared to the other approaches discussed so far, and contrary to expectations, the ID concept is least related to our own concept of direct participation. In the ID concept, categories like power, influence, autonomy, individual freedom, self-determination etc. are used and investigated only to determine the extent of democracy within a company in a descriptive way. Working conditions, work organisation or economic efficiency are merely treated as variables that enable or hinder industrial democracy. Although the ID debate is aware of other theoretical approaches and changing management styles which accommodate more participation in the workplace, it does not focus on them. It prefers to compare different types of legal and institutional solutions, such as workers' self-management, producer co-operatives, co-determination, works councils, collective bargaining or institutionalised rights of trade unions - concepts that are excluded from our research interest by way of definition. There is some research that provides additional indirect information on de-facto participation of employees (IDE 1981, 1993), thus giving some information on problems which are relevant to the EPOC project.

Human Resource Management: Motivation by Participation

Human Resource Management (HRM) covers the very wide field of theory and research on human motivation at work and how to stimulate it, both for the benefit of companies and employees. It investigates the relationship of work content and circumstances, work motivation, work satisfaction and work performance. Although this has been a topic since Taylor (1911), it gained considerable momentum in the 1930s, when the famous Hawthorne experiments (Roethlisberger and Dickson 1939) showed the considerable influence of social factors on individual and collective work performance. The *Human Relations School* which resulted from these experiments was then extended by additional theories about individual work motivation of which the various *motivation theories* of Maslow (1954), Argyris (1957), McGregor (1960), Likert (1961) and Herzberg (1966) became 'classical' approaches. Common to all of them is the idea of a basic human need for self-realisation in work on the basis of integrated tasks which permit the use of higher skills. Under the label of *corporate culture*[3], a further debate in the scope of Human

---

[3]   Cf. the international bestsellers by Deal and Kennedy (1982); Peters and Waterman (1982).

Resource Management originated in 1982: When employees identified with their companies and their goals, when they shared common values, symbols, and intra-company behaviour, they could be expected to fully engage themselves in their work. Intrinsic motivation and self-control to meet deadlines and production goals would replace external controls by superiors - a line of thinking which is prominent in the concept of direct participation as well.

It is important to note that the early motivation theories concentrated mainly on white-collar workers: their more diffuse job descriptions could not be controlled through Tayloristic or bureaucratic measures, and the increase of work performance needed more elaborate, motivational approaches. Blue-collar workers came into play in the 1970s, when it became apparent that through value change, through the average increase of qualifications, and through a tendency towards organisational decentralisation, intrinsic work motivation would play an increasingly larger role for blue-collar workers as well (Sisson 1994).

Organisational Research: Structure, Functionality and Development of Organisations

Organisation Research is somewhat related to Human Resource Management and general management topics. But its major interest centres around theory development, neglecting practical advice for managers. One prominent theoretical frame is the 'contingency approach' (Kubicek and Welter 1985) which stresses the variability and dependence of organisations on internal and external possibilities and constraints. In this context, participation - often operationalised in a number of hierarchical layers - is frequently investigated: does participation affect the efficiency of an organisation in a certain situation? Does it accelerate the process of decision making and is the outcome suitable to organisational needs? Is participation conducive to better conflict solution in an organisation?

Within recent years the concept of power and politics has been integrated into organisation Research. Following e.g. Crozier and Friedberg (1979), an organisation must be seen as a political arena where actors engage in 'micro-politics' to gain power and to influence decisions, where they form coalitions and struggle to defend their interests. This pertains to all actors, regardless of their position in the hierarchy or division of the organisation. In addressing these questions, inter alia, Organisation Research has somewhat 're-invented the human factor' (Türk 1989) and moved away from treating humans as rationally functioning elements.

A practical result of this human oriented approach towards the organisation is the Organisational Development approach (OD), which deals with problems of organisational change and the management of change (French and Bell 1977). The basic assumption of OD is that Organisational change cannot be achieved by formal actions and decisions. Change mainly results from the modified behaviour of members. Behaviour is modified by applying the concept of action research: with the help of external advisors, organisational problems are identified by organisational members, a common solution is sought and tested, and is continuously reshaped in case it proves ineffective. The core idea of OD is a double role for the members of an organisation: they are simultaneously both researchers ('What does not work in the organisation and should be changed?') and developers of the new concept ('What should the organisation look like?'). These processes are typically carried out by forming 'project groups' or 'task groups', which reveals striking parallels between Organisational Development and direct participation as we have defined it.

New Production Concepts: Direct Participation and Productivity

In the mid 80s several studies reported a "fundamental change regarding the use of labour" within companies (Kern and Schumann 1984). Work rather than technology was now regarded as the main factor in national and international competitiveness. Most important, organisation was no longer seen as a measure to arrange work around an existing technology, nor was work organisation only treated as a means for humanisation and motivation. It was now considered the major factor to enhance productivity and maintain competitiveness.

Discussion of this 'paradigm change' in Germany began with the publication of the aforementioned book by Kern and Schumann. This emphasised the role of human qualifications in the production process and generated the term 'Neue Produktionskonzepte' (New Production Concepts). Another important study at this time was the publication of 'Fabrik 2000' (Factory 2000) by Brödner (1985). The author not only stressed the outstanding role of human capabilities in work, but developed a concept of 'group technology', which presented a new view on the organisation of production processes and outlined organisational prerequisites for group work. A third influential study (Piore and Sabel 1984) demonstrated how changing markets demand increased flexibility of production processes and the need for many economic sectors to give up mass-production techniques in order to survive.

The MIT-study of Womack, Jones and Roos (1990) looked at different versions of New Production Concepts in the car industry: the authors compared Japanese automotive factories with European and US car companies and identified that the Japanese style of production organisation ('Toyotism') was much more efficient in that it achieved car production in half the time, half the space and with half of the costs. The authors attributed this efficiency lead not to the use of advanced technology but to the new forms of work organisation that pervade the whole firm. The public and scientific debate following this study can be taken as one origin of the EPOC project, and various (critical) arguments, hypotheses, questions and expectations deriving from the worldwide debate went into the conceptual approach of the EPOC project.

1.4   The Organisation of the Literature Study

A review of research on direct participation in Europe, Japan and the USA faces at least two obstacles and problems: The most obvious one is the language question. In case the authors of this report would master all languages involved, the problem would be mainly confined to time. As contributors to the EPOC conceptual discussion there was a shared understanding of the study's purpose and its conceptual and theoretical implications, of content problems to be aware of and of indicators to note. Yet, at the same time, such an author-centred approach would necessitate authors' intimate knowledge of research traditions and specific scientific approaches and debates in each of the countries concerned. As this intimate knowledge was lacking and, of course, the language problem remained a fact, we had to rely on foreign expertise.

Our problem solution centred around the following questions: how to find suitable foreign experts to inform us about research results in their countries? How to assure a common frame of reference for the task, which means (a) a shared understanding of our conceptual intentions and a common view of the salient features of the topic, (b) the selection of important studies in each of the countries, and (c) a unified structure of the separate research reviews to assure completeness and comparability of results. These problems were tried to solve as follows:

Selection of reviewers: The reviewer(s) for the different countries are academic experts in industrial relations and organisational sociology in their countries who, as university teachers and researchers, undertook the reviews themselves or engaged co-workers or graduate students to work under their supervision. Three research group members engaged themselves directly. The following experts contributed to the literature study:

Jörg Flecker and Brigitte Schramm, *Austria*; Michel Albertijn, *Belgium*; H. Hvenegaard and J. H. Pedersen, *Denmark*; Aarne Mattila, *Finland*; Robert Tchobanian, *France*; Dieter Fröhlich, Ulrich Pekruhl and Annette Schnabel, *Germany*; Maria Petmesidou, *Greece*; Linda Doyle, *Ireland*; Anna Lisa Tota, *Italy*; Koji Okubayashi, *Japan*; Jos Benders, *Netherlands*; Maria Louisa Cristóvam, *Portugal*; Andreu Lope Peña, Antonio Martín Artiles and Reyes Verella, *Spain*; Pia Juhlin and Åke Sandberg, *Sweden*; John Geary, *United Kingdom;* Judith Biewener, *USA*.

To assure a common understanding of the task and its implications, there were several meetings with the external experts in Germany in spring 1994. In all meetings, instructions followed an identical procedure: The concept paper of the EPOC study and an outline of the literature study, which both had been mailed in advance, were presented again, and additional details were given. All materials and problems were discussed.

As to the *selection of important studies in each country*, we had to rely on the expertise and the knowledge of the foreign contributors, in principle. From a *content point of view*, the selection and review of the studies were supposed to be grounded on the EPOC concept (Geary and Sisson 1994):

* All studies should deal with direct participation in the scope of our detailed definition, *regardless whether the term 'direct participation' was used or not*. Any popular labels were unimportant.

* The *actors* (management, workforce, unions, employee representative) should be specified, *and their motivation*, their positive interest or reluctance should be recorded.

* The *process of introducing direct participation* and problems arising in this process should be recorded.

* As to the *effects* of direct participation: What is the outcome of various types of direct participation? What are the economic effects? How are different actors affected? What does direct participation mean for working conditions? In which way are industrial relations affected?

* Particular attention should be given to *representative studies* investigating the spread of direct participation in the separate countries. In this context,

the reviewers were asked to focus on the *coverage in companies* as well: what percentage of employees in companies are affected by direct participation schemes?

Then, additional dimensions and/or limitations were outlined to either define or narrow the search process:

* There were *no limitations as to the different social science disciplines* the studies originated in, e.g. sociology, management science, etc.

* There were *no sectoral limitations*. It was suggested not to review research in the production sector only, but to consider research in the service sector and in private and public administration as well.

* There were no limitations as to the *research universe*: the research universe might be employees, managers, employee representatives, companies or others. There were no limitations as to company size.

* Only *empirical studies* should be analysed, not secondary analyses, studies on studies or theoretical texts.

* All *quantitative studies* should be reviewed as long as they were not of extremely poor methodological value.

* *Case studies* should be reviewed only if they conform to essential standards of social research. This was to avoid journalistic case descriptions and success stories.

* *'Grey literature'*, i.e. not officially published research, should be considered as long as it conformed to the above criteria.

* Further limitations were given as to the *relevant time span*: before 1980 only classical studies should be considered; between 1980 - 1985 emphasis is on quantitative, comparative and well-explicated case studies, while from 1985 on all studies conforming to the above criteria should be considered.

* Finally, *the number of reviews were limited for each country* to concentrate on important research and to assure manageability of information: about 20 reviews for the larger countries and about 10 reviews for the smaller countries.

To assure completeness and comparability of results in the single reviews, a common structure of the reviews was agreed upon, and the reviewers were asked to add an overview on country specifics in regard to research traditions and central topics, the possible influence of cultural peculiarities and industrial relation systems on the topic of direct participation.

1.5   The Potential and the Structure of the Report

The proceedings of the meetings with foreign experts, various bilateral discussions and the reviews submitted clearly testify that a common understanding of the problems and the task was achieved. Yet in spite of this fact, the material and the overall literature report based on this material suffers from various handicaps that must be kept in mind:

The information given for each country is far from complete, given the fact that there are different research universes (workforces, managers etc.), qualitative and quantitative studies, different sectors, and a multitude of topics covered by the label 'direct participation' (see the list of hypotheses in the EPOC concept paper; Geary and Sisson 1994:31-49), and a limited number of reviews. The above enumeration of schools of thought (with own research traditions) further adds to the abundance and complexity of material. Accordingly, the reviews can only inform us of important research results in each country, and we must be aware that our base material only covers a small segment of research.

Further, we must consider the enormous complexity of the topic. 'Direct participation' has been conceived of in a variety of ways by a great number of authors, working in different disciplines. Although we succeeded in ensuring a common frame of reference for the literature study, the report has some limitations. While each reviewer was to review the most important studies in each country, the requirement to confine this to at most 25 studies has meant that the review cannot claim to be totally comprehensive. Nonetheless, we are satisfied that this review captures the state of the current debate in each of the countries reviewed and offers both the new and informed reader a detailed and informative account of the importance of direct participation.

The report is organised around a discussion of the four main types of direct participation. Each type of direct participation is explored, followed by an analysis of the background factors leading to its introduction and problems associated with its implementation. In general, the data are analysed cross-nationally, with national references used only when advisable or necessary. An overview of direct participation measures in each country is provided at the end of the report. Direct participation's effects on the role of middle management and on industrial relations issues are treated in separate chapters.

Finally, the question arises as to what can be achieved from this literature report. Given the many limitations cited above, it can hardly be considered to be a problem-solving report. For the most part, this report can be conceived as a problem-raising study to enlarge our understanding of problems and issues. Its problem-raising capability should also become apparent by pointing to gaps in international research and, thereby inform our own research in the scope of the EPOC project.

In the following section, we discuss the four main types of direct participation and point to the historical contexts, their present functioning and problems arising therein. Chapter 2 covers unobtrusive, 'low-impact' forms of individual direct participation. Suggestion schemes, workforce surveys and employee appraisal and development schemes are such 'soft' forms where individuals are consulted, with management retaining the right to act. At the individual level, the topic of job enrichment as a form of delegative participation is addressed. We discuss the knowledge gained from its first phase of application in the Quality of Working Life phase, as well as the experience and problems of job enrichment in its second phase of application (i.e.: with the introduction of New Information Technology).

Quality circles were the first Japanese managerial concept widely applied in Europe and the US. In chapter 3 we analyse their popularity, their functioning in companies, their strongholds and pitfalls, and the reasons for their demise in the late 1980s. 'Group work' receives much attention in chapter 4. Self-directed working groups are considered to have the highest impact on organisational change, and are the most popular form of direct participation. We compare European and Japanese group work solutions, analyse what intermediary types of group work are applied in European and American business life, and consider their merits and demerits, both from a management and workforce point of view.

As direct participation has the capacity to change organisations and to eliminate some levels of organisational hierarchies, direct supervisors and middle managers can be severely affected. Chapter 5 discusses problems of middle management and ways of dealing with these issues. Chapter 6 takes up the relationship between direct and indirect representative participation. Task participation in terms of increased employee involvement in daily work and self-steering of employees, either as individuals or in groups, might create new needs for the protection of workforce interests. But it also might conflict with established structures of workforce representation through unions and employee representatives. We analyse emerging work hazards and union responses to them. We investigate the impact that direct participation might have on the principle of representative participation.

Finally, in chapter 7 we present survey results on direct participation for each of the 16 countries that contributed information. The data are meant to give an impression of how direct participation is discussed and how widespread certain applications are in the countries. We end the chapter with some European comparative data that permit some 'benchmarking' with 'low-impact' measures of direct participation in the European Union.

2   Individual Participation

Our analytical scheme to differentiate types of direct participation (cf. table 1) holds two forms of individual participation: (1) schemes to encourage individual workers to make their opinions known, but which leave management the right to decide and react, and (2) schemes that increase the rights and responsibilities of individual employees carrying out their daily work. The first type of individual consultative participation has received little attention in present political and scientific debates and will be referred to very briefly here. More emphasis is put on the delegative type of individual participation: under the label of 'job enrichment' it has been widely discussed in the 1970's, and it was 're-discovered' in the 1980's when New Information Technology (NIT) based on micro-electronics created considerable problems in firms applying it.

2.1   Upward Communication as Consultative Participation

'Direct participation' is about new organisational climates, about the re-discovery of the human factor and 'open management styles'. More than ever, employee work motivation and commitment to the firm's goals are regarded as main assets of the 'transformed' organisation. To win employees as active participants of organisational life needs a climate of trust, and increased communication is a minimum requirement.

'Communication' is a two-way process by definition; it involves information exchange, where all actors have the chance to submit information, to voice own ideas and to receive feedback. In organisation literature, the concept is often treated under the headings of downward and upward communication: the downward approach basically means information giving through newsletters, bulletins etc. On a group level we find measures such a team briefing or 'cascading information down the line'. The most frequently named types of upward communication are suggestion schemes, workforce attitude surveys and employee appraisal and development schemes, with quality circles as a suggestion mechanism on the group level.

In the scope of our own concept of direct participation which focuses on transformed organisations, schemes that rely on information only are excluded by definition because their intentions are too 'conservative' to fit the present debate about direct participation. Bottom-up communication fits our concept much better, but it is problematic if employees receive no feedback and their voice remains unheard.

When we take up suggestion schemes, workforce surveys and methods of employee appraisal and development as types of consultative task participation, we cannot present substantial recent information about these types, for various reasons: Our own conceptual thinking and our instructions to the foreign experts did not explicitly highlight these schemes as separate forms of individual consultative participation. But this omission seems to reflect a general trend: the present international debate about direct participation and organisational change rarely mentions these themes. Cotton, in his comprehensive overview of employee involvement research in the USA (1993-US), does not cover the topic at all. Hyman and Mason (1995-UK) who systematically investigate research on employee involvement and participation in the UK and in the USA, devote substantial space on the themes without reviewing much recent research. Private communication confirmed that systematic evidence is missing, in spite of the fact that all three communication schemes have long been practised and researched. The problems and possible explanations for their neglect in the recent participation debate might best be exemplified by a brief examination of each type.

Suggestion Schemes

Suggestion schemes are time-honoured ways for management to learn from interested employees how work processes and technology can be improved. In the most highly industrialised countries, suggestion schemes date back to the last century, with national associations spreading the idea and administering their application. In Germany, their details are highly regulated both by legislation and by company agreements, with works councils controlling their proper functioning. Suggestion schemes are comparatively widespread in Europe: The Price-Waterhouse/Cranfield study (1993-UK) undertook a comparative study of suggestion schemes in Europe and found that they operate in an average of 28% of all companies in ten European countries (cf. chapter 7). They are particularly popular in Northern European states, but are less so in the Mediterranean countries. In the UK, Hyman and Mason (1995-UK) report that due to a revival of the concept, the UK Association of Suggestion Schemes (UKASS) recently broke lose from a larger UK association and that between 1984 and 1990, the proportion of companies applying these schemes rose slightly from 25 to 28%. The authors speak of a "re-emergence of this type of involvement method" in the UK (ibid.:83).

Is such a positive assessment of suggestion schemes justified, and if so, why then did it attract so little attention in the 'direct participation' debate? One reason for the 'revival' can be seen in the Japanese interpretation of organisation: When European and American observers became interested in the 'secrets' of Japanese economic success, they were surprised by the large number of suggestions that Japanese employees working in teams put forward. One might say that the *kaizen* principle of 'continuous improvement' and the quality circles (cf. chapter 3) represent the institutionalisation of employee suggestions. In *kaizen*, the suggestion mechanism is 'built' into employees' jobs.

It seems to be this awareness of Japanese organisational strategies that has altered European and American attitudes towards employee suggestions. Traditionally, companies regarded suggestion schemes primarily as a cost-saving mechanism. Employee engagement in suggestions was seen as being motivated mainly by the anticipation of financial gain, a motive that was not highly rated in theories of work motivation. Herzberg's two-factor theory (cf. section 2.2) in particular regarded financial rewards as just a work hygiene' trait, something secondary that helped to prevent work dissatisfaction, but which failed to motivate employees to commit themselves to their work and to their organisation. Western observers then noticed that the Japanese strategy did not combine employee suggestion schemes with financial incentives.

If the 'revival of suggestion schemes' really originates from Western interpretation of Japanese organisational strategies, a problem appears: if suggestions have the potential for employee task involvement and if the idea is built into future jobs via the *kaizen* principle, the revitalisation of traditional suggestion schemes would be inadequate. It would miss the point by not being integrated into the every-day work role. Such a revitalisation would be a misunderstanding of Japanese principles, as was the case with the Western conception of quality circles (cf. chapter 3).

Workforce Attitude Surveys

For the same reasons as stated above, we can present only little information on workforce surveys as a means of individual consultative participation. These surveys are popular in European organisations. According to the Price-Waterhouse Cranfield Project (1993-UK), 24% of all companies in ten European states carry them out once in a while or regularly, while the Nordic countries use them more frequently (cf. chapter 7). Workforce surveys were a popular Human Resource Management concept in the 'company culture movement', one of the management fads of the 1980s, which aimed to inform management and to stimulate intra-company communication and participation.

The value of attitude surveys as a type of employee participation cannot easily be determined. Hyman and Mason (1995-UK:82-83) point to two key principles that such surveys must adopt in order to be meaningful. Firstly, surveys must not be designed to cover peripheral topics and to elicit answers that management wants to hear. Management must be ready for critical answers and assessments on a broad range of company problems and policies. Secondly, there has to be feedback on survey results. Unless such feedback is given employees will eventually lose interest in surveys as a meaningless activity which ends up in the company files. In regard to the functions of surveys, the authors point to a recent trend in the 'open management' context to use attitude surveys as a method for employee appraisal of management.

A positive example of the use of attitude surveys as a means of upward communication which comprises serious information gathering, feedback and manager appraisal is that used by the German Bertelsmann Corporation (Bundesmann-Jansen and Pekruhl 1992-D): among other 'company culture' schemes, this large media firm conducts four-yearly surveys with all employees. Topics covered include: employees' assessment of the company's image, the work situation and the conduct of their superiors. In addition, employees are encouraged to voice suggestions and complaints. The survey results are always analysed, published and discussed at firm level as well as at department level. Apart from stimulating communication, these surveys have two distinct aims: to alter workplaces and work organisation when serious criticism arises, and to control middle management. To give an example from this company, one survey revealed a clear rejection of newly installed open-plan offices. Top-management reacted to this criticism and had the offices rebuilt immediately, spending several million German Marks. A further example relates to the role of middle management. At Bertelsmann, this management group is considered a serious bottleneck for a company culture based on open communication and mutual trust. The company's codified basic operating principles, the 'Ten Commandments', include one paragraph according to which all superiors must explain and justify their decisions to their subordinates. In so-called 'January talks', all superiors must arrange discussions that permit employees' assessment of superiors' management behaviour. The regularity of these discussions is tightly controlled by top-management, and workforce assessment of their immediate superiors is controlled by regular surveys (for a similar example cf. Baisier and Albertijn 1992-B).

Employee Appraisal and Development

Employee appraisal and development schemes can be seen as another type of direct, consultative participation that seems to attract increasing attention in organisational change strategies. Traditionally, they were confined to managerial grades and "focused largely on subjective (and often vague) assessments of past performance or, even more subjectively, on the extent to which staff possessed desirable qualities" (Hyman and Mason 1995-UK:84). The rediscovery of appraisal and development schemes is said to have gained more attention in Japan and in the USA than in Europe so far. It is accompanied by an application of the schemes towards all sections of a company's workforce, to white and blue collar workers alike. Such an encompassing approach underlines the strategy to view employees as a strategic resource in the organisation.

In theory, immediate managers or supervisors and employees should have open discussions on the employee's past performance, on his/her strengths and weaknesses, on employee's future career goals and on whether these goals have been achieved. While being unable to go into detail, we will at least point out to some problematic aspects which arise in practice as discussed by Hyman and Mason. (1) According to the authors, such schemes can only function properly when they are closely linked with policies and practices in other areas such as manpower planning, training and pay. They need to be sufficiently resourced to enable an employee to attain his/her goals and to become confident, both in himself/herself and in the appraisal procedure. (2) In order for an employee to talk about his/her weaknesses, successes and failures, a considerable climate of trust and openness must exist. Once appraisals are coupled with promotion chances and performance-related pay, such schemes are in danger of becoming distorted and of degenerating into traditional exercises of employee self-presentation. Finally, Hyman and Mason (1995-UK:87-88) highlight basic problems in applying such schemes: They need 'trained' supervisors and employees as well as organisational techniques that are sophisticated and simple to administer simultaneously. Keeping in mind that such schemes should spread across the whole organisation and affect both white and blue collar workers in the 'trust organisation', the problems of introducing and operating company-wide appraisal systems become obvious.

All in all, suggestion schemes, attitude surveys and appraisal schemes have met with rather critical and very ambivalent comments by social science commentators. Hyman and Mason (1995-UK) treat them as 'soft' types of workforce involvement, with low impact on employee performance. They can quickly lose their charm and may result in cynical employee attitudes if they are not organised as feedback processes, and function as a 'one-way road' for simple information gathering by management without any feedback mechanisms. Similarly, Applebaum and Batt (1994-US:75) criticise such consultative measures as being "designed to elicit employees' ideas while retaining control over decision making".

2.2 Job Enrichment as Delegative Participation - the Older Approach

Whereas one can debate the merits of the consultative type of individual participation as it does not increase the decision-making power of employees, job enrichment clearly has the potential of increased autonomy, responsibility and work discretion. In what follows, we use the term 'job enrichment' somewhat imprecisely as a general term to cover three subdimensions which are kept apart in theory: (1) *job rotation*: rotation among equal skill requirements, (2) *job enlargement*: carrying out tasks of different skill requirements at the same level of hierarchy, (3) *job enrichment*: carrying out tasks of different skill requirements at different levels of hierarchy. As can easily be seen, job rotation ranks lowest among the three measures as it only adds tasks of the same kind. Job enlargement already entails a skill increase, and job enrichment means task extension on both the horizontal and the vertical dimension of rights and responsibilities. Enrichment somewhat touches upon the organisational power structure by blurring traditional divisions of planning, commanding and executing in the workplace. Of all three measures, job enrichment is clearly the most encompassing and a truly participant management strategy. In the following paragraphs, we discuss how the concept originated, why management became interested and then subsequently lost interest in job enrichment, and how the concept then reappeared without the actual label of 'job enrichment' being used. We then explore its merits for both management and the workforce.

Job enrichment is basically an older social science 'invention', particularly found in Human Resource Management. Work motivation became a topic of theory and research to "increase the efficiency of the individual at the job". Motivation was seen as a problem in the "continuing dread of the mechanisation of people as well as of jobs". Improving 'job attitudes' was meant to increase productivity, decrease labour turnover and absenteeism, and to ease working relations. "To the individual, an understanding of the forces that lead to improved morale would bring greater happiness and greater self-realisation [at work]"(all quotations from Herzberg, Mausner and Snyderman 1959:IX).

Two theoretical models of job enrichment stand out as the most popular, and they are connected with the names of Herzberg, Hackman and Oldham. The older approach, Herzberg's motivation-hygiene theory, also called *'two factor theory'* (cf. also Herzberg 1966), maintains that job attributes causing work satisfaction are inherently different from attributes which cause dissatisfaction. Motivating job aspects centre around achievement, responsibility, recognition and the work itself, whereas job attributes such as working conditions, pay, supervision, interpersonal relations and company policy are secondary, 'hygiene' aspects of the job. The latter can only decrease work dissatisfaction, but do not lead to satisfaction and a high work motivation. These two sets of job attributes are not extremes on one continuum, but denote separate dimensions. They are also called *intrinsic* and *extrinsic motivators*.

Equally well known and perhaps the most applied theory of job enrichment is the *'job characteristics model'* by Hackman and Oldham (1976, 1980). According to this approach, five core job dimensions lead to critical psychological states which, in turn, lead to personal and work outcomes. The core dimensions are skill variety, task identity (the degree to which the job requires completion of a 'whole' and identifiable piece of work), and task significance (the impact of the job on the lives and the work on others). These three core attributes are said to lead to 'experienced meaningfulness of work'. 'Autonomy' in work is supposed to foster a sense of responsibility towards the outcome of work, whereas the fifth core attribute, job feedback, provides the individual with clear information about work performance which leads to 'knowledge of results'. All three effects: experienced meaningfulness of results, responsibility and knowledge, are then expected to generate internal motivation, work effectiveness, job satisfaction and satisfaction with personal growth in work. Both the core dimensions and the final outcome are moderated by personal characteristics like 'growth need strength' (a personality trait to continually improve oneself), by personal knowledge and skills, as well as by contextual factors.

We do not attempt to discuss the enormous research literature that has developed around both theoretical concepts.[4] The bulk of this tends to be rather academic oriented, and shows that Herzberg's two-factor model is not supported on theoretical grounds and through research. For similar reasons, the job characteristics approach rests on shaky foundations as well. However, it is advisable to present the basics of both approaches. They developed some conceptual ideas that have become commonplace in all analyses of direct participation (like the devaluation of extrinsic, hygiene work variables such as pay and remuneration). Further, by pointing out the mediating variables, Hackman and Oldham remind us of additional influences on work attitudes and work performance that are often overlooked in research. Both aspects are important in qualifying existing research results on direct participation in general, and group work approaches in particular.

---

[4]   For an overview in the scope of direct participation issues cf. Cotton 1993-US:141-172.

'Job enrichment' left academia and became applied to organisational life in the Quality of Working Life (QWL) movement: The early 1970s marked a period of workforce unrestrained resistance to Taylorist-Fordist working conditions. Most notable were the overt protests, strikes and the vandalism of General Motors workers against products and tools in the GM-Lordstown plant in Ohio (Work in America 1973-US:19) and a series of strikes particularly in Italy and France against meaningless mass-production jobs. In other countries, indirect workforce protests were expressed through high rates of absenteeism, labour turnover or simply through a refusal to enter into dull mass-production jobs at all. A case in point is the Swedish car producers who, in a period of an overheated labour market were unable to recruit sufficient manpower and who faced extremely high rates of absenteeism and turnover.

Management and Job Enrichment in the QWL Phase

Management reacted to these challenges in various ways: it tried to re-design work through job enrichment or semi-autonomous group work; it automated production processes to reduce health and safety hazards of mass-production, and it also pursued some technological solutions to gain independence from an unwilling labour force. It is safe to say that management motivation in the QWL phase was overwhelmingly reactive, trying to pacify an unsatisfied labour force, keeping other (technological) options in mind. In his study of 'adaptive organisational changes' in 14 Italian companies, Butera (1988-I), for instance, found many instances of job rotation, enlargement and enrichment schemes, all dating from the early 1970s when management tried to comply with workforce resistance.

Such *reactive management motivation* when introducing measures of direct participation can still be found: Berggren (1992-S), who studied 20 Swedish car establishments over ten years, links management's offer of better working conditions through work re-design in the mid-1980s to the problem of recruiting employees to the automobile industry. In particular, young people had refused to work here because of strenuous and boring jobs. In another Swedish case, Steen (1991-S) explains management's interest in reorganising work procedures at ABB as an attempt to reduce very high rates of absenteeism and labour turnover in certain production departments. Banke (1991a/b-DK) reports the same for the Danish textile industry. He points to the declining birth rate and to the relatively greater appeal that the socially reputable white collar work holds for younger people compared to blue collar jobs which are often associated with dirty and unqualified work.[5] In Italy, too, we find this reactive management strategy in ITATEL, a large manufacturer in the telecommunication sector (Regini and Sabel 1989-I). In the early 1980s the company faced the problem of high absenteeism rates and numerous strikes. Internal research revealed that these difficult conditions resulted from work monotony, strain caused by the need for consistent attention and low work discretion through standardised tasks. Kauppinen and Alasoini (1985-FIN) link direct participation moves with the extreme strike activities of the Finnish labour force in the mid-1980s.

As in most other studies on direct participation, we have almost no information on how work re-design was introduced, regarding the *process of introduction*. As a concept intended to enhance the individual work role it is related to skill increase, as more skills are applied and needed in job rotation, enlargement and enrichment. *Vocational training* is the topic here. Teikari and Väyrynen (1992-FIN) give an example of the introduction process in a Finnish insurance company: Management wanted to allocate greater rights and responsibilities to all front-line clerical workers dealing with customers. The necessary changes entailed a new definition of the individual's range of power and responsibilities, new work premises, and training in new skills. These changes were jointly worked out in the planning phase, and this early employee involvement provided opportunities for a gradual adaptation of the new work model into the operating phase. As a result, office productivity improved markedly through shortened work chains and broadened skills. The total time required for customer service was shortened, turnaround time for compensation applications decreased, and all productivity parameters improved. Follow-up measures demonstrated that all employees involved totally favoured the new systems.

A very frequent handicap of studies analysing work re-design is that *its individual forms*, like job enrichment, *are not strictly kept apart* from group solutions. This makes the little information that exists on *effects difficult to assess*. Such is the case of ITATEL (Regini and Sabel 1989-I), where both job enrichment measures and semi-autonomous work groups were introduced successfully, i.e. work re-design decreased absenteeism and strike activities. Yet, this result does not allow the success to be attributed to one of the two measures of direct participation.

---

[5]   The attractiveness of white-collar work might endanger the future manning of new production systems which rely on the skills and qualifications of the workforce: industry will no longer need *any* workforce, but a *highly skilled* workforce, and the problem arises how to make such workplaces attractive when employement preferences tend towards white-collar work.

To somewhat repair this lack of information from a management point of view, we revert to the extensive overview of mainly US and British research on job enrichment carried out by Cotton (1993-US:141-172). On the basis of several hundred studies, the author tried to list the effects of job enrichment. The *results on workers' performance and productivity are confusing and often contradictory*. According to Cotton, it is rather safe to say that job enrichment somewhat reduces absenteeism and labour turnover, but there are no clear-cut results on job performance: sometimes job enrichment leads to higher worker performance in terms of productivity, quality and customer service, sometimes no effects were found, and there are instances with negative effects. Even where there are positive performance outcomes, Cotton refers to several authors who warn against interpreting such results in a stringent cause-effect relationship, to simply explain performance increases as a result of more stimulating complex work. "We have no definite idea why enriched jobs (sometimes) improve performance. Is it because the employees are more motivated and work harder or because they can change the job and work more efficiently?" (ibid.:171).

Employees and Job Enrichment

From a management perspective, research on job enrichment is scarce and results are inconclusive. Relative to the concentration of theory on employee motivation, *information on workforce reactions to job enrichment is broader*. We have ample research evidence on the widespread desire for autonomy and responsibility in the workplace. In Austria, a representative survey which has been repeated twice, shows the growing interest of the Austrian workforce for increased autonomy in work (Grausgruber-Berner and Grausgruber 1990-A). Swedish (Leion 1992-S) and Danish (Nord-Larsen et al. 1992-DK) surveys have supported this finding. In 1992, the Danish social partners and (later) the Danish government came to an agreement to reduce by half jobs with little self-determination and influence before the year 2000 (Hvenegaard and Haasing Pedersen 1994). The extensive comparative research carried out by Inglehart (1989-US:177-180) on nine EU countries and the USA testifies to this very strong need for more participation in task related matters. Thus, any direct participation offers to increase work autonomy are likely to be positively accepted by the majority of the workforces. (It should be noted at this point that these wishes referred to *individual* work autonomy only. This might have repercussions for group type offers of direct participation; cf. chapter 4).

According to the more academic oriented studies trying to test the 'job characteristics' model in particular, work re-design has its *main effects on job satisfaction.* Cotton (1993-US:163), in his review of research, concludes that "job enrichment efforts [and] job characteristics typically are related to intrinsic job satisfaction or satisfaction with the job itself". But the situation is more complicated and tends to be *confounded by moderator variables* such as personal growth need strength (individual's need to achieve something and to improve him/herself), by contextual factors and by individual knowledge and skills. According to theory and somewhat to common sense, not all employees want enriched, challenging and responsible jobs. Some people prefer routine jobs without accountability. Using the concept of *growth need strength* as a moderator variable, psychologically oriented research qualified this generally positive relationship between job characteristics and job satisfaction, showing that high need strength increases satisfaction with enriched jobs, and it also tends to improve work performance (Cotton 1993-US:159).

Job enrichment does not occur in an organisational vacuum. A relative *contextual factor* is company policy and the active role of management in measures like job enrichment. For instance, we find unskilled labour typically involved in job rotation, the most simplistic type of work re-design, whereas skilled workers experience the more demanding job enlargement and job enrichment schemes. A Danish example shows that management made this distinction a conscious company policy (Jørgensen et al. 1992-DK). This indicates that the clustering of certain work re-design measures on particular workforce groups holds elements of outside influence, and interpreting any outcome of measures on the workforce has to keep external factors in mind. In addition, interpretation of results faces further problems: bringing *knowledge and skills* as another moderator variable into play, there is strong evidence to suggest that employees themselves are very active in enhancing their work discretion and that the higher-skilled are more successful than the low-skilled workforce. Berggren (1992-S:225), in his study on the Swedish car industry, found "a remarkably consistent correlation between actual influence and desired influence", which describes the action potential of skilled employees. Nielsen et al. (1991-DK:28) support these results with their findings from a Danish example of organisational change: where self-determination in work was already greatest, "the greatest change has taken place, whilst at other places, where self-determination was rather limited, changes have been significantly more modest". The authors call this the 'Matthew-effect': "Unto every one that hath shall be given ...; but from him that hath not shall be taken away that which he hath." Based on a Quality of Employment survey and other data, Mortimer and Lorence (1989-US:259) found that "persons who are more involved in their jobs would want to take on responsibility and would mould their jobs in such a way that greater discretion is allowed". Similar Thomas (1989-US:129): "The greater the discretion, the more likely that workers would actively seek to create the means to desired goals" (cf. also Leion 1992-S).

These examples suggest that higher work discretion tends to be concentrated in those sections of the workforce that were already in a favourable situation, either through management intervention or through *processes of 'self-selection'* by active intra-company 'lobbying' and moulding of one's own situation. Needless to say that such successful employees generally express high work satisfaction. But if the self-selection hypothesis holds and the 'Matthew-Effect' is reality, *any simple theories about work satisfaction resulting from enlarged tasks must be viewed with caution.* It could well be that already 'satisfied' employees just added to their well-being and safeguarded their interests.

These interests are not as clear-cut as theory suggests. The dominant motivational theories point to the 'intrinsic' features of a job, to work autonomy, challenge, responsibility and others as being the most important for employees and in accounting for job satisfaction. *'Extrinsic' job features*, like income, working time, interpersonal relations with superiors and colleagues and company policy, do not add to job satisfaction, according to these theories. The narrow academic debate disregarded these topics to a large degree. In particular, the question of whether enriched jobs with higher responsibility should be more highly paid or whether this type of work is valued for its intrinsic benefits hardly was the subject of any attention: "Unfortunately, there is little research on this issue, only anecdotes" (Cotton 1993-US:169).

In line with these research gaps, only two of our own sources touch upon the role of extrinsic rewards, in this case pay, job security and intra-organisational status and power. Fenwick and Olson (1986-US) investigate the topic: who wants participation and why? In a Quality of Employment survey, 1,114 wage and salaried employees were interviewed about their wish for workplace participation. The analysis centred on their present job characteristics (meaningfulness, autonomy, extrinsic rewards) and their personal characteristics (age, gender etc.). It transpired that only workers' extrinsic evaluations affected their attitudes toward participation: support for the idea of participation increased when employees saw benefits in terms of improved pay and greater job security. Accordingly, support for participation is highly instrumental: "workers who negatively evaluate their extrinsic rewards want participation as a way of increasing these rewards" (idib.:513). The study suggests that management's efforts to satisfy intrinsic needs and personal efficacy have limited appeal for workers. The 'materialistic' concerns of workers about pay, job security and fringe benefits seem to be a greater motivator towards support for participation than dissatisfaction with intrinsic conditions of work. A study of organisational change in a small Portuguese firm with mainly academic personnel (Kovacs 1990-P) revealed that the level of responsibility in work involved and a good social climate induced employees to accept organisational change. The flexible organisation that resulted from the change activities was however heavily criticised for its lack of clearly defined responsibilities and the dilution of personal power, thus indicating that status and influence are an important additional dimension of work satisfaction.

Summary

Despite extensive research, our knowledge of the consequences of job enrichment as a type of individual delegative participation is rather disappointing. As a micro-approach that is geared to individual work places, its application does not really alter the organisation of work a great deal. This might explain why it is attractive for management which see a need for change, but hesitate to venture into radical solutions. We can only speculate about management's reserved attitude towards job enrichment measures: it might be that job enrichment as a distinct concept is not *en vogue* at present. Further, it might be that job enrichment is too closely associated with the Quality of Working Life movement, where management participated primarily in an attempt to cope with workforce resistance, whereas the present motivation for engaging in direct participation to be more pro-active, trying to solve problems of organisational flexibility and quality problems. Such pro-activity is popularly associated today with group-type approaches, such as quality circles and various other forms of group work. Finally, former experience with job enrichment might not have been convincing in regard to its effects.

Looking at the results of social science research on job enrichment, such management caution may be justified. Job enrichment is the best researched type of direct participation, based on elaborate theories. Yet, its practical, useful results are very disappointing. Our only positive knowledge is that job enrichment increases job satisfaction on average which, in turn, decreases absenteeism and labour turnover. This need not, however, result in better work performance.

Focusing on the workforce, we have learned that there are certain groups of employees, the higher skilled, who are drawn by management into the more elaborate schemes of work re-design (like job enrichment), whereas the lower skilled seem to be 'candidates' for job rotation schemes. This might point to the importance of employee *ability* for certain types of direct participation.

More research is needed on this topic. Other aspects which need to be examined are the *training costs* associated with job enrichment, the expectation of pay rises, the *introduction processes* of job enrichment, and the possible *role change of supervisors*. Further, any statement about the effects of job enrichment measures has to keep in mind the *fact of self-selection processes*: there are certain groups of employees who try to enrich their own work and succeed in occupying tasks with a high discretionary work content. This fact makes it difficult to make cause-effect statements on the benefits of job enrichment.

2.3   Job Enrichment and New Information Technology

Although job enrichment, as a concept, was not popular in the 1980s, it was applied to cope with the problems associated with the introduction of New Information Technology (NIT), *without the actors being aware of it*. As already mentioned, one of management's reactions to workforce unrest and to increasing labour costs in the 1970s was an intensified search for automated, technological solutions of production processes. The aim was not only to increase productivity but also to enhance planning flexibility and predictability. Such belief in automation was widespread throughout the 1980s. For a short while this view was even strengthened by the prospects that micro-electronics based NIT seemed to offer: the computer integrated, fully automated factory, popularly known as CIM (Computer Integrated Manufacturing). For some, it was regarded as *the* answer. Yet, within a few years filled with frustrating experience, this concentration on purely technological solutions was discarded and the value of human skills and a flexible organisation was (re-)discovered. Our international research evidence testifies to this. To outline the general problem we not only cite research on individual participation but include group schemes as well.

Bonazzi (1993-I) reports that in the Italian FIAT plants in the early 1980s, automation of the CIM type was regarded as the best solution to increase the efficiency of production processes. In the mid-80's, the attempts to establish a largely unmanned factory had failed completely: instead of the expected 2,700 engines per day, the plant produced less than 2,000 units. The problem was identified as a mismatch between new technology and old forms of work organisation. This insight led to a reversal of organisational policies that relied on the engagement of skilled workers through various forms of what we call 'direct participation'. Experiments with direct participation measures led to very promising results, and Fiat's managing director declared the new concepts of work organisation not only to be the solution for the company's technological problems, but a 'strategic choice' for the further development of the entire company. For the Swedish ABB company, Steen (1991-S) gives a similar example: in the mid-80's the firm installed robots to increase, *inter alia*, flexibility of production. Management soon found out that flexibility had not increased, however. This failure revealed the importance of new organisational structures, based on a skilled and motivated workforce to make new technology function. Further evidence that NIT led to the application of direct participation supports this conclusion (Lope Peña 1993-E, and Balog 1991-A).

Banke (1991a-DK:10) points to the particular problems of small enterprises running high risks when investing in costly automated and specialised machinery, "as this means that the production of this type of enterprise becomes more capital-intensive and inflexible. It is very likely that such enterprises would benefit from procuring equipment which increases the possibility of utilising the qualification of the workforce". The author suggests the integration and development of workforce qualifications. The enterprise would benefit from increased flexibility and employees would get more varied and involving jobs.

NIT is extremely flexible; it permits a variety of different applications and has the potential to affect many, hitherto separated functions in the firm. At the same time, this flexibility and its potential for cross-functional application is the very problem. There are no ready blue-prints for technology application, and its cross-functional effects might endanger the traditional work organisation. Both production processes and work organisation have to be reconsidered, and new solutions have to be found out in trial-and-error processes. In such situations of uncertainty, management has to rely on the expertise, co-operation and active engagement of the workforce affected. It has to grant employees the chance to apply their own judgement, something that 'job enrichment' is all about. Applying NIT, management depends on a committed workforce and has to give up control to a certain degree. Such employee participation assumes the character of a bottom-up approach, based on a high-trust intra-company climate. This is one of the messages of New Production Concepts (Kern and Schumann 1984-D) and of Flexible Specialisation (Piore and Sabel 1984-US).

Wheras in Europe NIT introduction is just *one* explanation for the spread of direct participation, the Japanese debate seems to explain the need for direct participation almost exclusively by the characteristics of NIT, micro-electronics in particular: For the Current Information Research Committee (1987-JP) it is 'quite natural' that New Information Technology causes higher workforce participation as the design and operation of new technology is only feasible when taking the experience of rank-and-file workers into account.

Kawakita's (1985-JP) research found that micro-electronics was the driving force behind workers' increased chances for participation in decision-making (similarly Takaki, Kondo and Fujii 1987-JP, Shimada 1990-JP). This new 'technological determinism' is emphasised in Okubayashi's (1988-JP) work, which points out that micro-electronics is the prerequisite for departing from mass-production systems and to run flexible small-batch production. In this process, the traditional one-man-one-job work organisation has to be changed to a group work system. The designers of new work systems are 'forced' by micro-electronics to a new 'organic' work organisation that operates on the principle 'one-task-one-team'. Other Japanese authors argue along the same lines (Ito 1988-JP, Ko 1989-JP, Shi 1991-JP, Okubayashi et al. 1994-JP).

The authors of the Japanese Current Information Research Committee Report (1987-JP) indicate an additional motive for actively involving employees in the design phase of new technology's application. The early involvement of the workforce in introducing new technology has been a debated topic in Europe as well. Such early participation was seen to be essential for two different motives: first, there is the tactical motive to forestall workforce resistance to technical change and second, the need felt to involve employees from the very beginning to enable the introduction of new technology from a practical point of view.

The 'tactical' motive is mentioned by Clausen and Lorentzen (1986-DK:24-25) when they refer to Danish companies and write: "when management not only carry out the necessary alterations to production, but in fact want to involve employees, this can be due to the following reasons: it may be that they want to break down 'resistance to change'; a need to build up employees' motivation and engagement". Yet, it seems that workforce resistance did not play a prominent role in recent technology introduction. This follows from the comprehensive British survey by Daniels (1987-UK) according to which technical change is overwhelmingly welcomed by the workforce.

The second motive, according to which management needs employee participation in the implementation phase to be able to cope with the changes new technology entails, is self explanatory. Yet, we have no data on how intensively employees participated and contributed to the implementation phase of technology introduction. Given the new management dependence on employees' skills and commitment, such early involvement should be widespread, and indirect evidence testifies to this: in Belgium (Baisier and Albertijn 1992-B), the Dutch and Flemish institution of work consultation (werk overleg), a quality circle type of group participation, was revitalised with particular regard to the requirements of NIT to have multi-skilled workers who are able to adapt to different production processes quickly. At case study level, we know of an Austrian industrial firm that involved its employees in the service departments in technology planning and implementation to adapt this technology to the companies' needs (Volst and Wagner 1990-A).

The process of enabling employees to cope with the intricacies of NIT involves skill enhancement, which necessitates additional *vocational training*. Whereas research on job enrichment in the older QWL tradition rarely focused on training, new skills and vocational training became a necessity when NIT was introduced. The European survey on New Technology and Participation carried out by the European Foundation (cf. Fröhlich, Gill, and Krieger 1993; Gill et al. 1993) shows that management attached great importance to this topic (unpublished figures):

Table 2: The Importance of Skills and Training for Implementing and Operating New Information Technology According to European Managers

	'great importance':	
	acquiring new skills*	training**
average of all EC Managers	55%	55%
electrical engineering	60%	53%
mechanical engineering	56%	58%
food retailing	57%	58%
banking and insurance	45%	53%

*   Answers from 2,878 managers in Denmark, France, Germany, Italy and United Kingdom.
** Answers from 3.870 managers in all 12 EC countries.

Source: European Foundation for the Improvement of Living and Working Conditions, Dublin: Survey on New Information Technology.

Table 2 shows that these skill and training needs were considered very urgent not only in the production sector but in the private service as well. We have indications to assume that training is likely not to be confined to the higher skilled groups only. Bottrup and Clematide (1990-DK:13) give an example of how even unskilled workers were trained for using greater discretion to use technology in an optimal way. Employees underwent training courses to cope with machine standstill and to improve the performance of the technical equipment: "the operators, through participation, must have the ability and the courage to undertake more and different tasks than previously - after the necessary supplementary training in the enterprise. To a large extent, the work remains machine-controlled. In many cases the operator cannot leave the machine whilst it is running. But now that the operators have learned how to stop and start the machines, they now have, in principle, the possibility of stopping them if special conditions make this necessary, for example break-down." As a result, 'job enrichment' to cope with NIT quite obviously entails much costly training activities. We can only speculate whether such expenses pay in the end. At least all surviving and prosperous companies quite obviously managed to compensate their training investments.

Effects on Employees

So far we have focused on job enrichment in conjunction with NIT, from a management perspective. What are the effects of NIT and job enrichment on the workforce? Such effects can be analysed from two perspectives: (1) what are the overall repercussions on the safety of workplaces? Did NIT live up to its reputation of a 'job killer' and destroy jobs, so that perhaps positive job enrichment effects could only be enjoyed by a minority of the workforce? (2) What are the individual workplace repercussions of NIT for employees who work with these new technologies? Did this kind of 'job enrichment' result in a more extended work-role, in greater rights and responsibilities, in more discretion for the individual employee? The first issue, the high productivity and the labour saving potential of New Information Technology and the possibility of large-scale job abolition was a hotly debated topic in the 1980s. Research has shown that, in regard to NIT, such apprehensions were largely unfounded. The aforementioned European Foundation survey found that from the EC data, the employment of additional personnel was the foremost reaction of firms to NIT introduction (according to the answers of 43% of both managers and employee representatives interviewed). In 38% of the firms, NIT introduction had no repercussions on the firms' workforces at all. 30% reported that personnel problems were solved through in-company movements; 10% reported voluntary leaving of personnel, and only 7% of the firms indicated dismissal of personnel (Gill et al. 1993:60). In terms of *quantities* of employees affected or unaffected, in absolute figures, NIT application impacted positively rather than negatively: of all employees affected by NIT (in absolute numbers), 39% were hired, 26% were hired or moved around, 17% were only moved around in the firm, and the remaining

18% were affected in various ways (both positive and negative) of which dismissals and voluntary leaving only form the smaller part (ibid.:66).

For general and specific methodological reasons these figures must be viewed with some caution. Employment effects are difficult to measure, and a more comprehensive and in-depth investigation of the topic in terms of the methodology employed indicates that the figures reported are likely to be too positive (Fröhlich, Krieger and Gill 1992-D). However, even regarding other research results to be less positive, the overall effects of NIT on employment were positive.

The repercussions of NIT for individual workplaces is another dimension: did NIT 'enrich' daily work by creating more complex work procedures, by enlarging individual employee's rights and responsibilities, and did employees evaluate their new work circumstances positively? Most studies interested in task changes due to new technology treat such questions superficially. There are only a few researchers trying to investigate what job attributes have changed and whether these changes have positive or negative effects for the employees involved. Research findings suggest that job enrichment in conjunction with NIT enables the input of high skills and leads to a variety of positive changes. But - contrary to what is often stated - it does not increase the discretionary content of work.

In Germany, Fröhlich and Hild (1991-D) investigated the work of 320 skilled workers in mechanical engineering after they had received off-the-job training in CNC-technology. At their workplaces, the majority applied their newly acquired skills in a holistic way, thereby conforming to the concept of intelligent use of new technology. According to the interviewees, work has become much more interesting, their responsibilities and the necessary input of mental abilities has increased. Their gratification from work - job security, promotion chances and social contacts - were rather unaffected, but remuneration had increased. Working time did not change; supervisor control decreased. The most significant change was a distinct decrease in the physical effort needed and an equally distinct rise in mental effort. Yet, as to the discretionary content of work, there was no change in the nature of discretion on the shop floor: the chances for making decisions regarding daily work (Entscheidungsspielraum) as well as the variability of daily work (Tätigkeitsspielraum) remained unaffected. Thus, while the range of duties and responsibilities increased, it was not accompanied by greater decision making power. This finding - the considerable change of working conditions in several dimensions while not altering work discretion in German mechanical engineering firms applying CNC technology - is supported by a German nation-wide survey (Henniges 1987-D) as well as by smaller studies (Frese and Zapf 1987-D; Weibler 1989-D; Schumann 1990-D). Looking at these results in a theoretical perspective, it seems that the introduction of NIT has not so much enriched jobs, but has tended to enlarge them, i.e. added more job elements on the horizontal level without altering vertical structures. It has to be added that the new work situation was, on the whole, very positively assessed be the workforce affected, and very few would have wished to return to former work structures.

On a very different data base and in regard to all forms of 'advanced' technology, Daniels (1987-UK:275) reports a "generally favourable picture ... of the impact of new technology upon the content of jobs applied to both the manual and to office workers". The balance of change was towards job enrichment; the range of tasks and responsibility was increased, as well as job interest. But "these changes appeared ... to have a more neutral or even slightly negative effect upon the autonomy of workers as measured by their control over how they did their jobs, the pace of their work and the degree of supervision they were subject ... there was little doubt that workers derived much less benefit in terms of control than in relation to other sources of satisfaction" (ibid.:276). The results reported from Germany and Great Britain are largely supported by studies in Italy. Ambrosini (1989-I) presents the answers of 190 blue and white collar workers in regard to job changes in 24 large metal processing establishments who had experienced technical change during the last three years. Between one quarter and two fifth of the respondents indicated that they enjoyed more autonomy at work, the work had become more interesting and that they had more responsibility. But at the same time, three thirds complained about more isolation in work, and 63% experienced more control from supervisors. On the positive side, again, one third of these employees said that they were consulted by their superiors "always or almost always" in matters concerning their jobs, and the large majority of employees indicated that they would like to have these consultative procedures extended.

A somewhat comparable case is reported for the Netherlands (Vieveen 1994-NL). Six companies were studied. Each had introduced a 'quality care' programme, applying the ISO 9000 norm. These initiatives were also aimed at improving the quality of working life. The employees reported that in the process they were burdened with more responsibilities without higher discretion to regulate their work. In addition, the ways of working were judged to have become more uniform, with more 'sticking to the rules' and less opportunity for improvisation. In spite of these somewhat negative assessments, the overall organisational change was positively evaluated by the workforce, as the new production regime provided a better information flow, better chances for problem solving and involved them more intensively in their daily work.

56

For two FIAT greenfield sites in Italy, Bonazzi (1993) reports workforce reactions to new technology. Although in these cases we are dealing with group work, the author refers to the evaluation of job changes due to technology as well. In general, employees accepted the increasing mental strains as the price for the considerable reduction of physical efforts that was so common in traditional automated work. In addition, they pointed to the increased 'labour dignity' that working with new technology entailed. This tendency has also been noted by Kawakita (1985-JP), when he concluded from a Japanese employee survey in five highly automated steel producing factories, that when work content shifts from manual to intellectual and conceptual work, the social distance between workers and the engineering staff shortens.

Summary

With the introduction of New Information technology, we notice that the term 'job enrichment' was hardly ever mentioned. The concept, however, was applied without the actors being aware of what they were doing. Whereas older research on job enrichment in the QWL tradition was often based on elaborate theoretical reasoning, no such claims have been made in the NIT context. Quite significantly, Clausen and Lorentzen (1986-DK) classified this research as 'empirical', meaning that it does "not keep explicitly to any theoretical background". Except for sweeping generalisations about the need for workforce commitment when running NIT, which is one message of New Production Concepts and Flexible Specialisation, organisational changes were initiated as a necessary response to cope with the intricacies of NIT.

'Job enrichment' was one answer to a technology option that failed. Management had to take on a sometimes new, positive attitude towards employees to make NIT effective. It was intended to pacify workers and to reduce absenteeism and labour turnover. Without ready blue-prints for NIT application, management sought the active co-operation of their employees, and job enrichment of this kind took on a bottom-up character. As the workforces, in general, welcomed 'advanced technical change' (Daniels 1987-UK), there was little need for tactical considerations about how to talk employees into acceptance. Research also shows that management was well-aware of the greater training needs to operate NIT, and generally, this training was provided.

Focusing on employees: first, the most important and hotly debated threat of mass-scale job loss proved premature. Secondly, NIT confirmed many theoretical expectations: it made work more complex, interesting and 'intellectually' more challenging; it reduced physical strain distinctly, yet at the expense of mental stress which grew in like proportion; NIT work took on a more abstract character, blurring distinctions between blue- and white-collar employees in firms. Further, we are safe to say that such work did not yield one important outcome: it did not really increase decision-making power and autonomy in the job. It seems that job enrichment through NIT has increased responsibilities without granting enlarged rights that accompany such new duties. In a narrow sense, we found more enlargement than enrichment. Yet, on the whole, employees positively accepted their new workplace.

These limits to individual job enrichment have been identified before. In contrast, group work is often identified as a significant corrective to the limitations associated with job enrichment experiments. 'Real' job enrichment, it is claimed, can only be achieved in 'semi-autonomous' work groups - this is the tenor of most research on the topic (DTI 1978-DK, Merli 1986-I, Butera 1988-I). And the present public and scientific debate on direct participation focuses exactly on these delegative types of group work (cf. chapter 4).

3 Group Consultation: The Experience of Quality Circles

'Quality Circles' is a summary term for a variety of measures that come under diverse labels and assume very different practices, both nationally and internationally. In principle, they hold some common elements: quality circles are voluntary groups, composed of workers or employees of a section or department. They meet regularly to discuss problems relating to their immediate work tasks and work environment, mostly under the chairmanship of their immediate supervisor who should adopt a moderator role. The meetings are meant to identify quality and workplace problems and to develop solutions to these problems. The proposed solutions are then passed on to higher management which is free to accept, modify or refuse the proposals. This characterises quality circles as a consultative group concept. The regular group meetings should take place during working hours, and attendance should not be remunerated financially. According to 'theory', a quality circle programme should not be hastily drafted and introduced, but should be conceived as a medium-term task which requires careful preparation and training of participants.

3.1 Management's Motives for Quality Circle Introduction

'Quality circles' was the first managerial concept to be 'imported' from Japan to the USA and Europe. They were considered to be the main factor explaining the remarkable Japanese success in producing highly competitive goods in terms of price, quality and time needed for product development, actual production and product change. Accordingly, quality circle adoption was strongly motivated by *competitive needs*, best exemplified by the implementation motives of a US electronics company which was doing fairly well financially, but "was also quite sensitive to the inroads foreign manufacturers were making in the electronics industry. In response to that threat, the company was quite actively keeping abreast of new management techniques and practices, especially those associated with the Japanese" (Griffin 1988-US:342). We frequently find such proactive management motivation in countries competing in the global market (cf. Beriger 1987-D, Kunzmann 1991-D). In Europe, the constraints of the Common Market and planning for the *Single European Market* in 1994 had a similar effect, particularly for the late 'joiners' in the Mediterranean: in three Spanish companies, the topic of product quality was enforced with particular reference to competitive factors of the European market (Carrasquer, Coller and

Miguelez 1993-E), and in Portugal (Cristóvam, Efertz and Jorge 1993-P). Elorriaga Achutegui (1991-E), the quality director of a Spanish bank, extends this argument to the banking business as well.

Formal quality norms and standard specifications like ISO 9000 or its national equivalents was another reason for management interest in quality circles. Such certified quality standards are increasingly considered excellent means of sales promotion (for two Greek companies cf. Xirotiri-Koufidou and Vouzas 1993-GR). They are often required when a company operates in a supply chain and when powerful customers force their suppliers to apply those standards (cf. Bratton 1991-UK). Legal regulations may pose a similar need for quality control, as was the case in an Italian pharmaceutical company (Carpo 1994-I). ISO 9000 not only prescribes certain standards for final product quality, but simultaneously regulates the processes and procedures of permanent quality production and quality control, thereby affecting the production process itself. Thus, quality circles have to be embedded in an overall concept of quality production, most often labelled as 'Total Quality Management' (TQM). In many cases TQM comes in tandem with other forms of direct participation at both individual and team levels.

Looking more closely at the quality circle concept, this managerial tool is about people; it is a way to engage the company's workforce or to get employees to care about problems in their immediate work environment and the company's products and services. Accordingly, quality circles in the West were not narrowly conceived in cost-benefit terms but rather as a suitable approach *to improving human resources and motivation* in firms. A survey by the Italian National Quality Circle Association (ANCQUI 1987-I) testifies to a mix of motives:

Table 3: Reasons for Introducing Quality Circles

human resource development	43%
quality improvement	43%
improvement of competitiveness	35%
gratification of employees	34%
improvement of communication	29%
cost saving	13%

Source: ANCQUI 1987-I

This list illustrates that 'quality' problems play only *one* role, and looking at the list in perspective, workforce motivation is the paramount reason for quality circle introduction. This is exactly the official rationale for applying quality circles in Italy: "to improve quality, not only as quality of products, but also and in particular as quality of the work environment in a broad sense, as this affects, first of all, the results and processes and activities within a firm" (ANCQUI 1987-I:33; similar for Italy: Nicoletti 1986-I; for Germany: Greifenstein, Jansen and Kißler 1993-D). A survey of the 100 largest German companies demonstrated that quality improvement of products was rated highest among all possible reasons for quality circle introduction. However, it was closely followed by increasing co-operation, satisfaction with work, working conditions and qualification (and competition; Antoni, Bungert and Lehnert 1992-D). Here again, we find a strong focus on workforce motivation. As a side-effect, quality circles are sometimes expected to serve not only management goals but to improve the *quality of working life*, and to improve employees' abilities and responsibilities, to offer challenging tasks, to improve health and safety as well as functional and social contacts. Such additional goals seem to be very prominent in the Netherlands (cf. Van de Water, Goessens and de Vries 1988-NL; Vieveen 1994-NL). Finally, we must be aware that many companies considered quality circles as a *'fashionable'* *topic* which one simply had to have for image reasons, sometimes hoping for some unspecified positive outcome (cf. Martin Hernandez 1993b-E).

Management reasons for introducing quality circles do not only centre around quality issues but try to achieve a number of different objectives. Cotton (1993-US:78), in his review of US quality circle research, is less positive in his conclusions about motives when he indicates that quality circles have been used for "solving almost every problem but ozone depletion in the upper atmosphere". In general, the main focus is on workforce motivation, stimulating inner-organisational communication and gaining increased flexibility which, in the end, might result in quality awareness and quality improvement. If conceived as an indirect tool that operates via changed employee attitudes, quality circles quite naturally assume a medium to long-term character with consequences for planning, training and budgeting.

3.2 Quality Circle Implementation

When quality circles appeared in Europe and the USA, they quickly assumed a very formalised set of rules which were fostered and supported by national Quality Circle Associations. There is a common understanding that seriously implementing quality circles means striving for organisational change in which top management act as the driving force or at least give credible support to the departments which apply circles.

The FIAT car company is an example of a serious attempt to introduce quality circles systematically (Merle 1986-I): After a company board decision to include all employees at each organisational level (management, service departments and production), a 'sensitising programme' aimed at making 250 higher level managers receptive to the quality issue and the need for organisational change was implemented. Parallel to this, a similar pilot programme was started for 250 blue-collar workers in a FIAT establishment in the Palermo region. As a second step (1981-1982), a similar programme involving 350 middle-managers discussing the possible changes in their role, communication problems between departments etc., was introduced. Simultaneously, top management continued to 'sell' the scheme to blue-collar workers by carrying out 'quality days' which consisted of three to eight hours of training for circle work. In 1983, foremen and front-line supervisors were familiarised with quality circles (step 3), and in 1984, the final move was towards blue-collar workers again. At the end of that year, about 25,000 blue-collar workers had been involved in circle training. The author gives additional information on five other Italian firms which have a similarly thorough quality circle programme.

A serious quality circle programme, particularly when it is part of an encompassing Total Quality approach, is often introduced with the assistance of outside consultants and (inside) facilitators. Companies can feel too insecure, or anticipate problems beyond their expertise and hope to overcome this with the help of outside moderators (Marks et al. 1986-US; Griffin 1988-US; Vermeulen and Gevers 1989-B). One finding of six case studies in larger Dutch firms, van de Water, Goessens and de Vries (1988-NL) identified that insufficient advance information on the new management measures is likely to cause irritation, even resistance by all target persons and groups. This includes middle and lower management, as quality circles may affect their power and authority. Based on their findings, the authors also advise management to create a non-obligatory atmosphere about circle participation. This might send out the wrong signals, or down grade the importance of quality circles in the organisation from the very beginning, and endanger their future success.

The few literature sources on implementation problems exemplify different points: a serious circle strategy needs planning and organisation. It must not only include front-line employees but different levels of management as well. Accordingly, in large companies such a strategy necessitates considerable bureaucracy in itself. It is a programme extending over several years, often supported by outside consultants. Advance training is needed for all participants, and the costs might be considerable. But as was pointed out before, not all companies pursue such 'textbook' strategies. Management motivation for engaging in quality circles is very mixed, and so are the implementation procedures.

3.3   Training for Circle Work

As to training needs, two types of skills are usually addressed: problem solving skills and group process skills. In regard to problem solving, intuitive-associative methods such a brainstorming or the Delphi-method are sometimes taught. Systematic-analytic methods and statistical analysis to find optimal solutions from a multitude of possibilities (such a Ishikawa diagrams to analyse cause-effect relations or Pareto analysis to form rank-orders of problems to solve; cf. Beriger 1987-D) are also used. In addition, the quality concept stresses record keeping of discussions and reporting of group results as formal skills needed. This illustrates the amount of paperwork involved in quality circles.

The learning of group process skills or 'social' skills is the second aim in circle training. One of the novelties of quality circles is the social dimension which is added to the traditional work role. Many employees experience for the first time that acting in groups where equal rights are accorded to all members can create new problems. Such problems range from simply not knowing the basic rules of discussion, misunderstanding arguments, misinterpreting other's motives without being able to clarify them in discussions, to being an actor and a target in the struggle over status and power in groups - in short, being part of what is popularly called 'group dynamics'. The ability to cope with such situations and to communicate efficiently with other organisation members and outsiders is called 'social skills'. These are needed to create and maintain a co-operative work climate. It is this climate of co-operation and trust that is envisaged in the quality circle concept, and the one which, in fact, is often its backbone and main goal.

The FIAT example of training about 25,000 employees for three to eight hours points to a considerable input of time and money. US surveys report that 89% of companies applying quality circles provided four or more hours of training, the mean time being between 9 and 12 hours (Seelye and Sween 1982-US). There is a surprising common trend in European and US research findings about the skills needed for employees to participate, not only in quality circle programmes, but in all other measures of direct participation as well. In highly developed countries social skills are considered the bottleneck, and most training programmes concentrate on developing these. Applebaum and Batt (1994:85-US) summarise the US training requirements: "although conventional wisdom based on human capital theory links gains in productivity to basic education and job-related training, the case studies make clear that training in soft skills [meaning: team building and group process] is a critical part of organisational change. Employers and managers indicate a much greater demand for training in process and behavioural skills than in technical skills". For Just-in-Time and TQM applications in Great Britain, the greater importance of social skills over technical skills are also reported (Dawson and Webb 1989-UK; Wilkinson et al. 1992-UK). In preparation for the Olympic Games in Barcelona many regional companies experimented with quality circles and undertook extensive training, all centred around 'soft skills' like group dynamics, leadership and communication (Miguelez et al. 1993-E); (for a similar process in a Renault establishment in France, see: Bouche et al. 1991-F). Faust et al. (1993-D) point out that for organisational decentralisation, those 'soft skills' are a bottleneck both on the shop floor and among all levels of management (for similar commentary in the UK context, see: IDS 1992). Danish researchers go even further when they stress the need for employee flexibility, co-operation, motivation and sense of responsibility in organisational change to be seen as "core skills" (Bottrup and Clematide 1990-DK). There is a possibility that this emphasis on 'social skills' is appropriate in highly developed countries only. Less developed European countries face need to develop both social and vocational skills at the same time.

Whereas considerable training went into this area of 'soft' or 'core' skills in Europe and the USA, we have no indication if Japan faces the same training problem. Although training is a distinct topic in Japanese research, 'soft skills' as a scarce commodity are never mentioned. Vocational skills seem to be the bottle-neck: on the basis of twelve surveys and case studies with engineers, supervisors and employees (CIRC 1987-JP), the authors state that conventional on-the-job training and study manuals are no longer considered sufficient. Instead, considerably more weight should be given to off-the-job training promoted by the company or by outsiders and to self-study with colleagues. Nowhere is a special need for the so called social skills emphasised. This situation can be interpreted in two ways: in the 'cultural difference' tradition one might assume that social skills are simply given in Japanese society and therefore do not pose a problem. But a different interpretation is feasible as well: it might simply be that Japanese actors overemphasise the cultural difference and take 'groupism' simply as a given, without ever questioning this assumption. On such a base, group problems might appear to be non-existent and, thus, do not need special attention. As will be shown, there is strong indication that Japanese workforces do not conform to the problem-free image of social cohesion and group acceptance.

3.4 The Effects of Quality Circles

In a strict sense, quality circles can be properly assessed only in respect of their intended aims. As we have seen, the objectives of quality circle implementation vary tremendously, ranging from improving product and service quality, to improving the quality of working life. It must also be added that in most cases, measurable aims are not even specified, making precise cost-benefit analyses impossible. Such a diffuseness of effects is reflected in research as well: we get information on every kind of outcome, but rarely on what quality circles were originally intended for - quality of products and services. In the USA, Cotton (1993-US:70) found only one study (Freiman and Saxberg 1989-US) that examined quality itself as an outcome. The conclusion was that there was "no change in quality after quality circle invention". Our own material is not very informative on this topic either. Ackermann (1989-D) has evaluated in detail the output of quality circles in six German companies from different economic sectors. Information on the effects comes separate from plain circle members and from circle coordinators:

Table 4: Positive Effects of Quality Circles According to Circle Members and Circle Leaders

	members	leaders
increased communication	42%	70%
improved commitment of employees	33%	43%
improved quality awareness	15%	28%
better working conditions	10%	8%
cost reduction	6%	15%

Source: Ackermann 1989-D

From the findings that emerged, it is firstly important to note that circle members are less positive about results than circle co-ordinators. Secondly, the social effects clearly predominate: increased communication and improved employee commitment to work is by far the most important outcome of circle activities. Quality is mentioned, too, but it must be pointed out that we are not dealing with factual quality improvement but with 'quality awareness' which is something quite different. In addition, the circle members mention it rather rarely (15%), whereas circle co-ordinators are more optimistic (28%). According to both groups, neither working conditions nor the cost situation improved a great deal.

In a Swiss and German study of quality circles undertaken from a middle management perspective (Beriger 1987-D), 33% of the respondents saw positive results in regard to factual improvements (unspecified), but 61% identified improvements in the area of co-operation. A survey investigating 'work consultation', a Dutch and Belgian-Flemish concept which closely resembles quality circles, was undertaken among 1,578 randomly selected Dutch companies (Loontechnische Dienst, 1993 - NL). The findings revealed a multitude of positive effects, all ranging high in the 90% approval range. The highest scores related to employee motivation, employee commitment, employee input, quality improvement and co-ordination - in this sequence. We find such positive human centred effects of quality circles reported in various European and US sources. Martin Hernandez (1993b-E) found that the social climate considerably improved and human relations between both co-workers and supervisors eased in a Spanish firm. Such developments are not restricted to circle members alone, but sometimes seem to spread through departments and affect non-members as well. Such a positive effect is reported in five Flemish establishments where management had pursued a solid, systematic quality circle policy. Here, even 50% of non participants reported intensified contacts with colleagues due to the circle programme (Baisier and Albertijn 1992-B). From 776 employee interviews in six German production establishments (Ackermann 1989-D) we learn that 63% of the circle participants evaluated their experience positively, with non-members showing even more positive attitudes (84%). Both groups indicated increased communication and improved social relations at the workplace as the most outstanding achievement of quality circles (similar: Greifenstein, Jansen and Kißler 1991-D, Marks et al. 1986-US). In a very dynamic Portuguese company (Cristóvam, Efferz and Jorge 1993-P), 85% of the workforce was trained, mainly in social skills. It is reported that, as a result, 90% of the training participants developed high self-esteem. An indirect positive effect is reported by Muffels, Heinen and van Mil (1982-NL): work consultation reduced the level of absenteeism across 785 Dutch companies investigated by a representative survey. Research in an Italian case found that circle members were less inclined to leave the firm than non-members (Raffaeli 1985-I).

A survey of the top 100 companies in Germany may serve as a synopsis of the diverse effects of quality circles according to management answers (Antoni, Bungard and Lehnert 1992-D). Fifty per cent of these companies had implemented quality circles and rated the social effects of circles to be much higher than the direct and indirect economic effects.

Table 5: Quality Circle Effects in the Top-100-Companies in Germany*

co-operation improved	5.00
motivation improved	4.68
work satisfaction improved	4.58
communication improved	4.50
working conditions improved	4.28
qualifications increased	4.20
suggestion schemes increased	3.95
quality improved	3.93
productivity increased	3.70
costs decreased	3.51
flexibility increased	2.76
absenteeism decreased	2.74
accidents during work	2.58
labour turnover decreased	2.00

*means of a scale between 1 = 'no effects' and 6 = 'total success'

Source: Antoni, Bungard and Lehnert 1992-D

We have two cases were management attempted exact cost-benefit analyses. In a large Spanish glass company with eleven establishments (Varela and Sener 1988-E), management estimated that savings through quality circle activities amounted to 5.3 million Pesetas, but admitted that when taking the up-front costs for training etc. into account, the overall balance is negative. Yet, management hoped for positive results in the course of time. Over a four year period, quality circles in a US electronics firm (Griffin 1988-US) developed 122 formal recommendations for product improvement, of which 81 were adopted by management. The programme costs amounted to $142,520. There were initial savings of $65,000 and yearly savings of $20,000, thus, there was about an equal balance of costs and savings. Again, management hoped that programme benefits would accrue for the foreseeable time.

Reviewing these effects, our sources tell us very little about quality improvement and the tangible economic effects of quality circles. There is a variety of positive results which centre mainly around the 'human side of enterprise': an improved intra-company social climate, improved co-operation and mutual information, not only between circle participants, but between the non-members as well.

3.5 Problems of Quality Circles

On balance, and despite detailed criticism, our analysis has portrayed quality circles in a positive light. Yet, the picture is too positive. Quality circles are said to be of little us unless they are incorporated in wider schemes of organisational change such as Total Quality Management (TQM). Different reasons account for the too rosy picture of quality circles as isolated measures: there is an overall trend to present only success stories of management schemes, particularly if information comes from management anxious to justify its own actions. Very often, social science research helps to support these positive images: generally, positive results are published more often than negative findings which do not match expectations. Consequently, success stories are likely to be over-reported. The reasons for quality circle failure are manifold and can be attributed to the problems that both management and workforce have with the concept.

The Management Perspective

When we presented information on the introduction process, training activities and effects of quality circles, we were dealing mostly with serious attempts of circle application. But it is questionable whether all companies attempted to apply this strategy in a serious manner. Quality circles had the image of a ready, off-the-shelf, low-cost management tool that promised quick results without really affecting organisational structures. Castillo, Jimenez and Santos (1991-E), for instance, report that in a MNC car engine factory in Spain, quality circles were adopted because they do not need high investment, and because they are an easy-to-apply method that promised quick results, and which could be restricted to quality problems only and to personnel fluctuations. The authors reviewed a large range of Spanish research on a variety of companies in different economic sectors to find out that, as a rule, management quickly stopped quality circles when the first initiatives did not yield immediately visible benefits.

In theory, quality circles need the support of top-management, and this is not always given. Geary (1993-IRL) writing about an Irish firm, found that management was not committed to quality circles and could not even reach agreement on the type of projects that should be addressed by the circles. Bradley and Hill (1983-UK) indicate the same for a British firm and point out that in a US company, management introduced a training course on quality circles only one year after circle introduction, thus demonstrating the superficial attitude towards this strategy. Wilkinson et al. (1992-UK) present the example of a British engineering firm where top-management vetoed almost all suggestions of problem solving groups because of time pressure to meet yearly production targets. Sometimes, quality circles are proposed and started by enthusiastic employees, with management displaying a distant attitude. Van de Water, Goessens and de Vries (1988-NL) found such bottom-up approaches in Dutch firms, and in these cases proposed solutions had very few chances of being heard by management. Tang, Tollison and Whiteside (1987-US) concluded that management-initiated circles were more successful than workforce-initiated circles.

In addition, there are quite tangible, down-to-earth problems that endanger circle application. Merle (1986-I), in six Italian case studies on 'avant-garde' firms, pointed out the complicated procedures of decision making that burden circle application with much 'red tape' and bureaucracy. As the most obstructive feature of quality circles, 43% of Italian managers named "time for meetings" (ANCQUI 1987-I). In a survey of 46 Italian enterprises (Nicoletti 1986-I), managers were most ambivalent about quality circles for exactly the same reason. Perhaps the most important handicap from a management point of view is the fact that the introduction of quality circles creates an organisational complexity that can confuse existing structures. Hill (1991a -UK), in his review of quality circles and TQM, points out that the circles created a parallel organisational structure which was generally not accepted by management, and particularly not by middle management. It created additional work and was not integrated into the current system of rewards and penalties, as it diluted responsibilities and threatened established power positions. As a trend, middle management is said to have a defensive, uncooperative and destructive attitude towards quality circles. This is basically the result of the German Top-100-Company survey (Antoni,

Bungard and Lehnert 1992-D), where the greatest problem was lack of "support from middle management". Whether the role of middle management is properly defined by these findings will be left open for the moment (cf. chapter 5).

The Workforce Perspective

When we looked at management's motives for introducing quality circles in Europe and the USA, we noticed a strong emphasis on human resource and workforce motivation reasons, and sometimes even Quality of Working Life goals. The main positive effects of quality circles, according to management, were precisely these social and 'climatic' improvements. Generally, such a positive view exists among workforces as well. But we must be aware that, on the whole, only small sections of firm's employees were affected by the circles. In addition, circle participation should be voluntary, and it therefore attracts a particular type of employees, mainly habitual activists, highly work-committed people. As is the case for management, we are dealing with mixed motives on the workforce side as well. Problems arise when certain 'rules of the game' are violated and expectations are not met (e.g., when the principle of voluntarism in circle membership is not respected, and when circle activities are part of the normal working time), and that management is seriously interested in circle suggestions. Then, there are additional drawbacks to circle work due to conflicting interests between groups of employees.

Most of our sources tell us that, in accordance with theory, circle participation was voluntary, activities took place during working time and were remunerated symbolically. Such symbolic rewards were e.g.: presentation of outstanding circle suggestions at the US or Japanese headquarters of European establishments by circle representatives (Baisier and Albertijn 1992-B, Stavroulakis 1989-GR), dinner with top management or being praised in company publications (Beriger 1987-D, Carrasquer, Collier and Miguelez 1993-E, Carpo 1994-I). But there are sources which throw some doubt on the proper functioning of voluntary participation: Martin Hernandez (1993a-E) reports some management pressure on Spanish employees to participate. In five Flemish companies with a systematic approach to quality circles, Baisier and Albertijn (1992-B) found hesitant participation and a low rate of membership in the firms. Members pointed to identified informal social pressure at workplace level and indicated that only 56% of membership was really voluntary. We, therefore, have instances where membership is officially voluntary, but a 100 percent membership is reported at the same time (Xirotiri-Konfidou and Vouzas 1993-GR).

Membrado Martinez (1991-E) reports a similar case of a Spanish IBM subsidiary where 95% of employees are circle members.

In such cases of almost complete participation of a company's workforce in circles, common sense sheds doubt on the level of voluntary participation. An extreme example of mandatory membership is given by Grenier (1988-US) for the USA: in a production unit of a large company with a predominantly female Hispanic workforce, circle membership was expected, and for employees it was advisable to comply, as pay rises and promotion chances depended on the interest shown in circle activities. Japan has developed and adopted quality circles on a mass scale. About 95 percent of the largest companies apply them systematically and involve practically all of their core employees (Okubayashi et al. 1994-JP.). In theory, circle membership is voluntary in Japan, yet research shows almost the reverse to be the case: Koumura (1986-JP) interviewed personnel directors in 186 larger companies (with a mailed questionnaire) about the problem. According to these respondents only 20% of the workforce take part "willingly", whereas the remaining 80% participate "unwillingly, under instructions from the staff". Here, it is worth noting that we are reporting a management assessment, with workforce opinion likely to be even more sceptical. Direct responses from personnel supports the largely mandatory character of circle work: in a Japanese Bank, 202 male and 168 female employees were interviewed about their circle experience (Maemura 1990-JP). Only 18% of males and 5% of females stated their autonomous attendance, whereas 55% of males and 74% of females explicitly indicated that membership was not at their discretion (the remaining employees gave ambiguous answers). This concurs with the findings of Lillrank and Kano (1989-JP) which show that in Japan, participation in quality circles is not voluntary and that considerable informal pressure is exercised to ensure total coverage (similarly: Michio 1988-JP).

When circle activities are not confined to regular working hours, management seems to face the problem of employee resistance. Overtime circle attendance leads to extra payments for circle members in an Italian company (Nicoletti 1986-I; similar for Spain: Carrasquer, Coller and Miguelez 1993-E). In 186 larger Japanese manufacturing companies (Koumura 1986-JP) only 42% of circle meetings took pláce during regular working hours; 40% of the companies have quality circle sessions both during and outside normal working time, and in 18% of the firms these meetings take place exclusively after or before normal working time without extra payment. The majority of Japanese workers are reported to object to this practice and thinks that the additional time-input should be remunerated separately. It is further reported that companies have reduced out-of-normal time-input recently.

A comparatively frequent complaint is about management disinterest which reduces motivation on the workforce side. This complaint is understandable, given the common 'quick-fix' mentality that exists in relation to circle installations. But even well planned and systematic circle policies risk running into problems. In particular, a lack of feedback to circle suggestions is a source of frustration as it demonstrates management's disinterest and unmasks the whole approach as just another management trick (Martin Hernandez 1993a-E; Baisier and Albertijn 1992-B). In trying to explain the breakdown of circle activities, Collard and Dale (1989-UK) report the following: circle activities didn't result in useful suggestions; all immediate problems were solved and new problems couldn't be identified; suggestions were made which management thought too far-reaching in their consequences; or new problem solutions were put forward without management ever reacting to them. This reluctance among management seems to be quite prevalent: according to union representatives of 195 Belgian companies, only 31% of their firms seem to take employee suggestions seriously. Most companies are reported to be reluctant to implement changes that are put forward by participation teams (Dielen 1994-B).

White-collar employees seem to be very outcome-oriented: as long as they see real results in circle participation, they seem to be strong supporters of the concept. But when they get the feeling of being engaged in shadow-boxing, interest fades quickly (Nicoletti 1986-I). In a different context, the loss of interest in voluntary participation through experiencing a play-ground situation is demonstrated: qualified white-collar employees who voluntarily engaged in union programmes to participate in solving workplace problems discontinued their engagement when they learned that their suggestions were not taken into account or even rebuffed because they did not fit into union policies (Fröhlich, Kindler and Sombetzki 1996-D). Baisier and Albertijn (1992-B) quote circle members who complain about meetings which they often see as a mixture of shadow-fights and diplomatic manoeuvre where employees are cautious to really voice their opinions about colleagues and supervisors.

According to theory, circle membership should be motivated intrinsically to improve working procedures and product and services quality. Yet, varied sources point to extrinsic motives for joining quality circles as well: the proximity of quality circle activities to the direct supervisor forms an excellent arena in which to pursue very down-to-earth goals, particularly in regard to promotion chances and subsequent pay rises. Marks et al. (1986-US) report such extrinsic motivation with US assembly line workers in batch processes who hoped for advancement in the organisation. A German case study (Bednarek 1985-G) revealed better promotion chances as the foremost reason for circle membership. Although evidence for extrinsic participation motives is scarce, common sense leads us to expect such goals to occur more frequently. Non-members sometimes suspect even outright negative motives for others' participation in quality circles: Baisier and Albertijn (1992-B) quote non-members as saying that members joined the circles simply to avoid working while sitting in meetings. The same authors point to quarrels about the uneven workloads of members and non-members, the latter complaining that they have to take over circle members' workload while circles are in session (similarly Horman 1991-B).

Thomas (1989-US) reports hidden conflicts at shop-floor level among members in US voluntary consultation groups which are composed of different skills: unskilled workers feel that they cannot properly contribute to the discussions; semi-skilled look down on unskilled workers because of their incompetence, and highly skilled workers look down on both groups because of the 'kiddie-stuff' topics they raise and want to discuss (similar for Germany, Greifenstein, Jansen and Kißler 1991-D). Stavroulakis (1989-GR) reports intra-circle conflicts over the degree of activity of the participants. Bradley and Hill (1983-UK) produce evidence that both members and non-members are critical of quality circles as they create tensions between colleagues at workplace level. At the Nissan car plant in Greece, conflicts arose between both groups because of the greater prominence of circle members within the firm (Stavroulakis 1989-G). Another source of conflicts is cited by Baisier and Albertijn (1992-B): circle members might come up with solutions for workplace change that affect all employees there, including the non-participants included. In a German VW car plant (Greifenstein, Jansen and Kißler 1993-D), a written agreement with the works council stated that quality circles should not be disadvantageous for either members or non-members.

Finally, we know of cases were workforces reject quality circles for very fundamental reasons and exercise informal social pressure on their colleagues not to participate on the grounds that they only serve the company's interest. These examples are from the US, the UK and the Mediterranean countries (Cotton 1993-US, Bradley and Hill 1987-UK, Hill 1991a/b-UK, Varela and Sener 1988-E, Castillo, Jimenes and Santos 1991-E, Petmesidou and Tsoulouvis 1990-GR). For the Mediterranean countries a 'low trust climate' between the workforce and management is often reported as a cultural trait: Greek management is characterised by "uncertainty avoidance" which needs to "maintain their share of control" (Veiga and Yanouzas 1991-GR), and employees are said to have a "long established distrust in their employers" (Raftis and Stavroulakis 1991-GR, similar for Spain: Price Waterhouse-ESADE 1992-E). For the US and the UK, workforce rejection of quality circles is explained by traditional adversarial labour relations and a low-trust climate between management, the unions and the workforces.

3.6 The Role of Quality Circles in Integrated Management Strategies

In the light of results that mainly rely on 'soft' indicators, the likely over-representation of success stories in the literature, given the many problems that both management and the workforce have with quality circles, it is not surprising that - as an isolated management tool - quality circles are considered an unsuitable organisational strategy. They can be effective over a short period of time, but their positive effects disappear after a while (Van Fleet and Griffin 1989-US, Wilkinson et al. 1992-UK). Even in Japan they were not as successful as popularly believed in Europe and in the USA: Cotton (1993-US:78) refers to an early study (Metz 1981-US) according to which only one third of Japanese quality circles were successful (similar: Koumura 1986-JP). They are said to have an average life-time of one to two years, "the greatest period of quality circle success is probably between 6 and 18 months" (Cotton 1993-US:76). For Spain, Martin Hernandez (1993a-E) reports that one third of quality circles did not survive more than two years, another third two to four years, whereas 25% existed longer than that. The author reports that the surviving circles are all embedded in a more encompassing strategy of organisational change, such as Total Quality Management (similar for Spain: Castillo, Jimenez and Santos 1991-E, Lope Peña 1993-E). In Italy in 1987, 61% of the surviving circles were part of a TQM programme (ANCQUI 1987-I). Nowadays, quality circles are considered as fore-runners, as a *transitional technique* for more integrated approaches (Lawler and Mohrman 1985-US, Griffin 1988-US, Hill 1991-UK, Carpo 1994-I).

Looking back, the rise and decline of quality circles in the Western nations can be explained as a misunderstanding of the original intentions of this group based 'suggestion scheme'. Shea (1986-US) calls the original quality circles a methodology for identifying quality control problems and for decentralising quality control without any further intentions regarding workforce motivation etc. According to the MIT study on the world-wide car industry (Womack, Jones and Roos 1990-US) quality circles developed at Toyota out of the group work process, as *an additional task of work groups*: after the teams were trained in cleaning and repairing their machines as well as in controlling the quality of their own products, their were allotted time for periodical meetings to find ways for improving their own work process. These group meetings were part of the line organisation, not a separate structure like they assumed in the West. But it was these meetings which were picked out in isolation from a different system of organisation (TQM, Lean Production) and were overburdened with a variety of goals which we outlined at the beginning of this chapter.

At present, quality circles are said to have their positive functions as one element within a wider, encompassing system of organisational change towards an integrated concept of the organisation. The most general label for such a concept is Total Quality Management (TQM), another highly ambiguous term. TQM is difficult to define by enumerating its common elements, simply because of the fact that TQM literature points out to various 'essentials' which do not always conform with each other and which sometimes contradict each other. In the absence of a single theoretical formalisation, Hill (1991-UK) tries to organise the main TQM ideas along the works of the American and Japanese 'quality gurus', Deming (1986), Juran (1988) and Ishikawa (1985). According to their writings, total quality is a management philosophy which institutionalises planned and continuous business improvement. Quality could be translated as 'excellence', as the "ability to satisfy customers in the market place. Total quality assumes that quality is the outcome of all activities that take place within an organisation; that all functions and all employees have to participate in the improvement process; that organisations need both quality systems and a quality culture" (ibid.:554).

Hill then proceeds to outline some basic principles to substantiate this rather vague definition: first, top management is the main driver of TQM. It treats quality as a strategic issue, determines quality priorities and establishes the rules and procedures to be followed. In this sense, TQM is clearly a top-down strategy. But at the same time it is a concept of how management ought to behave.

Second, quality improvement occurs in two dimensions. Quite in line with the top-down principle, many activities take place within the existing hierarchical structure. The principle to treat other organisational units as internal customers points to new arrangements on the horizontal level. The use of *ad hoc*, multi-departmental and inter-departmental project teams is a way of organising across both horizontal and vertical lines. In this sense, "cross-functional management is an essential feature of TQM" (ibid.:554). A further principle is the strict reliance on systematic techniques of issue identification and problem-solving which all employees should master. When problems are defined, all steps to problem solution are quantified and made measurable. The principle is to rely on data, not on personal opinions.

Finally, the intended process of continuous organisational change creates and depends on a new 'climate' and culture within the organisation. It can be characterised by high-trust relationships and open communication across all levels, employee awareness for quality and customer needs, by everyone feeling responsible for his/her own performance and being committed to the 'common cause'.

But these principles might give an unduly clear picture of what TQM is like. Some authors concentrate more on the 'hard' aspects of TQM that centre around systematic problem solving techniques. Others focus more on the 'soft', motivational factors and see the human resource changes and the new 'company culture' as the essence of TQM. Whereas the mainstream literature stresses its top-down, management driven character, other sources point to a complete reversal of the traditional hierarchy which, under TQM, stands 'upside-down'.

Without trying to clarify the concept any further, it should have become clear that TQM allows for a variety of types of direct participation as they were defined in this text: TQM permits consultative and delegative forms of employee involvement; it includes individuals and may include groups, and it may operate all diverse forms of participation in one organisation at the same time.

'Lean Production' is a somewhat similar broad, 'integrated' concept and is related to TQM. Lean production gained recognition through the MIT study on the car industry. This study revitalised and popularised the concept of group work world-wide. Such groups are created around relatively complex tasks (cf. the Japanese principle: 'one task - one group'). Within these groups, quality circles are an additional means of improving the work process, aiming at standardisation of procedures. Such standardisation should lead to a continual decrease of variability in products and services to achieve quality at low cost. The 'lean' principle and the 'Just-in-Time' (JIT) approach add to the cost effectiveness of procedures: a procedure is 'lean' when indirect labour (like planning and administration) is minimised and paramount attention is given to direct labour that creates new value. JIT is not just a tool to ensure that suppliers deliver just in time when a producer needs supplies, it is not only a way to reduce stock or to supply products and services at the exact time the customer needs them. It is conceived as a process to reduce all kinds of waste and to accelerate through-put time.

Like in TQM, quality is not something to be checked or corrected at the end of the production process, but an element in each production step. Employees are sensitised and trained to deliver flawless work results at each step in the work process. In a certain sense, quality is built into the process continually, with little need to correct mistakes later.

In Japanese versions of TQM and lean production, the role of the workforce is outstanding and secondary at the same time. It is outstanding as management strongly invests in training employees, transfers much responsibility towards them and relies on their expertise and commitment in a general trust climate. The secondary role of the workforce comes from management's primary commitment to quality and customer wishes, from the fact that training reaches front line employees latest in the implementation process, and through the fact that workforce suggestions aim at standardising procedures which considerably curtails workforce discretion.

In New Production Concepts, another integrated approach, we find an important parallel to TQM in regard to a new division of labour, but at the same time a somewhat different solution concerning workforce autonomy. Brödner and Pekruhl (1991-D), in their outline of principles of advanced New Production Concepts, describe this overlap and difference as follows: as to labour division, traditional *functional orientation should be replaced by an object orientation.* All areas of manufacturing (e.g. design, order management, production) should be structured in an object-oriented way, by splitting orders instead of dividing labour. Multi-level hierarchies and their high interface losses in co-ordinating traditional decision-making procedures should be replaced by work teams. Through the principle *'planning of results rather than planning of activities'*, work teams are given a wide range of discretion to carry out their work. The work results (what is done) are subject to central planning and control, rather than specific activities and operations (how it is done). Instead of merely executing exactly prescribed operations, skilled workers should carry out complete tasks co-operatively, and co-design and control their own working procedures. The aim is to use and continually develop employees' professional and social competencies in the work process. This latter principle of wide work group autonomy and flexibility differs considerably from TQM and lean production approaches that aim at standardising of procedures. This difference is likely to structure the functioning and evaluation of various kinds of group work to which we turn in the following chapter.

Summary

Quality circles is an institutionalised group suggestion scheme that functions on a voluntary basis. In Europe and the USA they were (wrongly) identified as the secret behind Japan's success in international markets. Accordingly, competitive needs were the first motive behind implementing quality circles outside Japan. But further motives were added quickly: quality circles were seen as a suitable way of helping to establish to formal quality norms and standard specifications. They were extended to develop human resources, work motivation and the Quality of Working Life. But often management considered this suggestion scheme an easy way of solving the firm's problems without having to alter established organisational structures, or simply regarded them as something 'fashionable' to have.

If adopted seriously, quality circle implementation requires top management's commitment, a longer time perspective and financial input for training employees at all levels of the organisation. Training referred to problem solving techniques and group process, 'social' skills. The social, 'soft' skills proved the greatest bottleneck and the most important skills in Europe and in the USA, whereas in Japan they are never mentioned.

In Europe and in the USA, the emphasis was clearly on fostering employee work motivation and commitment to the company, and it was in meeting these targets that quality circles clearly had their greatest positive effects. 'Hard' economic effects were rarely measured, and the improvement of product and service quality was never seriously checked. Cost-benefit analyses in money terms are rare, and their results were not encouraging.

There is a common understanding that the positive effects of quality circles are over-reported and that the circles have a number of handicaps: under pressure to meet production dead-lines, quality circle suggestions are likely to be ignored by management. Management with a short-term perspective on the circle idea suspends circles quickly when it does not see immediate results. Bottom-up approaches, employee initiated circles had fewer chances of being accepted by management. Textbook applications trying to live up to the enormous amount of 'blueprints' generated by quality circle congresses and national Quality Circle Associations easily led to complicated procedures and bureaucracy. Most significantly, quality circles did not directly affect existing organisational structures, but created parallel structures and confused existing work roles, responsibilities and power arrangements, thus touching structures negatively in an indirect way. This created resistance from supervisors and middle management in particular.

Workforces had their grievances as well: circle participation was not always as voluntary as prescribed by theory. Particularly in Japan, but not only there, social pressure to join is widespread. Then, there was colleague pressure not to join for various reasons. Such pressure was most likely to occur in the USA, UK and in Mediterranean countries. When circle activities were not restricted to normal working hours, resistance and the claim for extra pay set in. Management not taking circle suggestions seriously - a frequent occurrence - leads to workforce disinterest in circle work. In particular higher skilled and white-collar employees want to be taken seriously and to see results. When circle membership is taken up in expectation of profane, 'extrinsic' benefits, such as improving promotion and pay chances and exercising power, the result is co-worker counterpressure. In addition, employees can be afraid of altered workplaces due to their colleagues' circle activities.

By now, quality circles are considered a dead-end road of direct participation and organisational change if applied as an isolated measure. In their original Japanese settings, such circles were only one approach in an array of management strategies, most generally known under the label of Total Quality Management. TQM is a set of integrated measures, often strongly relying on a group work approach, with groups having 'real', delegated rights and responsibilities. Both in theory and in practice, quality circles can play a positive role here. Whereas most isolated circle application 'died' after 1 - 2 years, they survived as part of a TQM strategy, indicating their potential as a transitional technique for more far-reaching concepts of organisational change.

4   Group Work Between 'Volvoism' and 'Toyotoism'

The present public and scientific debate about direct participation focuses on group work as the dominating concept: not only within the production sector, but in the service sector as well, working in teams or in groups is widely considered to be the core element of new forms of work organisation. The rationale behind group work is the departure from task fragmentation and labour division which have often reached their limits or proved sub-optimal in their consequences, both regarding productivity and the quality of working life. The new goal is task integration and the decentralisation of decision making to gain higher flexibility in work processes, higher quality of goods and services, a better use of human skills, attractive workplaces, and an improved quality of working life. As the various activities and skills needed in complex work procedures generally surmount the capacities of individual employees, task integration necessitates the pooling of human skills and task commitment in a group. Group members can complement one another; they can identify their optimal work procedures, and they are responsible for their products or services.

The concept of group work dates from the 1950s. It attained popularity for the first time in the Quality of Working Life movement in the 1970s, and lost public and scientific attention thereafter, leaving the scene for other fashionable management fads and research topics. Its present popularity was supported by the widespread reception of the lean production study (MIT study) by Womack, Jones and Roos (1990-US) on the world automobile industry. This book established group work as the core concept of direct participation with sentences like: "the dynamic team work [is] the heart of the lean plant" (103). At assembly plant level, a "maximum of tasks and responsibilities is given to those employees who really create values at the assembly line" (103). Employees are characterised as "motivated generalists who are ready to learn many skills and apply them in a team" (263). Each member is requested to invest his/her knowledge in improving the work process, to eliminate faults and unnecessary procedures and to deliver a flawless product. To achieve this, all necessary information is given by management. The team concept is not restricted to assembly line only, but pervades the whole company: it is applied in design and construction as well as in the relationship of the firm to its parts suppliers.

The stunning economic advantages of the Lean Production (LP) system based on team work in the automobile industry contributed to popularising the group concept:

* The number of hours to assemble a comparable car is about half the hours needed in a US mass production plant; assembly faults are down to about one third; through 'just-in-time' practices parts stock is down to two hours whereas in mass production it amounts to two weeks.

* The quality of car assembly is lower in US and European firms than in Japanese firms.

* High-quality European cars need up to 30% of the overall assembly time for finding and eliminating faults.

* Japanese cars are - on the average - easier to assemble than US and European cars - a consequence of better design and construction principles.

* Under lean production conditions the time for designing a new car is almost halved.

* (Among other indicators:) after model change, Japanese manufacturers are 'back to normal' in regard to productivity after 4 months, US firms after 5 months, and European companies after 12 months; 'back to normal' regarding quality of car: Japan: after 1.4 months, USA: after 11, and Europe: after 12 months.

* Worker absenteeism amounts to about 5% in Japanese car firms, whereas in Europe one often finds an absenteeism rate of 25%.

* Japanese transplants yield almost the same positive results in productivity, quality, etc. in the USA as at home.

The last result carries the message that we are dealing with a universally applicable type of organisation, not just with a national and cultural singularity. This message went around the world, giving the group work concept the outstanding role that it now plays.

In the following, we want to look deeper into the work group concept. We are going to show that 'group work' is another general label that needs closer scrutiny. By contrasting two types of 'group work', the Scandinavian and the Toyota type, we want to point to the different shapes 'group work' can assume. We discuss their rationale for being shaped differently, and the preconditions, effects and problems that various group work types pose for management and for the workforce.

4.1   Two Contrasting Types of Group Work

The first group work principles date back to the study of Trist and Bramforth (1951-UK) on technical change in a British coal mine. To increase productivity, management had invested considerable technology and devised specialised jobs to replace the traditional system of working in groups. Contrary to expectations, the new technology and work organisation lowered productivity. Analysis of the 'old', more productive system revealed that workers had developed a system of job rotation that depended on a profound knowledge of the overall job and optimal work processes, and on an intimate knowledge of personal capacities and individual differences of group members which was taken into account. These findings were then 'codified' into what later became known as the 'socio-technical systems' approach. According to this approach, both the technical and the social systems have to be adapted to each other to make them work and be productive.

The Scandinavian Concept of Group Work

In the early 1970's, group work applications gained prominence worldwide. General Foods in Topeca, Kansas (Work in America 1993-US) and the Swedish experiments with self-directed teams at Volvo and Saab-Scania are examples of this. In particular, the Swedish and Norwegian applications, the 'Scandinavian' model, set the frame for group work experiments in the QWL movement of that decade. In Swedish car production, assembly lines were modified by the introduction of buffers and other technical solutions to break away from machine pace. Coherent tasks that allow longer work cycles and the application of different vocational skills were given to work groups that regulated their own work proceedings. The further development of that system finally resulted in small work groups that assembled whole cars at the Volvo Uddevalla plant which operated into 1993 (cf. Sandberg 1995-S).

In its *ideal* form, the 'Scandinavian' type of semi-autonomous work group has certain traits:

1.   Membership in a work group is voluntary. Employees are not forced into group work.

2.   Group members can chose the fellow members they want to work with.

3.   Members can chose their 'leader' or speaker from their own ranks to deal with the rest of the organisation.

4.   Group members can decide on the internal division of labour and work rotation.

5.   Group members have different skill levels that permit them to help each other and to learn from each other. This enables the group to carry out all necessary tasks.

6.   The tasks should be rather complex and conceived as a 'rounded whole' to allow for variability of work, different degrees of task difficulty and to allow identification with a 'whole' product.

7.   In regard to technology, the performance of the work group should be as independent of machine pace as possible.

These are high standards. But many of them were achieved in certain instances. Gardell and Svensson (1981-S:36-37) wrote about a management-union agreement on the internal 'constitution' of work groups in a Swedish firm in the metal sector, dating from the mid-1970s. They state:

"1.   The group makes its own decisions after consulting all actors affected.

2.   All parties must co-operate.

3.   Supervision and division of work is decided within the group.

4.   The group itself plans its own work rotation.

5.   The group decides over temporary overtime and grants shorter leaves. Leaves without wage reduction and leaves of absence are granted by the production manager.

6.   The group can handle certain developments in working methods and further training of group members.

7.   The group members themselves choose their formal contact person.

8.   The group is collectively responsible for their undertakings.

9.   When the needs of personnel is not in accordance with the plans, the production manager should be consulted for joint action.

10. The production manager should be consulted when production problems occur that endanger monthly deliveries or other plans.

11. When a conflict arises which cannot be solved in the group, any of the members can talk to the union representative or the production manager about his/her problem."

The description of the ideal Scandinavian type of group work as well as the Gardell and Svensson example of management-union regulation of group work highlight its QWL potential and indicate the societal conditions in which the Scandinavian model originated. In our discussion of individual direct participation of the job enrichment type (cf. chapter 2.2), we mentioned that since long, job rotation, enlargement and enrichment has been long regarded as difficult to achieve on a strictly individual level. Most practitioners and writers indicated that these three measures could best unfold their potential in a group set-up, and that only work groups could really guarantee the functioning of job rotation, etc. Looking both at the blue-print of socio-technical group work and the practical example of how it was regulated in one firm, the chances for improved working conditions, more complex tasks etc., become evident. In addition, the Gardell and Svensson examples tap the general industrial relations atmosphere in which the project originated. It was a joint union-management undertaking which aimed at increasing industrial democracy in parallel with productivity improvements. This and all other Scandinavian efforts to enhance the Quality of Working Life took place in a period of full employment or even in an over-heated labour market, when it was difficult to recruit employees for certain industrial jobs and to motivate them to stay in their firms (cf. chapter 2.2). In sum, the general economic situation made such organisational changes necessary while guaranteeing their success at the same time.

Group Work in Lean Production

Looking at the Japanese group concept, we are confronted with a very different type of group construction and functioning. Inevitably, we are referred to the MIT study again. But although the group concept occupies the central role here, we learn very little about it in detail, how it functions and how it is embedded in the organisation. The description is very sketchy and indirect, and the reader has to assemble information from the context. The principles of Lean Production (LP) form the general frame of reference and can be summarised as (Roth 1992-D:5): teamwork, kaizen (continuous improvement), zero-defect principle, just-in-time/ zero-buffer time principle, customer orientation, efficiency of research and development, enterprise culture, integration of suppliers. According to Jones (1991-US), one of the co-authors of the study, these principles form a whole. He states that "lean production is fully functional only when all its elements are in place and working together ... nothing can be accomplished without the organisation of work groups consisting of individual members who are all capable of carrying out the various tasks particular to their area of responsibility in the production process." The study itself tells us that group members are generalists without portable skills between firms, except their flexibility to adapt to new work procedures. We further read that the LP team "eliminates any discretion - therefore it is lean" (ibid.:106), and that the groups work at higher speed than in traditional mass production, with 'creative tension' as a result. The authors indirectly characterise the Japanese groups when they criticise the Volvo Uddevalla concept on the basis that, here, group members can change their internal division of labour on their own. Obviously, Japanese group members do not have this discretion. Altogether, the study conveys the impression that in Japanese group work, work pace depends entirely on machine pace, that tasks are highly standardised and repetitive, and that vocational skills permit changes between short-cycled operations only.

Although the MIT study concentrates on the Toyota model as the 'leanest' of Japanese LP approaches and explicitly points to other, somewhat 'softer' applications in Japan as well, a brief look at the rationale of LP discloses certain features of Japanese-type group work as necessarily following from basic LP principles. Klein (1991-US) reminds us that LP is about 'process control' which involves "eliminating unexpected consequences, uncertainty, or variability from an operation. This, in turn, implies a high degree of standardisation throughout the manufacturing process, in both the technical and social systems" (ibid.:25). The author notes that standardisation is a 'cornerstone' of the continuous improvement process (kaizen). In a group, "individual team members can suggest changes to the production process [in quality control circles] but must gain agreement from the other team members before the design is actually changed. Once the task has been designated, however, there is little autonomy in task execution, and this is where standardisation comes into play" (ibid.:33). Klein points to the functioning of such teams in an American company: "if a team member wants to introduce a change which impacts on other members of the subgroup, that person must gain consensus from the group before making the change. If, however, the change affects the entire team, the person must raise the suggestion at the weekly team meeting, where a collaborative decision is made" (ibid.:33). In Japan, such group decisions are sometimes formally signed by all members and thereby become binding for all. Under such conditions, collective *autonomy is limited to task design* as opposed to task execution. The next group activity in regard to task design follows this scheme again and reduces the degree of freedom at each operation: even "when an operation is done at the outer tolerance limits, the variation allowed in subsequent tasks is narrowed" (Klein 1991-US:31).

The Just-in-Time (JIT) system further supports standardisation and reduces individual and group autonomy. JIT is essentially the elimination of inventory and buffers. Without the chance to buffer tasks, a batch process effectively becomes a continuous process. Individuals or teams have to synchronise their activities with each other constantly, and this reduces autonomy as well: "people [can] no longer shift to vertical tasks (problem solving activities or other assigned duties, like safety, quality, or materials) whenever they chose" (Klein 1991-US:27-28).

Further details complement a picture that conveys the message of very little autonomy and unfavourable traits of group work from a workforce point of view: Altmann (1995-D) reports that at Toyota, job rotation is restricted to narrow process areas and is ordered by supervisors. Contrary to LP folklore about 'flat hierarchies', supervisory levels at the shop floor are numerous and control is tight. Needless to say, supervisors are selected by management. Vocational training is company-, process-, and even machine-specific, derived from experience rather than based on formal instruction. There is limited off-the-job training of short duration for core workers only. The payment system is almost independent of workplace requirements, and rests on an appraisal system that is only "partially oriented to potential individual performance in the long run" (ibid.:345). More important are behavioural traits, such as co-operation, competitiveness, generating suggestions, identification with group and company etc.[6]

Comparing both the Scandinavian and the Japanese type of work group conception, the differences are evident, and all traits and regulations are juxtaposed (cf. table 6, p. 86).

Looking at these two extreme types of group work, both approaches have very little in common, except for the single fact that people are working together in groups. For some European authors, the differences between the Western and the Japanese concept of group work are so distinct and fundamental that they want to reserve the term 'group work' for the Scandinavian high-autonomy type of groups only, whereas the Japanese solution should be named 'team work'. As such distinctions are generally not

---

[6] The Toyota personnel assessment system has been changed recently, stressing individual performance more strongly at the expense of 'climatic' factors (cf. Grönning 1995-S).

made, and as both terms only denote the extremes of many possibilities of group application, we suggest the use of 'group work' as the general term and specify it in accordance to needs.

Table 6: Contrasting Types of Group Work

Dimensions:	'Scandinavian'	'Toyota', 'Lean Production'
entry/exit	voluntary	mandatory
qualification	mixed	unitary, 'generalists'
task complexity	rather complex	little, short cycled
technology dependence	rather independent of machine pace	dependent on machine pace
autonomy	large; task design and task execution	narrow: task design only
internal division of labour	voluntary	largely prescribed
selection of group members	by the group	by management
selection of group leader	by the group	by management

The QWL and the Productivity Aspects of Both Types

Any evaluation of both group work types depends on the perspective taken. *From a QWL point of view*, the Japanese LP solution contradicts all Western notions of 'good work', likely not to be attractive to European and US workforces at all. But they found their personnel in Japan facing external constraints similar to which the Scandinavian solution of enriched jobs and large group autonomy had been invented for. These labour shortage constraints including an unmet labour demand. Since World War II, the

Japanese labour market had been continually overheated.[7] To recruit employees to the group work that was slowly evolving as a system after the war, companies granted life-long employment for its core workforce, called 'regulars'. High wages were paid, based on seniority (which makes leaving the firm after some time a risky, costly affair, as employees again begin with low wages in their new companies), on superiors' rating of general group behaviour, and on annual bonuses (cf. Okubayashi 1993-JP). Such benefits are restricted to the 'regulars' who amount to max. 20-25% of the Japanese workforce. The remaining great majority of the workforce are either marginal workers, mainly females in the supply industry, or seasonal, unskilled workers who function as an employment buffer in Lean Production. Further 'regulars' are recruited immediately after leaving high school and are carefully trained and socialised into company culture and the specific work requirements (cf. Altmann 1995-D). Thus, in addition to Japanese 'groupism', working conditions were made attractive through 'extrinsic' benefits, such as job security, high income and identification with company. 'Work itself' in our sense has never been a Japanese concept, not for the weak company unions either, which concentrated on regulating pay and working time.

There is a sometimes passionate debate about the *productivity effects* of both approaches. Following the MIT study, the answer is clearly in favour of the Japanese type of group work. But critics point to various indirect negative effects such as health hazards and stress through dense work processes and irregular working time due to frequent and sudden request to work overtime. Altmann (1995-D) quotes sources which show that in the economic boom of the 1980s employees left car manufacturing companies on a large scale, thus indicating their discontent with their work circumstances. He quotes survey results according to which only 4. 5% of the car workers would advise their children to enter such firms. Thus, finding employees for such highly productive, but stressful and hazardous work heavily depends on the general economic situation. As the MIT study admits, the working of the 'Toyota system' entirely rests on the life-long employment guarantee. If this cornerstone is endangered, the highly productive system could not be upheld. In the past, Japanese companies always used employment buffers to adapt to business cycles which affected the employees negatively, such as deploying surplus workers in the supply chain or through early retirement. However, for a few years now, many Japanese companies face serious economic difficulties

---

[7]   Only recently (April 1995), the unemployment rate reached its peak with 3.2%, which is considered very high. In the Western countries, such a rate would signalize full employment, the low percentage attributable to normal labour market fluctuation.

that can no longer - in regard to workforce size - be straightened out through buffer solutions. Dismissals of core employees, of 'regulars', are already reported. As a consequence, we might expect that in economically threatening times, employees' appreciation of such work circumstances will rise. But in general, workforces are either ambivalent or negative about lean production work, thus making LP applicability and success a matter to be dictated by the labour market conditions.

The Scandinavian group solution is already showing such a reaction to labour market conditions. It is well known for high group autonomy and various other positive traits, but its productivity potential is very contested. The MIT-study is very definite on the success conditions of the Volvo type group organisation: it is unsuitable to produce efficiently for a mass-market, but might have its place in low-volume/high-value car production. In the meantime, both Volvo factories producing on the group principle (Kalmar and Uddevalla) have been closed down, officially for productivity reasons, thus supporting the MIT evaluation. But the reasons for closure are contested, with critics of this measure pretending that both establishments had reached the 'normal' productivity level. Considering the fact that the Uddevalla plant had been the company-wide benchmark factory for all European Volvo plants in regard to quality standards, we may assume that a combination of economic factors and other 'political' reasons accounted for the closure of this factory (cf. Sandberg, ed. 1995-S).

Japanese Inspired Production Systems - JIPS

Unfortunately, we do not have hard efficiency figures *for the automobile* industry to discuss the economic viability of the 'pure' Scandinavian type group work applications in this industry. In general, the discussion has reached a point where, from a productivity point of view, such pure applications are not feasible. In Europe, there is a felt need for a third way that is between Volvoism and Toyotism, for a solution that combines as many positive traits and functions of both concepts as possible, yet tries to avoid their handicaps. There is often talk about Japanese Inspired Production Systems (JIPS; Nielsen et al. 1991-DK; Nørby 1992-DK) or 'para-Japanese' group applications (Bonazzi 1993-I).

Vanbuylen (1993-B) investigated five car establishments of different multi-national companies in Belgium and identified that Ford, Renault and Volkswagen still experimented with group work of different kinds, whereas group work was widely applied at the Opel and Volvo plants. At Volvo in Ghent, the personnel department developed teamwork as a mixture of Japanese models and the Swedish human-centred tradition. Pure Japanese teamwork was considered too rigid and imperious, whereas the Kalmar and Uddevalla approaches were seen as not productive enough. The Volvo Ghent work groups consist of about 10 employees which work within the boundaries of a stringent line assembly. Some task enrichment is accomplished through several channels: In addition to the team leader, each team includes a 'team man' who fulfils jobs associated with 'working in a team': he collects statistics, checks material, assists team members etc. Team members can take turns to be a team man. The functions rotate daily or weekly, according to team preference.

Secondly, teamwork equals job rotation. Any team member should be able to master at least three different jobs, with five jobs being the maximum. The actual job rotation schedule is determined by the team. For example, some teams change four times a day, others once or twice a day. Management takes its job rotation system very seriously. It developed a three-phase model, ranging from having 'introductory knowledge' to being 'fully experienced', and keeps track of where employee scales in on which job. Thirdly, management is trying to further enlarge tasks. Maintenance and quality assurance now form standard parts of employees' tasks. The company plans to carry the idea somewhat further. In the long run, workers should also be able to implement elementary modifications to robots. The assignment of technicians to the teams to facilitate a knowledge transfer from technicians to workers is also planned. Teams meet twice a month in short quality circle-like meetings.

The team leader is installed through management, but all employees can apply to this position. He is responsible for quality control and has 'coaching' tasks, e.g. he ascertains smooth job rotation within the team. His tasks can be described more as a go-between rather than a manager. He has no real management responsibilities and is, as an example, not allowed to sanction team members. This remains the prerogative of the first line supervisors, each of who are responsible for three teams. Although each employee can apply for the team leader position, most of these positions are filled by former foremen whose jobs were eliminated. Preparation for the job takes 18 months and includes courses on a wide variety of qualification, like e.g. public speaking. Continuous evaluation over a 12 months trial period serves to secure that only suitable candidates are appointed. Team members do have a say in this evaluation procedure, but do not possess final decision making power.

Although we do not get a complete picture of all details of the group work system, the Volvo Ghent example clearly shows a team work application that differs from both the 'Scandinavian' and the 'lean production' model, leaning more to the Japanese concept. We find these 'Japanese inspired production systems' throughout all indigenous European automobile firms. Under this general label, the actual applications do not follow a unified model. Each company is experimenting with or already applying own solutions. A homogenous concept cannot be detected even in one country, e.g. Germany (Schumann et al. 1994-D), not even in one company: Daimler-Benz, for instance, experiments with six different types of group application (Gerst et al. 1994-D). Siemens, a German electrical engineering firm, operates with at least seven different types of group work (Grob 1994-D). In Italy, FIAT has reorganised its production system in a 'para-Japanese' way, oriented at concepts of cellular manufacturing and group technology (Bonazzi 1993-I, Cerruti and Rieser 1991-I). The basic units are called UTE (elementary technological units) which correspond to work groups with limited autonomy. Each UTE is responsible for a complete segment of the production process, assures the quality of its own work, and treats the next UTE as a 'customer'. The group leader is chosen by management and has considerable supervisory power.

But we find one recently built greenfield Opel factory in Eisenach, Germany, which obviously seems to follow Japanese lines very closely. In the absence of social research in that establishment we quote a journalistic report on the system's functioning: "People on the assembly line are like a ballet group which always moves in the same rhythm, directed by a hidden organiser" (Gottschall 1994-D). This observation does not inform us about any organisational details, but it reminds us of the Japanese principle of aiming at continuous standardisation of the work process, even down to the smallest detail. The 'ballet group' metaphor makes a group solution with very little autonomy very likely. It should be added that this establishment is located in a structurally weak area with high unemployment, thus, making use of a negative labour market situation which seems to foster the acceptance of such working conditions.

Japanese transplants in Europe do not apply their home system in pure form but try to adapt to local peculiarities and traditions as far as possible (Groth, Kammel and Tsumara 1994-D). Such was the case in Greece and in Italy. Teocar, a greenfield establishment of Nissan in Greece (Stavroulakis 1989-GR) is reported to have a very thin hierarchical structure with loose supervisor control. Work assignments are standardised, and the foreman co-ordinates a largely automated work process. The company made these workplaces attractive by offering higher than normal wages and job security which surpasses normal Greek standards. Voluntary quality circles are the main instrument of workforce direct participation. Honda opened up an establishment for smaller motor bicycles in the agricultural Abbruzzo region in Italy (Signorelli 1993-I). Management attempted a mix between the original Honda model and the Italian context. One criterion for choosing this site was to recruit workers without any experience in industrial work in order to train them 'ad hoc' according to company's needs. A strict selection procedure failed because of 'clientelistic' local social relations: everybody knew everyone, and management did not succeed in recruiting employees that it wanted. As a rather small firm with just one assembly line, the workforce is controlled through 'management by sight'. Contrary to Nissan in Greece, supervision is said to be extremely dense, with a worker-supervisor relationship ten times higher than in normal European and American companies. The system operates a soft implementation of JIT, depends on a low degree of automation, and keeps stocks and production buffers. Job rotation, team work, and multiple skilling are said to be very poorly applied. But we also know of other Japanese transplants that operate much closer to their home system, such as Nissan Sunderland in the UK (Garrahan and Steward 1991-UK) or NUMMI, the General Motors-Toyota joint venture started 1984 in the USA (Klein 1991-US). Here, collective autonomy of work groups is limited to task design as opposed to task execution, as was described above.

Closing our overview of group work in the automobile industry, we can conclude that both the Scandinavian and the Japanese approach are not applied in pure form in Europe and in the USA. JIPS or 'para-Japanese' solutions that try to combine the strongholds of both systems, while avoiding their negative traits, are sought.[8] One might summarise that Scandinavian influenced group type applications tend to be more frequent in existing 'brownfield' companies trying to change traditional structures and coping with an existing workforce. For more Japanese-type group applications with more restricted group autonomy, new organisations are typically created, and are staffed with a carefully selected workforce. The fact that such 'greenfield sites' are all located in structurally weak regions with high unemployment rates indirectly testifies to problematic workplaces that the majority of employees obviously find difficult to accept.

4.2 Problems of Group Work

We used the automobile industry as the most widely discussed example to clarify basic concepts of group work and point to some problems. But the

---

[8] Recent developments in the German car industry show a confusing trend, with some companies moving more strongly towards Japanese type group work whereas others give up the group work concept altogether (Willeke 1995-D).

group approach is not limited to this line of production. The concept is seen as the most important stepping stone, suitable for changing all organisations: in all production branches, in the private and public service sector, even in public administration. Yet, looking at *research* (not reality) we get the impression that group work is applied and discussed only in the production sector (cf. Cotton 1993-US:190). There is either little reorganisation in the service sector or there is little research interest there.

In the following, we want to discuss some important problems of work group organisation in a more systematic way. Although our examples are almost exclusively based on manufacturing, we are unable to give an overview over the different types of group work applied and the problems surrounding these particular applications. As was said about the car industry already, there is a multitude of group work applications that might differ even in the same company. In addition, all research focused on different aspects of group work. Attempting a rough classification, group work applications might look like this:

(1) The older *QWL work group* applications are heavily influenced by the Scandinavian tradition, first of all aiming at improving working conditions, without too much reference to productivity problems. Many of these group applications were funded by government programmes that alleviated the productivity issue considerably, but which made the experience gathered here hardly transferable to everyday business life.

(2) Workgroup application in *mass production*, using assembly lines - this is a rather small segment of overall production processes - , and as 'brownfield' sites, they experiment with or apply various forms of group work, leaning towards Japanese approaches.

(3) Newly created factories in such *mass production*, 'greenfield' sites, especially if owned by Japanese companies are likely to tend towards Toyotism as closely as national culture and the labour market permits. Their very creation in structurally weak regions indicates a rather low-autonomy, high-stress group concept.

(4) The majority of firms are *not mass producing*, and we assume that they try to find their own applications, which may or may not resemble the Scandinavian or the Japanese model.

Against these rather broad classifications, we want to discuss problems of introducing group work, personnel selection, training and skill issues, the remuneration problem in group work, labour market problems internal to the firm and external labour market effects due to the 'lean' organisation, and the productivity outcomes of re-organised firms. We have to state in advance that most of these issues are poorly covered by the research sources available.

Introducing Group Work

Systematic group work introduction aiming at decentralisation is one of the most radical approaches to organisational change, and organisational change is hard to achieve. Existing organisations have their traditions and their power structures, with members defending their 'vested interests' and struggling for influence. From Daniels (1987-UK) we learn, for instance, that the British workforce has a very unfavourable attitude towards general organisational change (as opposed to advanced technical change which is welcomed). Because resistance from actors on all levels is to be expected, management often prefers to create new organisations, particularly when aiming at group work and decentralisation (Emery 1980-US). General Motors devised a car plant in Austria as a 'greenfield' site, as all actors were aware that "this would distinctly reduce the resistance potential of established and hardened technical, organisational and social factors" (Scheinecker 1988-A:168). Japanese companies are said to only open transplants as 'greenfield sites' for this very reason. In Great Britain, the North-East has a large number of Far Eastern Companies, reputedly the highest concentration in the country (Beck and Stone 1992-UK). National governments and regional organisations often encourage the creation of new facilities by offering subsidies and other advantages, which was the case of the Honda plant in Italy (Signorelli 1993-I) or Pirelli Cables in Wales, Great Britain (Clark 1993-UK). It is in such new facilities that Japanese models of group work are most successful.

In existing organisations, introducing group work is said to be a very difficult, time consuming and costly process. Careful management starts out with pilot projects and experiments with small projects. Only when all problems are seen and solved in experiments are staff trained on a larger scale (Dawson and Webb 1989-UK). In an Italian food processing company (Citarella and Vitale 1988-I) the introduction of semi-autonomous groups in a TQM programme took five years, the time having been used for training middle management, line supervisors and workers in seminars. At BICC Cables, a British 'brownfield' manufacturing company, it took nine month to organise production into four cells (IDS 1992-UK). The reorganisation of one ABB department in Sweden took eight years altogether to reach the effects every actor involved expected (Steen 1991-S). As many interests are affected and much resistance has to be overcome in 'brownfield sites', organisational change is often only possible when external advisors and consultancies are engaged. As outsiders, they can analyse intra-firm problems, moderate the change process and help overcoming resistance to change. It is in these established organisations that the inclusion of outside consultants is reported as necessary (cf. Wall et al. 1986-UK; Bottrup and Clematide 1990-DK; Steen 1991-S; Wilkinson et al. 1992-UK).

Looking at the time-perspective of organisational change, the costs of external advisors and the training necessary, it is immediately evident that management ventures into a very costly process, where positive outcome is by no means predetermined. Organisational structures cannot easily be changed by defining formal rules and regulations. The 're-drawing of the organigram' is not a sufficient prerequisite for introducing profound organisational changes such as group work. The so-called 'soft' factors in organisational structures, i. e. non-technical and non-(formal)-organisational factors, turn out to be the real 'hard' ones and thus can be severe obstacles to any change. These soft factors are for instance: individual requests and habits; interests in gaining individual negotiating power within the firm; practices of co-operation and communication; traditions of dealing with conflicts; aversions between individuals; bundles of formal and informal agreements between work council and management; grown hierarchies; conventions of co-operation of work council and management etc.

All these conventions, traditions and practices are attached to patterns of interaction, implicit assumptions, attitudes, ways of thinking, norms, values, symbols etc. When all these elements have been in place for years, they form a structure which is very resistant to any change. Research shows that, in order to overcome this resistance all relevant actors have to be involved in the entire process of change. However, as for example Teixeira (1984-P) reports from his case study in Portugal, such participative processes are open ended and cannot rigidly be determined by top management.

Clematide and Bottrup (1990-DK), who have been involved as consultants in organisational development processes in five Danish companies, emphasise the importance of the introduction process. According to them there are several barriers which have to be overcome:
- existing traditions,
- arguments about the advantages of divided jobs may be prevalent,
- employees with 'narrow jobs' may have difficulties in believing that they are able to acquire the new qualifications required,
- the existing qualifications in the enterprise may be insufficient,
- groups sticking together may impede the creation of broader jobs across existing groups,
- insufficient communication and lack of trust and misunderstandings.

According to the authors, employees must have knowledge about general strategic objectives; individual persons in management and among employees must keep insisting that changes are of use; changed work organisation must be followed by training initiatives; new principles must be tested during trial periods, and it may be of advantage to get outside help in the start-up phase. All these prerequisites can only be achieved by comprehensive participation of employees in the change process.

The successful introduction of group work in ten Danish enterprises investigated by the DTI (1978-DK), revealed one general feature: although the change was mostly initiated and, in all cases, introduced by management, employee representatives and other practitioners from all levels of the enterprise participated intensely. Various committees and consulting groups had been established, and employee surveys and other means were carried out in order to discuss and manage the implementation process.

Etlinger, Gruber and Scheinecker (1987-A) emphasise the role of participation, too. Using an Organisational Development approach (OD) they emphasise the importance of involving all relevant organisational actors. These actors
- "have to be critical regarding the actual situation and must have ideas of the goals that shall be achieved (real utopia);
- must use their own working capacities in order to foster this change process;
- have to be ready for change and must be accepted by their colleagues;
- must believe in the problem solving abilities of people affected and must be unprejudiced about how to cope with certain things" (137).

A completely different concept of participation in the introduction of group work, is described by Fixari, Moisdon and Weil (1991-F). In the early nineties the French government subsidised a programme on new qualifications which was aimed at the simultaneous development of employment, training and work organisation. The programme, adopted in a Renault plant, was directed at assembly line workers who would enhance their qualifications by improving and reshaping their immediate work organisation. This qualification concept came close to the principles of OD, as described above: groups of operators who co-operated in daily work met in training sessions which were moderated by experienced organisers. Both the operators' know-how and their knowledge gaps had been identified to enable the employees to find new solutions for work organisation. The change process was successful as several problems of work operations could be solved, and the qualification programme resulted in a new form of work organisation. According to the authors, this transformation of work organisation was feasible only through involving the operators and their direct supervisors. Not involving them would have meant severe resistance to any change. Similar findings and conclusions are reported by Kalliola et al. (1994-FIN), Elorriaga Achutegui (1991-E), Kovacs (1990-P), and Clausen and Lorentzen (1986-DK).

Vermeulen and Gevers (1989-B) and Laville (1988-F) point out to the important role of corporate culture for participative change processes. A so-called 'low-trust-culture' of distrust and conflicts between actors on all company levels is not conducive for discussing new forms of work organisation. The move from a low-trust-organisation towards a high-trust-culture, however, is a complex change process in itself and cannot be realised easily.

Selection of Employees

One of the problems often neglected as a success factor for group work is the careful selection of employees. Whereas traditional methods for selecting employees concentrate on vocational training, specific job skills and general aptitude and intelligence, working in groups necessitates additional personality traits, such as a liking for work with others - a characteristic which Hackman (1975-US) has termed 'social need strength'. This need must then be made operational as 'interpersonal skills', the ability to operate easily in a group. One way to gain such a potentially co-operative workforce is through personnel selection. The Japanese companies have an 'extremely selective' recruiting process in regard to employees' abilities for co-operation (Altmann 1995-D), not only in their own country, but also abroad: in their German transplants, for example, Japanese management tests all applicants for their capacity *and readiness* for working in groups (private communication from Koji Okubayashi). For staffing its Georgetown Kentucky, plant, Toyota employed an assessment centre focusing on interpersonal skills. For staffing the NUMMI GM-Toyota joint venture with returning UAW members, management developed new selection tests to find out which employees would work together and which would not (Cotton 1993-US:197). One of the first examples of highly productive group work that went around the world in the 1970's was the case of General Foods at Topeka, Kansas. Here, too, a highly selective recruitment process preceded the manning of the greenfield site: out of more than 600 applicants, management carefully selected 70 employees for their interpersonal skills and their readiness to work in groups (Walton 1977-US). Similarly, when Pirelli established a greenfield site in Wales, management "was able to select the most suitable employees" (Clark 1993-UK).

In group work, selection of members has always been an important aspect for team functioning and success. Its significance has not always been fully grasped by the social science literature. The 'first' group concept in the socio-technical tradition described a working group that operated on the traditional right of British miners to form their own work group, to recruit colleagues they knew and could depend on (Herbst 1962-UK). Under such conditions, any positive effects of such group work can partly be attributed to the self-steered selection of 'reliable' group members, a topic that was never given proper attention in socio-technical systems theory. Further, all group applications in the QWL phase were experiments, with voluntary group membership and many drop-outs in the process (Fröhlich 1983). Because of this principle of voluntary participation and its experimental character, any positive conclusions about the ease of group work and group work effectiveness based on these early QWL findings have to be viewed with caution.

When contrasting the Scandinavian and the Toyota models of work groups, we characterised the Scandinavian model as having voluntary group membership, as opposed to mandatory membership in lean production approaches. This contrast is important considering that serious group work approaches in TQM and lean production are a pervasive strategy to affect and change the whole organisation. In such firms, group membership is often mandatory. When we learn that group work is the norm in 93% of all large Japanese manufacturing firms and in 83% of all large non-manufacturing firms as well (Okubayashi et al. 1994-JP), mandatory group membership comes as no surprise. The extremely selective personnel recruitment processes in Japan as well as in Japanese transplants obviously helps to ensure that group work will operate successfully. But the question remains: how can *established* firms that try to reorganise their work structures motivate their workforce to support such changes. If serious organisational change based on the group work principle is considered an appropriate and necessary solution, and if the principle of voluntary group membership cannot be upheld, then this will pose great personnel problems in 'brownfield' companies. Unfortunately, there is little research available to us on this topic.

Personnel Training

Most of our sources mention training needs in conjunction with group work, with two types of skills usually addressed: vocational and group process skills. As was pointed out in chapter 3.3, social skills are particularly important whenever we talk about groups, as group work adds a new social dimension to the work role. Many researchers and commentators consider these 'soft skills' to be important, not only for shop floor employees, but for also for management. Dawson and Webb (1989-UK) report that in a US transplant in Scotland, *all staff* were trained after a successful experimentation phase with TQM and JIT practices. Brady et al. (1993-IRL) tell us that in 12 Irish based companies, a large degree of training was initiated, the vast majority of which focused on interpersonal skills, problem-solving skills, communication, administration and planning, which were considered to be essential for team success. The authors point to one firm where 80% of employees were involved in team working, and each employee received an average of ten days training in one year. In a medium-sized Danish electronics factory employees working in semi-autonomous groups were provided with training (Olsen 1993-DK): 18 hours for co-operation and psychology, 7 1/2 hours for discussion techniques, 7 1/2 hours for planning, 6 hours for systematic trouble-shooting, and 2 hours for ergonomics. This schedule highlights the particular importance of 'soft skills'. Alasoini (1992-FIN) maintains that in Finnish companies employee training was more a question of moulding attitudes than actual professional training. New social skills were considered particularly necessary for middle management and front-line supervisors as their work roles were most heavily affected (see chapter 5).

But vocational training is needed as well. When discussing group work in the automobile industry, we mentioned that team members sometimes differ in the number of operations they are able to carry out to become an experienced worker. This was the case at the Opel Antwerp plant where it takes an employee two years to reach full wage and who can function in different teams. A similar scheme is reported for Volvo Ghent (Vanbuylen 1993-B). In the Austrian GM greenfield plant, group members have to acquire 'flexibility points' through training: "To get the flexibility points, the training necessary is organised by the group members themselves. There is sufficient know-how to train new team members. Such training is carried out on the basis of co-operation and mutuality" (Scheinecker 1988-A:174).

Asendorf et al. (1988-D) describe an extensive 20 month in-house training programme for group members in a mechanical engineering plant. The process started with an on-the-job training exercise on machines that the workers were already familiar with, followed by training on new machines. Half a year later, continuous job rotation was introduced for training reasons. Then, all group members practised the role of group leader, being mainly responsible for co-ordinating the 'pilot' working group. In addition, group members went through ten special courses on maintenance, CNC-programming, work organisation etc., ranging from 6 to 40 hours and totalling more than 130 hours. The whole programme ended with a two-and-a-half-day seminar on co-operation within groups. The company were able to afford this extensive programme as a consequence of government funding. Yet, the authors still report shortcomings in the training process, mainly due to time constraints.

From their own experience in five Danish companies, Bottrup and Clematide (1990-DK) emphasise that extensive employee training is the *conditio sine qua non* for successful organisational change. They enumerate various training methods and training locations, but indicate that many core qualifications to master new work roles can only be obtained within a participative development process: "Experience from several of the sub-projects shows that particularly with respect to these qualifications, solutions are to be found within the enterprise by letting employees have an active role in the renewal process and in the work re-organisation initiatives" (ibid.:59).

Two sources on German car plants exemplify the negative repercussions of poor training for the group work concept. At a Northern German VW establishment, a box system of car assembly was introduced, with four self-selected co-workers doing complete tasks on an equal base (Wehner et al. 1992-D). No special training took place. Although team members had chosen themselves as colleagues, there was no mutual help and co-operation, but constant conflicts. Work burden increased and work satisfaction decreased. Output quantity and quality was lower than on the conventional assembly line, and the company moved to cancel the box system. Minssen (1994-D) reports that half of the workforce as Opel Bochum work in groups, but that conflicts increased among members and that more group process training was needed for conflict resolution.

The Pay Issue

The way group work is remunerated is a very important issue for the functioning of teams, their productivity and the evaluation of team work from a Quality of Working Life point of view. Lack of consensus on the pay system can even lead to the ending of group work, as was the case in two Danish clothing firms: group work was discontinued because of remuneration problems that could not be solved (Banke 1991a-DK). Unfortunately, the importance of pay in work groups has been a neglected topic in the socio-technical research tradition (Kelly 1978), and it has only been recently that its prominence has been realised and solutions sought.

Group work depends on the co-operation of individuals in a set of interrelated activities that aim at producing a relatively complete product or service. The outcome is the result of a group effort, and, "ideally the pay system should support and reinforce collective productivity by workers, efforts at group maintenance, and the taking of responsibility by workers" (Cotton 1993-US:193). Yet, a *team based pay* approach as the theoretically best solution for group spirit and cohesiveness has two handicaps: group performance is difficult to measure as it is also influenced by external constraints which the group cannot control. Further, treating the group as a whole presupposes that each member performs equally. This carries the risk that the group's slowest members will be pushed out by group pressure. Team based pay which treats each member alike is considered a very problematic approach as it creates too much group tension (Eyer 1994-D).

There are two pay models that try to avoid these handicaps: a salary plus bonus system and skill-based compensation. Following Cotton (1993-US) the *salary plus bonus* system is easy to administer. Yet, individual and group bonuses might be difficult to assess. They might also lead to competition between work groups. Accordingly, a company-wide bonus would be easier to regulate. The author points to the case of General Motors' Saturn plant where employees were paid 80% of their normal pay plus performance bonus dependent on Saturn's success. Many potential employees did not enter the plant as this scheme carried too many uncertainties as to their final income. *Skill-based compensation* is increasingly becoming the most popular concept. Employees start out with an hourly pay, calculated at beginners' skills. For each additional skill learned, the hourly pay rate increases by a certain amount. Mastering all skills needed for the group tasks, and perhaps learning skills to enable a person to work in another group would mean reaching the highest skill grade and the highest compensation possible. The concept of 'polyvalent' workers in Belgium car plants strongly reminds us of this system. Cotton (1993-US:194) points out that the proper functioning of this system necessitates opportunities for training and upgrading.

Skill-based pay is also becoming important in Germany. Eyer (1994-D) considers flexibility as the central employee capacity needed for group work. According to him, flexibility is the degree of mastering different skills which should be remunerated on a time basis, according to the Cotton example put forward above. In addition, the author opts for an individual performance bonus. But while skill-based flexibility is easy to assess, it is the individual performance bonus which poses the problem: who is to evaluate individual performance in a group? If the work group becomes really self-directing with little necessity for interference from the surrounding organisation, supervisors increasingly lose knowledge of internal work group proceedings. When the group's work becomes a 'black box', superiors cannot really assess individual performance. Proper evaluation can only be done by the co-workers in the group.

Such peer performance appraisals are already applied in group work (Grenier 1988-US). Cotton (1993-US:174-176) describes its functioning in a US production facility: the pay systems rest on the skill-based compensation scheme described above. About one year after the teams were set up, peer performance appraisal was introduced. An outside operations facilitator (without supervisory functions) hands out appraisal forms to each team member. Within a week they have to rate their colleagues on "safety/housekeeping, teamwork/participation, work habits, communication, and technical skills" (idib.:176). In a fixed procedure these results are fed back to the team. We quote Cotton in full on its functioning:

"Initially some employees were worried about other team members 'sticking it to them.' The appraisals have tended to be more rigorous and have produced lower evaluations than those given previously by supervisors. However, the team members feel that the appraisals are more valid and prefer being evaluated by people who know their work (the team members) rather than someone who does not see their daily work (the unit manager). These evaluations force members to keep a check on their own performance. On one work team one individual was voted out of that group by his teammates" (ibid.:176).

Our other sources do not contain instances of such clear-cut approaches and results. We need not look at the Japanese situation as the remuneration system rests on quite different premises (cf. 4.1 above). In Europe and in the USA we find very different schemes for remunerating group work, sometimes even within one company. Such is the case with Siemens, a large German manufacturer of electrical and electronic goods (Grob 1994-D). Roughly 10% of all employees work in groups of very diverse kinds. Compared to the average wage, group members are more often in the high-pay brackets, with more than half of the workers mastering four and more tasks. As to the pay system, 25% of the group members are paid individually for piecework, 35% for group piecework, and 15% are paid by group bonuses. In three US firms operating flexible manufacturing systems, Adler (1991-US) found a pay-for-knowledge system with salary increments for new skills acquired. In 12 Irish companies Brady et al. (1993-IRL) detected very different systems, ranging from strict group performance schemes to remunerating vocational skills. One US transplant had shifted its approach from solely paying for the acquisition of vocational skills to a system of remunerating the applied skills together with certain administrative and interpersonal skills. In two companies of the Finnish light electrical industry operating with flexible manufacturing cells, there was a trend away from individual-oriented piecework pay towards monthly salaries (Alasoini 1992-FIN). The GM transplant in Austria (Scheinecker 1988-A) operates with 'flexibility pay' which rests on time-based pay plus flexibility additions which are based on 'flexibility scores' given by the supervisor (*Meister*) in co-ordination with the team speaker. In case of disagreement, the works council is consulted.

The few examples point to a great diversity of attempts to tackle the difficult problem of remunerating group work. Although there is no systematic evidence, the trend seems to go towards skill-based pay schemes enhanced through various individual and/or group performance elements. If skills are to form the basis of future remuneration schemes, training will have to be provided for workers to improve their flexibility and, thus, their income and professional advancement. If management are interested in decentralisation through effective work groups, then they will need to invest in appropriate training.

Economic Effects of Group Work

When attempting to assess the economic potential of group work as the core concept of decentralisation strategies and lean production approaches, we are inevitably referred to the MIT study. One secret of the study's success is the reported tremendous economic effects of lean production. There are few other studies, however, which present such startling results. There are a number of reasons here: first, as has been shown in the preceding text, the older QWL experience is not too helpful as it largely neglected the productivity issue. Most of the serious, systematic group work approaches aiming at decentralisation have been taken up only recently and are often in a stage of experimentation. Second, many companies have not defined exact economic objectives and benchmarks to be met, and are thus unable to state accurately whether group work was successful in the end. Accordingly, many assessments are intuitive, expressing general evaluations. Finally, we have a few well measured and documented effect figures, but which reveal competing results.

Very positive and somewhat in line with the MIT figures are the effects of 'modern' Swedish group work that had been introduced in one department of ABB (Steen 1991-S). The approach is termed 'modern' insofar as it had a clear productivity perspective in mind from the very beginning and aimed at a far-reaching change of organisation. The figures are impressive, indeed (cf. tables 7 and 8).

The ABB case is one rare example of quantified effects of thorough organisational change. The productivity effects are stunning, and considering the traditionally high labour turnover and absenteeism in Swedish mass-producing companies, the positive changes cannot be overlooked. According to the study, the project costs of 1.7 million SEK was almost recouped one year later. Although we have no information about up-front costs in the five year planning phase, the message remains unchallenged: thorough organisational change 'pays' in the end.

Table 7: Productivity Effects of Group Work at AAB

through-put time decreased	from 12 to 1.5 days
faults decreased	from 15% to 1%
service degree improved	from 25% to 98%
stock and products in production decreased	by 80%
labour turnover decreased	from 39% to 5%
sickness absenteeism decreased	from 14% to 8%
productivity increased	by 15%

Table 8: The Balance of Costs and Returns at ABB (in thousand SEK)

costs:		returns:	
training	300	decrease of stock	400
layout	150	fewer products in work	200
work places	700	decrease in absenteeism	250
working environment	100	decrease in labour turnover	350
other	200	fewer extra employees	100
temporary production losses	250	decrease in indirect time	350
	total 1,700		total 1.650

Source: Steen 1991-S

Another example of the successful implementation of group work is the study of 12 Dutch companies that all operated with group work (COB/SER 1990-NL). The study tried to measure both effectiveness and efficiency with hard indicators.[9] But serious problems occurred in assessing the economics effects. Only in a few cases had clear goals been formulated in advance, and

[9] Indicators for *effectiveness* were: delivery time, quality (in terms of numbers of faults), technical flexibility (introduction of new products and new markets), use of time of managers; indicators for *efficiency*: productivity, stock costs, loss of material, personnel costs.

in just two cases had the results to be achieved been quantified within specific parameters. Further, in some instances new production machinery had been implemented at the same time which made it difficult to isolate the impact of work groups. Unfortunately, no systematic overview of effects is given, just remarks on different measures, such as:

* delivery time was clearly reduced in all cases, sometimes 'spectacularly';

* 'quality improvement' showed mixed results;

* technical flexibility had clearly increased, although two companies aimed to reduce it;

* productivity had improved and stock costs decreased in nine out of 12 cases, although this could not always be quantified;

* personnel costs decreased in all instances due to staff reduction on the side of management and support staff.

Some costs had increased: higher wages per employee due to 'heavier' jobs (5 cases), increased communication costs in two cases, and 'investment costs'. In six cases, a pay-back period had been calculated: in three cases it amounted to two years, in the remaining three cases it was one year. Overall, most organisations seem to have benefited from working with teams. For Denmark, Bottrup and Clematide (1990-DK) refer to group work in a medium sized firm for health equipment where management 'assumes' that, all in all, the productivity results have been positive.

A number of positive economic effects of 'manufacturing islands' in a mechanical engineering plant are reported by Asendorf et al (1988-D). As in most other cases, there are no concrete figures, only qualitative estimates: time for machine preparing, maintenance and standstill was reduced; reactions to fast-changing market demands were much more flexible; process and product innovations are easier. These 'primary effects' were followed by a number of 'secondary effects': higher reliability of delivery times; staff savings within the manufacturing islands, since hierarchies vanished and all workers could substitute for one another; staff savings in the 'indirect' sector, because many of these tasks were transferred to the islands.

Similar results are quoted by other reports estimating the economic effects of group work. Lavikka (1992-FIN) states that 81% of plant managers in the clothing industry who introduced group work indicated increased productivity, and 71% observe an increase of manufacturing flexibility. Group work in

Fiat's 'Elementary Technological Units' (UTE) is said to be one main reason for the company's recovery after years of deep crisis (Bonazzi 1993-I). Ito (1988-JP), who investigated the internationally most competitive Japanese enterprises states that the flexible organisation based on job delegation to lower company levels is the key for understanding the competitive power of these firms. 91% of all Belgian companies which introduced TQM reported clear positive results (PRACQ 1990-B).

Sometimes, 'success' is defined in much wider terms, as was the case of 12 Irish companies. In the study by O'Hehir and O'Mahony (1993-IRL), all of the companies were able to report significant productivity improvements. They felt that as a direct result of their success they were able to attract new investment and new products to Ireland. The authors also noted that management referred to an improved perception of the company among customers, employees, and the community at large.

There is Swedish research that throws a shadow on too optimistic expectations about the efficiency of reorganised production. Using the Osterman (1994-US) concept of 'transformed' organisations, the NUTEK study (1993-S) asks whether transformed organisations making (among others) strong use of group work, are more productive than traditional mass-production firms. The author selected 13 Swedish and 12 German enterprises in electronics manufacturing to compare them in a quasi-experimental way, keeping as many parameters constant and developing sophisticated 'benchmarking' measures to permit statistical performance tests and cross-national comparisons. The study found out that 50% of the Swedish firms could be considered 'transformed', but none of the German establishments. Contrary to expectations, the German firms were significantly more productive than their Swedish comparison group. The authors interpret this unexpected result in terms that, perhaps, the Swedish firms were not transformed enough or that positive benefits might accrue later in time.

In his study on group work in two companies in the Danish clothing and textile industry, Banke (1991b-DK) comes to an 'old-fashioned' conclusion about the merits of traditional mass production:

"The project has shown that group organised production can be a competitive way of achieving production flexibility. But compared to traditional large-batch production in line organisation, a group will most likely show inferior results when traditional efficiency measures are used, provided that the enterprise is able to recruit sufficient manpower for piece-work production. Therefore, in order that group-oriented production becomes economically profitable, it is a precondition that the flexibility requirements of the group are adjusted according to the needs created by the market situation of the enterprise." (ibid.:73).

The two studies by Nutek and Banke, indicating that group work might not in all cases lead to higher productivity, raise an important and neglected topic: group work is only *one* principle of restructuring organisations, and the question arises under which circumstances will group work lead to increased productivity. It might well be that the proper functioning of group work needs an appropriate supportive organisational environment and does not work within traditional structures. Accordingly, introducing group work would necessitate other organisational changes to complement this form of direct participation in order to make it productive. Like in the case of quality circles, isolated group work applications might prove suboptimal or even unproductive. It might well be that work groups function properly only in integrated approaches of organisational change and in new organisational structures.

But apart from the two studies cited above, the overall assessment of group work regarding their economic effects is very positive. Higher flexibility and increased productivity are considered to be the most important effects. Group work and related methods of work organisation are regarded as one of the major keys to gaining international competitiveness. However, in most cases we have to rely on general statements by top managers rather than on precise figures. Those investigations that provide us with precise data, such as the MIT lean production study or the ABB case, report stunning results. These two studies analysed companies that either operated with completely 'untraditional' organisational structures from the very beginning or a company that reconstructed whole business processes. In both cases group work formed the core element of a new organisation.

Kling (1995-US) who reviewed 17 US studies on high performance work systems, found similar results: different kinds of new work practices, ranging from training, communication schemes, job design, teamwork to gainsharing, are particularly effective in regard to productivity improvements when implemented together. The author was also able to present studies with very positive performance increases, but he points to some questions that largely remain unanswered so far, among them the question of causality and of financial outcome. In regard to 'causality' the open (methodological) question is whether changes in work practices precede changes in performance. The causality issue hints at the possibility that productivity improvements might have made new work practices feasible or that there existed positive intra-company factors that boosted performance increases to begin with. As to financial outcomes, the author stresses the need not only to concentrate on productivity but to take other firm outcomes into account as well. This would include looking at the up-front costs of implementing the practices, their likelihood of success or failure and the overall financial balance. In sum, Kling's findings urge us to be cautious in measuring and evaluating the economic effects of direct participation.

A Note on Labour Market Effects

Similar to new information technology, the lean production concept has the reputation of restructuring workplaces on a large scale, leading to 'lean employment'. The MIT study principle of 'half of everything' might apply to employment as well. Whereas such fears were hardly confirmed in regard to new technology, they seem to be justified when looking at lean production. But in discussing the labour market effects of new, work group based strategies, one has to take the topic of intra-company labour markets and workforce segmentation into account as well. For both issues we have only sparse and mainly indirect evidence. But we want to point out to some problems nevertheless.

A decrease in labour demand: the lean production message, 'half of everything', sets the frame for labour market prospects. In regard to such effects, this message has not been proven yet by research; lean production applications in Europe and in the USA are isolated and often only in their experimentation stage. But the concept itself has this capacity: it is about decreasing the share of indirect labour in organisations, so that employees who do not directly add value (i.e., employees in administration, support staff, supervision etc.), are most at risk. The term 'flattening of hierarchies' points in the same direction of making position holders of several strata superfluous. The introduction of group work can thus be expected to result in fewer employees, unless markets are won for more products/services.

In our sources we often find comments that these principles work in practice. For Europe and the USA we hardly found any instances of a 'Japanese' solution, i.e. granting life-long employment for the core labour force, the 'regulars', a solution that is gradually being withdrawn in Japan in recent years, too. In this respect, the British Rover example comes close to a 'Japanese' solution of granting life-long employment: since the 1980's the company engaged in a thorough TQM programme and adopted various kinds of participation measures, group work included. Rover's so-called 'New Deal' offered an employment guarantee for all employees who wanted to stay with the company. Necessary reductions in manpower were going to be achieved with the co-operation of employees through re-training, re-deployment, natural wastage, voluntary severance and early retirement programmes. In the past three years over 10,000 employees had left the company, 3,500 since the New Deal agreement (Harfield 1995-UK). We have a somewhat similar management strategy with the German Volkswagen company. Here, employment was guaranteed for a few years with the workforce accepting a cut in working hours and a proportionate cut in wages, as well as employees' consent for flexible overtime work in times of excess car orders.

The majority of our sources treat labour market problems rather indirectly. Castillo, Jimenez and Santos (1991-E) remark very generally that workplace restructuring is usually accompanied by staff reductions. The Dutch study on group work effects states that personnel costs decreased as the number of staff were reduced (COB/SER 1990-NL). Particularly in the automobile industry we find 'flat hierarchy' effects: at the Opel Antwerp plant (Vanbuylen 1993-B) management levels were reduced by four, and many jobs in product inspection disappeared in addition. Cerruti and Rieser (1991-I) report on the Fiat reorganisation where hierarchical levels in production were reduced to only three: the production manager, the head of operative management and the foreman. In the Honda Altessa greenfield plant (Signorelli 1993-I), 'indirect' workers had been reduced by 37%, reaching a ratio of indirect-direct work of 1:2, far less than the average Western European ratio of 1:3 that Oliver and Wilkinson (1988-UK) found out. A British study on team working (IDS 1992-UK) states that in all six companies investigated, team working resulted in a slimmer management structure.

Rarely do we find remarks like that by Dawson and Webb (1989-UK) who investigated TQM applications in two Scottish establishments to find out that "no jobs were lost". Taking these few examples, we are left with the question: what happened to the former position holders? At present, the mass media provide the best information on labour market effects where we often read and hear of actual or planned workforce reductions in major firms through organisational restructuring. Although many dismissals might be due to ordinary rationalisation measures, we may safely assume that job loss through lean production and lean administration is a fact.

The issue of *intra-company labour market effects and workforce segmentation* carries the problem of who is drawn into the new organisational practices. Are only certain segments of the firms' labour force selected to work under the new organisational schemes? Is there a trend that a firm's core processes are carried out by core employees whereas less central functions are either systematically 'outsourced' or undertaken by temporarily hired (and fired) additional workers? In the Japanese situation we have already highlighted LP companies' reliance on core workers, but these amount to only 20-25% of the total workforce. The bulk of the firms' workforce is unskilled and/or seasonal, with much work being 'outsourced' into the supplier chain:

"these marginal workers form the quantitative employment buffer for lean production" (Altmann 1995:332).

On this special topic our own sources are not very informative. For the 'Japanized' North Eastern region of Great Britain we learn that two thirds of the workforce working in Japanese transplants are temporarily employed (Beck and Stone 1992-UK). O'Hehir and O'Mahoney (1993-IRL) in their study of 12 Irish firms, cited increased employment levels in these companies, but they did not elaborate on whether these were permanent or temporary posts. In three British engineering companies, group work went with skill enhancement which was confined to the core group of skilled workers. In regard to labour segmentation, the findings of Alasoini (1992-FIN) from studies in the Finnish electrical, engineering and paper industries point to homogenised manpower *within* the companies, as a consequence of new organisational models. Unskilled jobs were lost in the process, and companies tended to have a high skilled homogeneous workforce. The author concludes that the new segmentation lines will run more between companies than within them.

We have to repeat that our sources on these important topics are very sketchy and can just give us examples to highlight problems. But even these few sources are alarming enough to call for more political and research attention to be focused on the labour market issue in the future.

4.3   Workforce Reactions to Group Work

In the preceding sections, we often referred to employee issues when discussing group work problems. We did this in relation to management problems in general, but mainly in regard to the behavioural side of workforce reactions (such as absenteeism and labour turnover). When we take up workforce reactions to group work separately, we try to concentrate more on attitudinal aspects: how do employees experience group work, and how do they cope with it? We have very little knowledge of such topics, mainly for two reasons: (1) whereas research on management and union motives are popular topics, research on employee attitudes are usually neglected in industrial sociology and industrial relations (Thomas 1989-US, Carpo 1994-I). Research of this type tends to be found only in Human Resource Management, and then relates mainly to job satisfaction and related issues. (2) Social science research investigating the world of work has not yet developed theoretical approaches to explain social processes and work performance in real-life work groups. At best, and inaccurately, they transferred theoretical concepts geared to individuals (cf. chapter 2) to the group concept, overlooking that a social dimension is added here which changes the picture. As a result of these shortcomings, the following section necessarily rests on a small empirical base. We are going to discuss the general evaluation of group work by employees, the problem of social pressure of control, the problem of 'inner segmentation' of work groups through skill protection, and employee expectations towards group work.

The State of Research

Not all workers are in favour of group work. The many survey results carried out in Scandinavia and Austria on the preferred workplace all indicate the great wish of European workforces for higher discretion at work, but at the *individual* level (cf. chapter 2. 2). Even if they would like to work in groups, this does not mean that they are able to do it in reality. Company practitioners manning their greenfield sites are aware of this problem: when we discussed workforce selection practices above, we gave instances of selection procedures that test both applicants' desire and ability to work in groups. Quite obviously, this problem is well known to practitioners.

Who, then, prefers group work and why? The extensive research carried out in the QWL phase does not answer these questions, as the situation was untypical in various respects. As we already pointed out, the management objective of introducing group work was to reduce problems of high absenteeism and labour turnover in physically strenuous, boring, and 'alienated' jobs. The unions were interested in high quality workplaces and in industrial democracy. In a situation of overheated labour markets, both actors could attach a secondary role to productivity issues and to group work operating under productivity constraints. In addition, most group work measures were experimental in character, mostly financed by government programmes. As experiments, group membership was voluntary, and companies often had to select among many applicants. We do not have much information on who volunteered and who stayed out or dropped out in the process. And, finally, many of these experiments generated much attention among social science researchers and in the mass media, thus creating an 'unnatural' situation that could not be compared to group proceedings in normal working life. The actors knew about their special situation. Any results from research in such situations are in danger of producing 'Hawthorne effects', results that cannot be reduced to the subject matter, but to methods applied. In particular, the QWL experiments are said to have generated such methodological artefacts (cf. Fröhlich 1983-D, Cotton 1993-US). As a productivity tool, group work gained wide attention only in recent years, and as there is still much experimentation and little research, we know very little about its functioning and evaluation from a workforce point of view.

General Evaluation of Group Work

As already discussed, Japanese employees who work in groups in the car industry, do not seem to like it. Altmann (1995-D) reports that in Japan's economic boom in the 1980s, when alternative employment possibilities arose, workforces left the car companies on a large scale. Perhaps even more telling: only 4.5% of all car workers would advise their children to look for employment with automobile companies. Unfortunately, we do not know whether this applies to the core workforce, the 'regulars', to the marginal workforce or to both.

We have little information on how group work is evaluated in European and American greenfield sites. Greenfield sites are typically located in structurally weak areas, where employees have few employment alternatives. In addition, employees are heavily pre-selected in regard to their ability and willingness to work in groups. Yet, we learn that at the German Opel Eisenach car plant, people left the firm just a few days after taking up employment, as they could not stand the work pace, and workforce unrest is said to be mounting (Gottschall 1994-D). The greenfield Volkswagen subsidiary in Belgium, after experimenting with group work, still had an absenteeism rate of 20%. While blue collar workers originally favoured teamwork, they quickly realised that management only headed for an intensified Taylorism. Through the constant reduction of dead time, work pressure increased steadily. The industrial relations situation was described as tense and resulted in several strikes (Vanbuylen 1993-B).

But we find many instances of employees being very positive towards their group work experience. Cotton (1993-US:174) quotes a team member at Johnson Wax in the USA: "Out of the 30 years that I've been working here, this is the best thing that ever happened to me. " The same author (ibid.:179) refers to the General Food Topeka plant and quotes Lawler, Jenkins and Herline (1974-US) who reported "the highest levels (of satisfaction and improvement) we have found in any organisation we have sampled". The author further supplies figures on group work in the Volvo Kalmar plant where 90% of the workers liked teamwork and job switching between teams (ibid.:180). The Dutch survey of 14 instances of group working in 12 companies had similar positive results: "with a single exception, nobody wanted to return to the old structure" (COB/SER 1990-NL). These are just a few examples which show that group work can be a very positive experience in daily work. Yet, such results are hard to interpret in the absence of details about company specifics, about selection and self-selection processes of employees, and about the actual functioning of group work.

The Dutch example touches upon the problem of work loads in group work. Although increased independence and decreased monotony were judged positively, at the same time work was felt to have become more intense, carrying more responsibility. On the question of health - safety hazards and stress caused by work - we have practically no information. In the absence of information relating to stress, we turn to research on new information technology (cf. 2. 3). This research showed that working with new technology and applying high skills such as CNC programming considerably reduced physical strain, but simultaneously increased the needs of concentration and mental stress required. Nevertheless, the evaluation of such stressful work by the employees was overwhelmingly positive.

Social Pressure and Social Control

Group work holds, however, another stress potential, known as 'informal social pressure' and 'social control'. Social pressure and social control is a universal phenomenon in all types of groups, but it takes on a more urgent shape in the world of work. In work groups, people have to co-operate for a common results. In such cases, we can expect strong mutual pressure towards conformity in regard to qualitative and quantitative work input. "Probably the most pervasive and powerful influence on compliance is influence from one's co-worker" (Walton and Hackman 1986-US:170). Such pressure increases when income depends on group performance. When discussing pay problems of group work, we indicated that the ideal remuneration scheme supporting and reinforcing the collective productivity of workers, the team based pay scheme, is considered too problematic, partly because of the group pressure problem. Weaker group members are pushed out, and only 'Olympic teams' will remain in the end.

But even without such performance controlling pay solutions, the general problem remains, and one might ask whether social pressure is one of the productivity secrets behind the work group approach, in addition to needs of interconnected tasks that can best be met by co-operation. Whereas continental European sources rarely discuss this topic, in Anglo-Saxon research we find frequent instances where management has a clear vision of the self-control attributes of work groups and their efficiency effects. When workers control themselves, management is relieved of control. A US management's assessment of groups is cited as a way "to create a sense of group responsibility in co-operation with management. To make it a matter of peer pressure, not management pressure" (Thomas 1989-US:138). At the Opel plant in Eisenach, one of the first team experiences was that often there is "group dynamics which is more stressful than an authoritarian boss. No superior needs to control presence at work and work performance. This is done by the groups, as nobody is ready to tolerate poor performance of a colleague over a longer period of time" (Gottschall 1994-D:246). In Great Britain, we have additional instances of peer pressure being used by management as a conscious tool to increase worker performance (cf. Bratton 1991-UK, Beck and Stone 1992-UK).

Some additional examples can be forwarded to substantiate the problem of group pressure. In Japan, Altmann (1995-D:340) reports "massive social pressure within the group". The management of a Danish medium sized electronics factory introduced autonomous work groups on a voluntary basis. In a series of research reports this attempt was documented by Danish social scientists who wanted to explore "the possibilities of developing a richer and healthier working life, and thus greater self-determination for the employees ('the good work')" (Olsen 1993-DK). Management invested about a week's time for intensive training of the voluntary participants, two thirds of this time being allotted to training in interpersonal skills and group dynamics. Here, again, some of the employees involved left the project before or during the project because of interpersonal problems and the appearance of "leaders". In the end, the groups had experienced "considerable drop-out". To overcome these problems, Irish workers in peat production who were forced into group working because of the company's severe survival problems, reserved the right to chose their own members (Faughnan 1991). In a detailed case study, Barker (1993-US) analysed the change process from hierarchical, bureaucratic control to what he calls 'concertive' control in the form of self-managing teams. The author shows how group members progressively control each other way in behavioural details, and he concludes that "concertive control did not free these workers from Weber's iron cage of rational control. Instead, the concertive system ... appeared to draw the iron cage tighter and to constrain the organisation's members more powerfully" (ibid.:408). In the U.S., Applebaum and Batt (1994, p. 153) refer to group pressure problems in a summary fashion; Fröhlich (1983-D) and Cotton (1993-US) give detailed examples.

From this evidence, we can see that group work has a problematic 'social' side. While there are instances of self-steering groups which function without problems, and are experienced as true job enrichment and a definite improvement of working life, this positive effect may be most common among employees involved in boring assembly line jobs group work. Unfortunately, however, our knowledge about the preconditions and smooth functioning of work groups, from both social and economic perspectives remains limited. We further have to consider whether the productivity effects of group work are solely due to a better execution of interrelated tasks from a task necessity point of view, or whether productivity gains are partly due to social control factors. Further research on productivity and stress in group work has to be careful to keep various potentially influencing factors apart.

Skill Protection - the 'Inner Segmentation' of Work Groups

There seems to be a general trend that group work is more favourably evaluated by semi-skilled and unskilled workforces than by skilled employees, the latter group mainly being afraid of skill loss when working in a group context. The IDS study (1992-UK) of group working in six British establishment reports cases where groups held different skill categories. One of the problems with this integrated form of team working was skilled workers' fear of losing professional status. This was so pronounced in one company which had introduced group working in 1979, that it took a further ten years before craft employees could be convinced to join integrated production teams. In Finnish electrical plants that introduced cellular structures with mixed skills, opposition to organisational change came mainly from the skilled male employees (Alasoini 1990, 1992; similar situations were found in Denmark in a job enrichment project in the furniture industry: Bottrup and Clematide 1990; in Austria, in a greenfield car plant: Scheinecker 1988; and in Portugal: Cristóvam, Effertz and Jorge 1993).

Sometimes this skill problem is characterised by the "Matthew-effect": Skilled employees working in groups managed to reserve more attractive and flexible tasks for themselves (Dawson and Webb 1989-UK; for a Swedish example cf. Berggren 1992). In an Irish manufacturing establishment practising group work in a Just-in-time (JIT) context where the groups had autonomy to regulate their own work, the same split between skilled and unskilled workers, between operators and assemblers, appears. One employee is quoted: "there are no autonomous working groups. It's not happening and nobody is doing anything about it. Operators don't do assembly and management and supervisors are not pushing it. Here, there is no team-work" (Geary 1993-IRL:527). In an Austrian car plant, maintenance workers resisted group work openly indicating that this concept was valuable for the semi-skilled and unskilled only (Scheinecker 1988-A; Similar findings have emerged in Denmark: Bottrup and Clematide 1990-DK).

On the other hand, low skilled workers with rather monotonous jobs seem to have a real chance of improving their working conditions through group work. In a German bank, the routine processing of records, employing low skilled workers, proved to be a problem (Brater and Büchele 1993-D). This task was subsequently reorganised to group work where employees received a very high degree of self-regulation. Interviews with 86 persons revealed extremely high approval rates, with high percentages reporting increased work motivation, satisfaction, increased self-confidence and increased decision power, rating between 61% and 91%. All interviewees (98%) recommended this type of work organisation without any reservation. In two Finnish clothing firms, the switch to group work was welcomed by the largely unqualified female workforce: despite various problems 88% wanted to continue it (Palmroth, Hanki and Kirjonen 1993-FIN).

These few sources point to severe problems and possibly even resistance to organisational change when employees with different skill levels are to be integrated in one group. This finding contrasts with the idealised concept of co-operation which assumes an atmosphere of mutual help where all participants can learn from each other. The reality is likely to be different, with pecking orders and vested interests to be defended, with employees carefully trying to guard their status and power. The existence of such problems seems be the underlying reason why greenfield sites are so popular when introducing new production methods on a strict group basis. They allow the careful selection of low-skilled personnel.

What do Employees Expect From Group Work?

It is important from both an academic and a QWL point of view to ask what employees expect from work in general and from group work in particular. Is it autonomy at work, the chance of taking over responsibility, being intrinsically engaged in the task itself, carrying out 'complete', meaningful tasks? Such theories have been outlined in chapter 2. 2, and they have been developed in the context of individuals only. An extension of these theories towards group work is problematic, and new group based theories are still missing.

Results from three Scandinavian studies challenge the thesis that *taking responsibility* on a group basis is always attractive to employees: A LOM project of the Swedish Work Environment Fund (Westerberg 1992-S) wanted to decentralise the handling of finances in Swedish day-care centres, expecting the work group to take over budget responsibility. The project organisers expected organisational advantages, like better allocation of resources and awareness of restrictions regarding time and other scarce resources. At the same time, they were looking forward to "better motivated personnel who are taking over responsibility" by improving work through participation. In her action research approach, the author noted an unexpected "resistance from personnel towards own budget responsibility" (ibid.:134).

Instead, the employees had other priorities on their agenda: firstly wage increases, and secondly, good human relations at the workplace. Own budget responsibility rated extremely low (cf. for a similar case in a Danish organisation for home helping: Olsen 1988-DK).

The motives that became apparent in the above example are called 'extrinsic' or 'instrumental', and they do not conform to theory. We frequently find this type of motivation related to participation. In their review article on the functioning of various participation schemes which covered different types of group work, Kelly and Kelly (1991:43) summarised research evidence from a workforce perspective. One of their outstanding findings was the dominance of instrumental, mainly financial gains, that employees might get from participation schemes: "Workers may see that it is in their interests to co-operate with managers in production and may support new decision-making and reward systems where they perceive that they are likely to experience financial gain."

A British study (O'Connel Davidson 1990-UK) examined the link between job content and employment conditions, testing the assumption that high-discretion work requires employees to exercise their discretion and initiative, which should be rewarding in itself. In a recently privatised public utility, clerical work had been characterised by a strict and detailed division of labour. Management wanted to correct such problems by introducing multi-functional team working. Under these new arrangements, as well as being primarily responsible for a particular set of tasks and duties, employees were also expected to acquire a broader range of knowledge and skills in order to facilitate functional flexibility. Based on this work structuring concept, management saw an inevitable link between functional flexibility and improvements in working conditions which should be self-rewarding. Although over half of the 53 clerks interviewed agreed that the new work organisation was more rewarding, varied and interesting, the vast majority also agreed that team working intensified their work and should be better remunerated, something which was not anticipated by management (for a similar case in a French Renault car plant cf. Fixari, Moisdon and Weil 1991-F). Pay problems often identified in relation to group work testify to the importance of material benefits in group based participation schemes. This forces us to question the theory which expects the enlarged work roles with higher discretionary content to be the most highly valued roles.

Another principle of work structuring claims a human need to accomplish 'whole', complex tasks, and, at the same time, blames job specialisation and fragmentation, usually accorded to mass production. With the possibilities of job rotation, enlargement and enrichment, work groups can offer opportunities to overcome fragmentation. That such needs do not always exist, is exemplified by Regini and Sable (1989-I): in Sicily, women wanted to keep their traditional assembly line work instead of a new work organisation that included group work. To keep their traditional tasks and to avoid group work, they even offered to work at higher belt speed.

As further explanatory information is missing, this piece of research should not be over-estimated. Much more to the point is a thorough study in three U.S. firms (Adler 1991-US). The investigation of flexible manufacturing systems (FMS) in a group set-up produced evidence of self-developed, rather tight divisions of labour, based on job specialisation, in the groups. Although individual and even group autonomy was low, satisfaction and motivation were high. In explanation of this unexpected result, the author suggests that job specialisation was perceived by workers as an effective way of getting the job done, "that when workers can establish a feeling of organisation-wide responsibility for the effectiveness of their work, sacrifices of individual autonomy and even sacrifices of work group autonomy can be accepted as long as these sacrifices are seen as effective ways to accomplish necessarily interdependent tasks" (ibid.:458). The author suggests that the key factor behind motivation and satisfaction might be efficacy, rather than autonomy or the absence of external constraints. He indicates that if workers identify with the broader goals of their work, autonomy may be less salient than efficacy: "This result is surprising when we consider the long history of sociology's critique of bureaucracy and other forms of standardisation and formalisation that turn the employee into a mere cog in the system" (ibid.:458).

Overall, our knowledge of workforce reactions to group work is patchy. There is clear indication that even in Japan, working in lean production groups is not highly estimated by employees. We do not know for sure about workforce reactions to working in JIPS type greenfield sites in Europe and the USA. Apart from the fact that, here, employees are intensively selected and establishments are typically located in high-unemployment regions with few employment alternatives which automatically increases the attractiveness of such workplaces.

But we find many instances of employees evaluating group work very positively. Such examples have to be carefully investigated to find out about the preconditions of 'good' group work to be able to generalise results and generate construction principles of positive solutions, applicable in practice. We found no clear evidence of particular health and safety hazards, but stress increase was reported.

Stress is not only a consequence of more complex tasks. It can follow from the social situation of mandatory co-operation as well. Such informal social pressure and social control has often been reported, most frequently in conjunction with group based payment schemes. But social control works in all instances, and management often sees the advantage of worker self-control which is more efficient than supervisor control could ever be. The question arises whether productivity gains of group work are actually due to an improvement in the processes dealing with complex tasks, or whether group pressure acts as a contributor.

In general, highly skilled workers are sceptical about working in groups, fearing the loss of qualified work, qualification, status and income. Many sources tell us that high skilled workers succeed in retaining the 'better' jobs in work groups, thus creating a form of 'intra-group segmentation'. The unskilled and semi-skilled workers seem to be the true winners in group work, and their positive reactions to these new work circumstances are distinct.

Many instances contradict theoretical expectations of intrinsic motivation for taking over more responsibility and enjoying complex tasks (although motivational theories on working in groups are still missing). There are strong extrinsic motives, to the point that working in groups must 'pay' and that the additional skills acquired and applied should justify higher remuneration. Then, there are instances showing that large-autonomy, self-directed teams 'invent' a rigid division of labour if that contributes to getting a 'job done' - a finding which is hard to explain using existing theory.

Summary

The present public and scientific debate on direct participation focuses on group work as the central concept. Group work represents a departure from traditional task fragmentation and labour division. It strives for task integration and the decentralisation of decision-making in order to gain higher flexibility of work processes, higher quality of goods and services, a better use of human skills, enriched workplaces and an improved quality of working life. The group work principle was originally developed in the 1950's and experimented with in the Quality of Working Life movement in the 1970's, particularly in Scandinavia. It gained its present prominence through the MIT study on the world-wide automotive industry that advocated group work as one of the main secrets behind Japan's economic success.

The present public debate often lacks a clear understanding of fundamental differences about the original European type group work and the Japanese solution which can be conceived as two extremes: Membership in *Scandinavian groups* is voluntary. The groups select their own members. The qualifications held by group members are diverse in order to enable members to learn from each other and help each other. Their tasks are rather complex and not very dependent on machine pace. They regulate their own internal proceedings and have significant autonomy in regard to task design and task execution. They elect their own leader. The *Toyota* or *Lean Production groups* display the very opposite features: Group membership is mandatory, and members are carefully selected and 'socialised' into group work. They hold company and workplace specific qualifications to operate in short-cycled, machine-paced tasks. Group members are expected to constantly streamline their task execution through the kaizen principle and in quality control circles: they are supposed to recommend further possibilities to eliminate any variability in their work, to streamline the design of tasks, and in task execution they have to adhere to solutions that were put forward and agreed upon by the members. The internal division of labour and any job rotation is prescribed by superiors who are nominated by management.

From a Quality of Working Life point of view, the 'lean production groups' defy all European notions of 'good work'. Group members have discretion only in task design, aiming at further standardisation of task execution. This type of work is highly disliked in Japan, but acceptance rests on the guarantee of life-long employment and a remuneration system that seriously inhibits changing employer. As the principle of life-long employment is already being eroded, we can expect this type of group work to change in the future.

The Scandinavian type of group work developed in a time of over-heated labour markets, with workforces unwilling to accept boring mass-production jobs. It has proven its worth for increasing work motivation and decreasing absenteeism and periods of sick leaves. But unlike the Japanese group solution, its productivity potential is very contested.

Under the label of 'Japanese Inspired Production Systems' (JIPS), European and US American companies are experimenting and applying group work concepts that try to combine the strengths of both systems while avoiding their handicaps. Japanese teamwork is considered too rigid and imperious, whereas the 'Scandinavian' approaches are seen as not productive enough. A unitary concept has not yet evolved: we find various types of group work in the same countries, even in the same companies. As a trend, 'Japanese' type solutions are typical in newly founded, 'greenfield' sites, whereas established organisations in 'brownfield' sites display more 'Scandinavian' elements of group work.

Japanese transplants in Europe and in the USA do not apply their home system in pure form, but try to modify their approaches to cope with local peculiarities and national traditions. To avoid resistance to organisational change, such transplants are typically conceived as 'greenfield' sites, preferably in structurally weak regions which offer few employment alternatives for the workforce.

Introducing group work in existing organisations is a tedious process which takes time, in one case: eight years. Internal company traditions, vested interests and power structures have to be altered and overcome, and low-trust climates have to be converted into high-trust ones. Such change processes are very often moderated by external advisors and consultants. The active inclusion of the workforces smoothened the change process.

In general, group members are carefully selected, both in regard to their willingness and their capacity to work in groups. Such personnel screening is easy to achieve in 'greenfield' sites. Unfortunately, we have very little knowledge about work group manning in 'brownfield' firms. For group work to function properly and be productive, additional training of employees is considered a necessity and is carried out in most cases. Companies apply different training schemes of various duration for their workers to become multiskilled. Rarely is vocational training left to the group members themselves. Many commentators point to the 'social dimension' of group work and the need for 'social skills'. The lack of such skills is often regarded as the real bottleneck in achieving smooth group work functioning, and the various training schemes and the time and money invested to foster social skills, testify to the fact that most companies try to cope with this problem.

The remuneration system is one of the most serious topics of group work, creating conflict and sometimes even breaking up group experiments. Ideally, the remuneration system should reflect the common group effort and responsibility, and would request a *team based pay* approach, with all group members receiving an equal income. But this system is not recommended due to various problems. A salary plus bonus system is easy to administer, but conflicts often arise about the proper bonuses. In Europe and in the USA, there is a trend towards *skill-based pay schemes, enhanced through various individual and/or group performance elements.*

The MIT study has set the key note in regard to the economic effects of group work in transformed organisations of the car industry: 'half of everything' on the cost side. Most of our information on productivity increase and economic benefits is very positive, and the Swedish AAB case is particularly encouraging in this respect. But most positive assessments were rather general. With the exception of AAB, we rarely found precise figures. Various reasons account for this: indicators for productivity, efficiency and effectiveness were poorly defined, and cause-effect relations are difficult to isolate. General assessments made by management regarded different dimensions and were positive. But in two instances, traditional production schemes proved superior to new work schemes in transformed organisations.

The labour market effects of group work are a 'forgotten' topic. We did not find any straightforward information on how the 'flattening of hierarchies' and 'lean' approaches affected companies' workforce size. Equally unsatisfying is our knowledge about intra-company labour market effects and workforce segmentation. From Japan we know that large companies often operate with a core workforce, heavily relying on additional, peripheral employees. Such core-periphery problems are reported for Japanese transplants in Europe as well.

Our knowledge of workforce reactions to group work is very patchy. In Japan, working in lean production groups is not positively assessed. There are indirect indications that working in JIPS type applications in Europe and in the USA meets similar 'scepticism'. There are very positive employee reports on group work, but the basis for a positive or negative assessment of working in groups is still unclear. We did not encounter particular safety and health hazards through group work, but stress increase is a fact. Part of this stress is attributed to the frequently reported informal social pressure and social control that exists among group.

In general, the highly skilled are sceptical in regard to working in groups, fearing the loss of qualified work, qualification, status and income. In groups, they often succeed in retaining the 'better' jobs for themselves. As a trend, the unskilled gain from group work and are staunch supporters. Contrary to theory, the extrinsic aspects of group work, income in particular, seem to play a more decisive role for work motivation that 'the task itself'.

5. The Debate Over the Role of Middle Managers

Direct participation was defined as a management driven strategy to encourage rank-and-file employees to engage themselves more strongly in task related matters and to self-organise work either as individuals or as groups. All of these strategies imply some form of organisational change, varying from small work role re-definitions to completely new organisations adopting lean production approaches. In normal change strategies, all levels of management operate as agents of change. Top management make basic decisions, the lower echelons operationalise them down to the shop floor or office. But the present situation to foster task participation and to achieve organisational decentralisation differs from the traditional norm: basic decisions are still made by the top echelon, but the middle management layers are no longer simply agents to execute such decisions. Middle management itself is a prime target of change. In theory, TQM approaches want to substitute strong hierarchies and top-down policies by a horizontal organisation and integration. In LP the elimination of some hierarchical layers ('flat hierarchies') is an explicit, additional aim. Thus, middle management functions are not only re-defined and altered; some functions are in danger of disappearing altogether. Middle management's problems are obvious. Our research sources testify to this, and references to middle management problems are numerous and repetitive. Yet, the problem of middle management remains to be qualified. There are good reasons, supported by research, that this managerial group can and sometimes does act as a facilitator of organisational change as well.

In the following we want to point to some basic problems and attempts to solve them, based on selected pieces of research. We use the term 'middle management' rather indiscriminately, and point to different functions only when necessary. As to problems and problem solutions regarding middle management in social research, we have to add in advance that descriptions and suggestions are very general and almost common-sensical, leaving many questions unanswered.

Our picture of middle management problems might have been painted in too dark colours, as the different forms of direct workforce participation and top management policies behind them clearly have different impacts on the organisation. Types of individual participation, such as suggestion schemes, workforce surveys or job enrichment strategies are said to be low-impact measures. Quality circles, were applied in Europe and in the USA, did not seriously affect the organisation either. But talking about group work changes the picture, particularly in conjunction with decentralisation goals. This radical approach to organisational change clearly affects not only the common employees, but their immediate supervisors and the middle echelons of organisations.

5.1 Middle Management Problems With Various Types of Direct Participation

Even 'low-impact' individual consultative measures such as suggestion schemes and workforce surveys might have an impact on middle management. When employees have innovative ideas about their workplace or about work procedures, this might negatively fall back on immediate superiors. Higher management might wonder why such suggestions were not put forward by supervisors themselves. Whereas this suggestion problem is more of a 'thinking game' with no empirical evidence behind it, workforce surveys can have a more irritating potential for middle managers. In chapter 2.1 we referred to the 'Ten Commandments' of the German Bertelsmann corporation, one of which states that all superiors have to explain and justify all of their decisions *vis-à-vis* their subordinates. One of the means in which top management can find out whether this rule has been applied are regular workforce surveys. Surveys results can be broken down to department level and discussed here, putting management at that level under pressure (Bundesmann-Jansen and Pekruhl 1992-D; similar for Belgian firms: Baisier and Albertijn 1992-B).

Whereas such measures are rather diffuse in their consequences, mainly creating an indirect control atmosphere, middle management's situation can be more directly affected through job enrichment of individual employees. As a reminder, job enrichment entails the re-definition of an individual work role, extending the range of tasks horizontally and vertically. Vertical task enrichment means that the employee gains more rights and responsibilities, and quite naturally the question arises: whose rights and responsibilities are touched in the process? Job enrichment was more often applied in the 1980s, when New Information technology made its inroad into manufacturing firms. Sandberg (1992-S) gives a vivid example of problems that can arise in instances of such technical change: in a Swedish engineering workshop, three CNC machines were introduced, the workers having been trained beforehand to programme and run theses machines. Programmers opposed the new work organisation as it did not follow agreed rules. The production technology department was opposed to it, as it could not provide advance information for a whole week and was unable to handle emergency planning. Supervisors were completely negative, as work planning, their most important task, was taken away from them: "It therefore happened, on occasion, that the supervisor retained the drawings for the week's work, and then apportioned the jobs. Management tried to discuss with SALF [the supervisors' union] what alternate functions the supervisors could assume. The problem was not entirely solved, but an agreement was reached to allow the experiment to continue as planned" (ibid.:169).

Among all types of direct participation, quality circles as a group approach with only a consultative focus was initially considered an easy tool for organisational change. It was welcomed by top management for various reasons: it could be tried out in pilot projects; it was often considered low-cost, and it left all decision making power with the hierarchy that was free to accept or reject circle suggestions. Thus, it appeared to be relatively problem-free, unobtrusive means of achieving potentially large effects. As already discussed, quality circles are nowadays considered to be ineffective, a frequently cited reason for their demise being middle management's opposition. There is ample survey evidence to suggest that top management considers middle management as the bottleneck for circle introduction and functioning: In a survey on German enterprises with quality circles, top management stated that middle management opposition was the main hindering factor (Antoni, Bungard and Lehnert 1992-D). Middle management's 'scepticism' about it being 'just a new fashion' and 'fear of loosing control' are the foremost reasons given by Italian top managers, with 57% of them indicating middle management opposition (ANCQUI 1987-I). Such negative evaluations could be quoted for many countries.

We get the same message at company level: At Teocar, a Nissan transplant in Greece that operated with quality circles, middle management and supervisors refused to support the circles, thinking them to be just 'a whim' that would pass (Raftis and Stavroulakis 1991-GR). In three Portuguese industrial firms, middle management and the skilled workforce first welcomed quality circles, but soon got the feeling that they undermined their authority and autonomy. Some middle managers are said to have left their firms because of circle introduction (Cristóvam, Efertz and Ramos 1993-P). The French *groupes d'expression*, consulatative groups based on law, were heavily contested among management: some saw it as a chance to dynamize the organisation, for others, they only created disorder in the firm. This conflict was particularly intense in middle management (Bernoux et al. 1985-F). Other research points to outright hostility of middle management and supervisors towards the circle idea (Vermeulen and Gevers 1989-B). We could cite numerous sources for most European countries testifying to middle management's dislike of quality circles at enterprise level.

Why are middle managers and supervisors so negative about circles? Middle management's main complaint is that circles 'confuse structures', that they create a parallel organisation, a 'shadow hierarchy' (Beriger 1987-D, Hill 1991-UK). Supervisors and front-line managers are faced with an additional body, making recommendations to change workplaces - normally their own task. Circles might come up with good solutions which supervisors should have had as part of their normal work role. Then, direct supervisors are at the same circle as leaders in most cases, which means additional workload in preparing and chairing circle activities. Laville et al. (1988-F) report from a German medium sized firm that supervisory staff resisted quality circles, fearing an alliance between the workforce and top management.

These are the most common complaints we hear. In the Mediterranean countries, an additional reason is quoted: holding discussions with 'inferiors' and listening to them is often considered inappropriate for men in power positions. For Fiat brownfield sites, Bonazzi (1993-I) points to a deep rooted culture where expertise is strictly linked to authority and where the bureaucratic model is considered the best. For Spain, Martin Hernandez (1993a-E) explains middle managers' aversion to quality circles as a consequence of having been brought up in an authoritarian management system where hierarchical leaders are never questioned. A Portuguese study on the *Meisterkrise*, the 'crisis of function' of middle managers in production, points out that this group is mainly male, older, with low schooling, and that the need for a new relationship with their employees often results in an 'identity crisis' (Freire, de Lurdes and Vito Peña 1994). For Veiga and Yanouzas (1991-GR), Greek management can best be characterised by 'uncertainty avoidance' resulting in a particularly 'assertive behaviour'. Spanish sources plainly speak of management's 'macho' attitude. The Mediterranean examples, characterising management in general, also apply to middle management. Thus, apart from sometimes well-grounded factual reasons for resisting employee task participation, cultural factors can come into play and aggravate problems.

So far, we only talked about middle management's recalcitrance when dealing with 'soft' forms of direct participation. Middle management's problems become very serious when it comes to group work, TQM and LP strategies. Whereas one could sometimes doubt the appropriateness of middle management's resistance particularly regarding consultational direct participation, middle management's fears are very often justified when looking at the consequences of delegative participation and 'integrated strategies'. The greatest, easiest to grasp and best-documented problem arises for front-line supervisors, when group work is introduced in manufacturing. The central idea of such groups is that they steer themselves and therefore do not need steering from outside. There is wide consensus that group work eliminates the traditional positions of foremen. The role of front-line managers (in German: *Meister*) is said to undergo a serious change at least, and there are initial indications that this position is in danger of becoming obsolete. Minssen (1994-D), in his study in the Opel Bochum plant, clearly states that supervisors (and maintenance personnel) are the 'losers of group work'. The *Meister* display a very negative attitude towards group work, as groups haven taken over some of their former functions. In addition, the elected group spokesmen constitute a new level of hierarchy *Meister* have to deal with without being able to really control it. *Meisters'* roles are blurred: they are still responsible for reaching production goals yet have only insufficient means to control the production process. The same author reports that in the greenfield Opel Eisenach plant, the new position of an 'area engineer' has replaced the *Meister* function, and this position can be reached by group spokesmen without any additional examinations. A newly opened chemical factory in former East Germany has been organised without any *Meister* positions: production groups deal directly with higher management levels (Minssen 1994-D:45). Scheinecker (1988-A) gives a similar poignant example of problems in an Austrian GM transplant: In two years, the integration of production, inspection and maintenance could not be achieved, due to *Meister* resistance who rejected a change of their work role and their numbers. In their opposition, the *Meister* were supported by their white-collar union.

The problems increase when more far-reaching strategies for organisational change are pursued by top management, when hierarchies are to be eliminated and cross-functional management is the aim. This is the case with Fiat. The reorganised company relies on group work, called UTE, as its basic units. But top management aims at the Integrated Factory (IF) which comprises the 'flattening of hierarchy' and 'product orientation instead of process orientation' in addition to UTE's. This IF is clearly said to affect middle management much more than the workforce, through dismissals and through changed work roles. We have little information about the actual labour market repercussions of such integrated strategies. However, we learn from a Fortune 1000 study in the USA, that companies' reliance on middle management dropped significantly between 1987 and 1990 (Lawler, Mohrman and Ledford 1992-US). The authors argue that this might reflect, among others, a job loss due to flattened organisational structures. Clark (1993-UK) reports a high turnover rate of middle managers in a CIM plant in Great Britain which made it difficult to develop coherent personnel policies and a system to audit the implementation of self-supervision.

5. 2 Middle Managers as Supporters of Organisational Change

The latter example shows that although middle management is an endangered group, it is not superfluous and is needed in the future. At this point, a word of caution about a general recalcitrance of this group is in order: In spite of the fact that middle management is affected by direct participation one way or the other, not all middle managers simply resist this change. Many of them see great chances for themselves and their organisation and have a positive attitude towards change, often actively supporting it. This 'deviant' information needs to be explained:

The bulk of our research evidence testifying to middle management's resistance is based on senior management's answers on change barriers. Interviewing middle managers directly changes the picture considerably. Such is the case in regard to quality circle introduction and functioning in Italy. From senior executives we learn that 57% of middle managers oppose these circles (ANQUI 1987-I). But we get a different view from middle managers: only 30% are reported to be hostile toward quality circles, the remaining 70% favour them (Nicoletti 1986-I). These contrasting data may point to senior management's negative perceptions of managers in the organisation's middle echelons.

The Italian survey on middle management (Nicoletti 1986-I) highlights a variety of attitudes towards quality circles: the most reserved, sometimes even hostile middle managers are said to be front-line managers and direct supervisors who felt their power positions endangered. Middle managers responsible for quality standards had a favourable attitude towards circles but did not actively promote them, whereas middle managers in the organisation and personnel departments turned out to be the active supporters of quality circles. These results are apt to differentiate the summary term 'middle managers' and point to various subgroups with differing interests. This indicates that support for direct participation measures among middle managers decreases when their positions are endangered.

We cannot decide whether this common-sense explanation can be considered a rule. There are contradicting instances where middle managers fully support organisational change. This was the case in five Danish companies where most first line/middle managers expressed the necessity to involve employees in order to increase organisational flexibility and quality. One middle manager is quoted as saying: "To involve the employees is simply a necessity. It is particularly important that the persons who are familiar with the work are the ones who bring forward ideas; and then, we must try to put into practice as many of their ideas to make them feel secure and enjoy working" (Bottrup and Clematide 1990-DK:32). Other sources report a general split in middle management attitudes towards direct participation. The application of French expression groups was particularly contested among French middle managers, some of them opposing this measure, whereas others fully supported them (Bernoux et al 1985-F). Bundesmann-Jansen and Pekruhl (1992-D) found a similar rift running through middle management in the Bertelsmann media corporation, with one part supporting and applying the company's participation schemes and another selection of management obstructing them. The latter group feels under heavy pressure from the top to produce quick results which, in their view, does not permit 'time consuming' measures of direct participation. In addition, a number of these middle managers lacked the communication skills to manage in a monitoring way.

Other sources tell us that middle management reactions largely depend on the engagement of senior executives when pursuing organisational change through direct participation. Geary (1993-IRL), in a study of two comparable foreign establishments in Ireland, found that in one firm, the implementation of quality circles met with middle management disinterest or resistance, while top management displayed only weak interest in the process. In the other establishment, senior executives were very successful in convincing their middle managers to support organisational change through group work. Top management had a consistent policy of change; it was able to convey to everyone that change was seriously wanted. All initiatives supporting group work were consciously supported, and line managers were rewarded for their specific efforts. In this process, first line managers came to appreciate their new roles as group facilitators as being more interesting and challenging than their traditional hierarchical work roles. Hill (1991-UK) who had pointed to widespread middle management resistance in regard to quality circles, found that middle managers displayed very positive attitudes towards TQM approaches:

"Middle managers appreciated the increased decentralisation and their greater influence over the decisions taken elsewhere in the organisation. Many also believed that TQM could advance their careers, by bringing them to the attention of more senior managers if they performed well on a major improvement project, and that it gave them a better understanding of the wider organisation. Decentralisation and participation ... can also promote more teamwork and flexibility within the management group. The literature on employee participation strangely has ignored the desire among managerial employees for more influence and involvement; yet the extension of managerial participation under TQM is a significant gain for people who, like the employees they supervise, have a real interest in a more participative system of managing" (ibid.:561).

Other sources give additional information about what kind of middle managers are more likely to support direct participation initiatives and which are not. We already quoted a Portuguese study on first line managers' resistance to organisational change where this management group was described as mainly older, with low schooling (Freire, de Lurdes and Vito Peña 1994-P). Following a similar argument, the Finnish social partners point out that middle management attitudes often vary from generation to generation, with young managers being more receptive to change (Mikola-Lahnalammi and Aloisini 1995-FIN:13).

The few sources that have been discussed give the general impression that middle management are unanimously negative about organisational change through direct participation. Most complaints about this employee group come from interviews with senior managers, and it might be worth considering whether 'middle management resistance' to change might be an easy way out for senior executives who themselves are afraid of change. It then depends very much on what type of organisational change is intended: when 'lean' policies and 'flat hierarchies' are the outspoken goal of change, middle management resistance will be greatest, whereas TQM approaches seem to hold less threat and more chances for this group. Further, middle managers' reactions will depend on their functions, with first-line supervisors being most affected. Needless to say, the younger generation is likely to be more flexible and may perhaps be keen to change their own narrow work role to one that is more participative.

5.3   Training for a New Role

All commentators agree that the work roles of middle managers will change in the process of organisational restructuring through direct participation. The extent of this change and the management functions affected will vary with the type of direct participation implemented: When low-impact, individual, consultative or delegative forms are applied, front-line supervisors and foremen will be most affected, whereas any systemic changes aiming at cross-functionality based on the group work principle will have more encompassing repercussions on all middle echelons throughout all organisational sections. There is a clear trend away from directive roles towards a coaching, facilitating role. Middle managers become team organisers and communicators between teams and senior management. As 'team managers', their 'social skills' tend to become more important than their technical, vocational skills. Dawson and Webb (1989-UK) tell us that in a Scottish subsidiary of an US electronics company that was organised around JIT and TQM principles, supervisors were chosen for their social skills, rather than their technical abilities.

But instead of selecting appropriate middle managers to fit new roles, the majority of sources stress the great need for training middle managers to enable them to adapt to their new roles and functions. In particular, the TQM approach always saw management as the prime target group for change. From a Belgian representative survey we learn how training for TQM was apportioned to separate groups within the firms: it is first of all directed to middle management (32%), followed by white collars (30%), top management (24%) and blue collars with 19%. The first training goal was team building skills. This training preceded or complemented the introduction of TQM and prevented middle management resistance from the very beginning (PRACQ 1990-B). In their survey on various participation strategies in 649 firms in the Barcelona region, Miguelez et al. (1993-E) found considerable training activities in group dynamics, leadership and quality control methods. They were, first of all, directed towards middle management, and much less towards plain employees (similar for four Spanish firms: Lope Peña 1993-E). In ten Italian companies, top management was aware that TQM introduction would affect all actors. In addition to training, most companies tried to overcome problems from the re-definition of all power relations by stressing the 'symbolic dimension' of the firm, by supporting company-wide communication, common company values, company culture and corporate identity (Carpo 1994-I).

Such training and 'soft skill' promotion activities are also reported for popularising the much less threatening quality circles. Top management in Nissan Teocar in Greece openly admitted that it under-estimated the need to train middle management (Stavroulakis 1989-GR). To make quality circles acceptable in Italy, some companies created temporary project groups, composed only of middle managers to discuss problems and to change attitudes (ANCQUI 1987-I).

Whereas the new role of middle management poses problems for European and American firms, we hear of no such problems in Japanese companies. First of all, companies starting out with a completely different LP organisation do not face such questions, as all actors are chosen and socialised into the other system to begin with. Still, there are problems, but they seem to be covered up by at least two strategies: the MIT study tells us that the supply-chain companies and even foreign transplants are 'parking positions' for managers to prepare them for future challenges. Altmann (1995-D) confirms such practices, but is much less positive in their evaluation. In particular, jobs in firms in the supply chain are very often 'dead-end roads'. In addition, there seems to be sizeable intra-company unemployment when superfluous employees are kept. Unfortunately, Altmann gives no details about the composition of this group.

Summary

Summing up, middle management's status as a problem group is obvious and a cogent result of direct workforce participation. Although the various types of participation affect this group in different degrees, already the low-impact participation schemes like workforce surveys and job enrichment have the potential to irritate some sections of middle management. Quality circles, still considered low-impact in regard to organisational change, generated considerable resistance, with middle management being afraid of parallel structures and 'shadow hierarchies' which confuse work roles and power relations within their firms.

Middle management problems become more serious with group work introduction and LP schemes, aiming at fewer hierarchical levels. Any strategy to flatten hierarchies means the direct threat of job loss. There is a common understanding that in manufacturing, foremen and front-line supervisor are the losers in group work. Many of their functions are taken over by the groups. We know very little about middle management behaviour in regard to cross-functional reorganisation and 'lean' approaches. We have some indication that labour turnover increases in such cases. The severity of job loss and the labour market problems of middle managers remain a blank.

However, middle management reactions are not as clear cut as they often seem to be. Senior executives who are the prime source for middle management, are much more critical about this group's resistance than middle managers themselves. If middle managers see a new role for themselves, if they are supported by senior management and can acquire new skills through adequate training, then the younger ones in particular might be active supporters of organisational change.

Middle management is still needed in 'transformed' firms. In many cases, this group is likely to be 'leaner', and its role will change: top-down functions will decrease, and moderating, coaching and facilitating roles are asked for. It needs determination and time to train middle management particularly in these 'soft skills', but such training is a necessity and the main solution to win over the hearts and minds of middle management.

6   The Impact on Employee Representation

Perhaps with the exception of the Scandinavian countries, for most unions and other employee representative bodies, management driven direct participation was something disturbing which put them on the defensive, and created the need to defend their own position and to react. The disturbing novelty was the fact that management offered various forms of task participation and increased work discretion to employees whose unions had sought, but never succeeded in obtaining, more industrial democracy. Employee representatives wondered about management's motives and about the possible repercussions of direct participation on their own role and functions, and on the future working conditions of employees. Unions were concerned that management might by-pass them; that direct links between management and employees might develop new trusting relationships between both parties at the expense of representative bodies; that such direct involvement might alienate employees from the idea of collective representation and collective bargaining (growth of 'individualism'); that representative bodies might lose standing when employees experienced quick solutions to workplace problems through direct participation which employee representatives had been trying but had failed solve; that the functioning of the dual representative structure of unions and works councils might be broken up when works councillors at firm level are drawn into direct participation measures; that, finally, the whole system of collective bargaining might be threatened. In addition, it was unclear what positive and negative effects on the workforces could be expected, and how unions and employee representatives could cope with a possible deterioration of working conditions and defend employees' workplace interests.

Very illustrative for the new, open situation and for the reactive position the unions found themselves in is the Irish case (O'Hehir and O'Mahony 1993): the Irish Congress of Trade Unions initiated research to investigate the union's problems and the possibilities offered by the new forms of work organisation. The researchers conducted empirical investigations in 12 Irish firms (including subsidiaries of multinational companies), which sought:

(1)   to review the implications for trade unions of introducing flexibility within the workforce and such systems as teamwork, world class manufacturing, quality ethos and human resource management,

(2)   to review and make recommendations on the response of trade unions to these changes in the organisation of work and in the management of such change,

(3)   to review and make recommendations on employer attitudes to trade
        unions, in the light of the above, and their implications for
        employer/trade union relationships,

(4)   to review and make recommendations on how trade unions can
        respond positively to the requirements of modern industry while
        safeguarding their members' interests.

Based on their empirical data, the authors concluded that these new work
structures are likely to become more widespread in the future and that their
introduction will revolutionise work practices and employees' experience of
work. They state that the main reasons employers have for supporting the
introduction of these techniques is that they deliver significant benefits to the
organisation. Therefore, unions should attempt to find a new role for
themselves in relation to these strategies. As to the strategic options which
would allow unions to respond to the new initiatives being undertaken by
management, the authors outline five possible responses which range from
total opposition to active promotion of the introduction of changes in line
with the union's own agenda. In regard to the benefits and risks associated
with these options, the authors point to increased job security in the long term
through enhanced productivity and to improved quality of working life. It
concludes that the development of a high trust relationship between
management, employees and their representatives is essential if these
initiatives are to succeed. They finally suggest that unions should adopt a
flexible approach and that a rejective, negative attitude is not a realistic
alternative.

The Irish case testifies to the seriousness of the new challenge to traditional
union policy and identity, and the research project of the Irish Congress of
Trade Unions describes the range of topics and offers a framework for
analysing the situation of unions and workforce representatives with regard to
direct participation. Based on empirical research, we want to discuss the
following five topics: (1) Why does management introduce direct
participation in establishments? Is organisational change only meant to
increase the competitiveness of the firm, or does management have other
objectives, such as using direct participation as a means of weakening
representative systems? (2) How do unions and employee representatives cope
with direct participation in their companies? How open are they towards the
new trend? Are they just defensive or do they actively co-operate? Which
problems arise when coping with the approaches? (3) Is direct participation a
potential source of conflicts between different bodies of workforce
representation, such as unions and works councils? Does it drive a wedge

between employee representatives? (4) Does direct participation alienate the workforces from the idea of representative participation? Do employees who experience more say at the workplace develop a critical attitude towards unions and works councils? (5) Finally, what hazards and chances do employee representatives see for the workforces they represent? What are the social consequences of organisational change and where do they see particular needs for protective action?

In this context, we encountered the difficulty of differentiating between unions as national organisations and establishment-based workforce representational systems. A precise analysis would have to take into account the very different national models of overlap and independence between both institutions of workforce representation, a task which cannot be solved here, as our material often was not detailed enough. Instead, we tend to treat both institutions in a general way.

6.1 Direct Participation - a Union-Avoidance Strategy?

Unions have had various forms of direct participation on their agenda for a long time, but this has gone unheeded by management. Thus, when management actively promoted such measures questions arose as to the motives behind this policy change: Is employee participation propagated and pursued solely for company performance benefits, to increase quality, international competitiveness and the like? Are there other, more 'political' reasons for propagating direct participation, such as weakening the representative system or even preventing the establishment of such systems where they do not yet exist? We can assume that such questions were considered in many countries, but it has only been considered by researchers in the USA and, to a lesser extent, in the UK. Here, we find a strand of research which investigates direct participation programmes as a means of 'union busting' and union avoidance.

The study of Kochan, McKersie and Chalykoff (1986-US) was primarily concerned with the reasons behind the decline of unionisation in the U.S. and asked how frequently innovative work practices were introduced as a means of avoiding unionisation. Data from a panel survey of 243 identical establishments show that keeping the firm union-free was management's main motive for introducing direct participation in non-unionised companies in 31% of cases in 1977. By 1983, this incidence had risen to 45%. This strategy was obviously very successful: "... a firm that engaged in ... innovation in its non-union plant reduced the risk of being organised by approximately 14.4 percentage points compared to a firm that implemented none of these innovative practices" (ibid.:496).

Such data suggest that workplace innovations should be concentrated in non-union companies, and that such firms should be leading in workplace innovations. Yet, there is other U.S. research which questions these results and, implicitly, the reasoning and explanations behind them: Based on interviews with a subset of 313 Fortune 1000 companies, Eaton and Voos (1992-US) challenge the notion that non-union companies are the progressive leaders in workplace innovation (which they should be if the union-avoidance hypothesis holds). The authors found innovative practices more prevalent in union firms than in non-union ones. According to the survey results, union firms make more use of all the types of direct participation practices than non-union firms, with quality circles and job enrichment most likely to be found in moderately unionised companies, whereas Quality of Working Life (QWL) committees are most prevalent in highly unionised environments. The non-union sector leads the union sector only in the practice of profit-sharing (which is not our topic here).

Based on two surveys, Cooke (1992-US) tried to show that union avoidance is not a clear-cut policy and that workplaces with employee representative participation achieve greater improvement in quality than more traditional workplaces. The first survey was carried out in 1986 with 350 large unionised manufacturing plants located nationwide (194 plant managers responded). For the second sample, 300 Michigan manufacturing firms employing fewer than 1,000 employees were randomly selected and surveyed in 1988. (Responses were received from managers in 70 unionised firms and 61 non-union firms in the second survey.) The author defines employee participation as "work groups, teams, circles, of committees eliciting the input of employees and union representatives" (ibid.:199).

In the nationwide sample of unionised firms, 57% reported having jointly administered programmes, 6% reported having programmes administered solely by management, and 37% had no participation programmes at all. According to these figures, the general union-avoidance hypothesis is not confirmed. But the hypothesis gains more support from the second survey of both union and non-union firms: only 32% of the unionised firms were reported to have formalised employee involvement programmes, whereas such programmes were found in almost two thirds (63%) of the non-union firms.

In addition to the topic of union avoidance, U.S. research sometimes investigates the success chances of workforce involvement schemes in union and non-union firms, asking whether direct participation in unionised firms can have productivity effects at all, under what conditions it might have such effects, and how these effects compare with non-union firms. Such questions rest on the assumption that unions are a handicap to productivity gains through workforce involvement. A case in point is the aforementioned study by Cooke (1992-US). With respect to the effect of joint labour-management participation programmes, the study indicates that improvements in product quality in unionised firms are equivalent to improvements achieved through participation programmes in non-union firms. The author contends that his "collective voice" thesis regarding more effective employee input through union representation is supported by the findings of this study, although under certain conditions: "... unionised companies appear to achieve their goal of product quality improvement when union leaders are involved in the administration of participation programmes, but not when union leaders are uninvolved. Taken together, these two findings suggest that positive collective voice effects are realised when unions are treated as partners, but negative restrictive union effects become dominant in the absence of such partnership" (ibid.:132).

Using a similar line of reasoning the U.S. Federal Government promoted Employee Involvement (EI) programmes to reduce 'fraud, waste and abuse'. A survey covering the 25 largest federal departments and agencies revealed that most agencies viewed union involvement from the beginning of implementation efforts as desirable 'in order to prevent any strain between labour and management' (U.S. Merit Systems Protection Board 1986-US:13). Where management has kept the unions involved, fewer problems arose.

The few U.S. studies cited here are not meant to answer the question whether direct participation *is* primarily used as a management tool to decrease union influence. They only serve as examples of the fact that this topic is regarded as a serious problem in the USA. In Europe, we find such research interest only in the UK, but the topic is considered not too urgent. As an example, Marginson et al. (1988-UK) report that in Great Britain, quality circles are likely to be found in companies that recognise unions. There were none found in non-union companies. From this finding, based on a quantitative survey of 143 large enterprises, the authors conclude that quality circles appear to be part of a wider managerial strategy to win over the hearts and minds of employees and that such policies seem to have an anti-union motivation.

Similar to the UK, Ireland once had the reputation of strenuous industrial relations and of union-avoidance. The results of the Irish study of 12 manufacturing establishments (O'Hehir and O'Mahony 1993-IRL) with which we introduced this chapter, point out that such a reputation is outdated: management undertakes organisational reforms for their expected economic benefits. Another Irish study (Brady et al. 1993-IRL) in nine unionised Irish establishments found that the unions had been involved, and had discussed the introduction of direct participation with management from an early stage in the process.

These few pieces of information on the USA, the UK and Ireland might best be rounded up by the summary review of several U.S. and British studies done by Kelly and Kelly (1991). The authors highlight attempts in these countries to create a new union-management climate under the label of New Industrial Relations (NIR). According to the authors, "the advent of workplace innovations coincided with the downturn of the 70s and the economic recession of the early 1980s" (ibid.:36). This coincidence suggests that management had come under strong external pressure to create new organisational structures hoping to reap economic gains, with union avoidance being a marginal topic.

In continental Europe, the problem of union avoidance has not been raised in research. The general lack of research in this area can indicate a very different situation, based on other structural prerequisites. It might be construed that the European scene differs from that in the US, based on the EPOC Social Partner Study: extensive interviews with leading representatives of both the trade unions and employers associations the national level in all EU countries as well as in the metal and the banking sector of these countries conveys the impression that both sides take the topic seriously. However, they put "more emphasis to assessment of reality rather to considerations of principle" (Regalia 1995-I:74). To underline the different European situation, and in anticipation of a topic to be discussed later (cf. section 6.4), an "unexpected" result of this study needs mentioning: "... although with relevant exceptions, in most cases [the European social partners] appeared to view the crucial and controversial issue of the impact of direct participation on indirect or representative participation respondents with a quite relaxed attitude" (ibid.:102). On the basis of these findings, we can conclude that, in general, direct participation in the European countries does not seem to be an issue for antagonistic policies between management and unions.

Given the great differences in European industrial relations systems and traditions, this rather relaxed attitude of most of the European social partners is surprising. It might indicate social principles that are more widely shared and more unifying in their consequences than one would expect at first sight. In this context, Spyropoulos (1995-G:3) points to common principles, such as the importance attached by European policy makers and social partners to better jobs and better working life quality, to shared "... fundamental principles as freedom of association and the right to organise and bargain collectively; the institutionalisation of the organisations representing the social partners and their more or less great involvement in the decision making process; the central role played by decentralised relations and collective bargaining at the level of the undertaking, and the importance attached to national systems of social protection". Enumerating such common features is not meant to imply that a harmonious 'European social model' exists in all 15 EU member states. But it may indicate a shared set of rules for smoother problem solving.

Aside from this common set of shared rules, and the general understanding that direct participation is not a management strategy for union avoidance, there is great diversity in how programmes of direct participation are implemented by management at company level. It is precisely this problem of implementation which - under the label of regulation - causes concern among European unions and works councillors: is management entitled, and does it implement organisational change unilaterally in their firms? Does it exclude existing bodies of indirect participation, and might it be doing this as a conscious strategy?

The EPOC research concepts distinguishes three kinds of regulation (Geary and Sisson 1994): (1) *unilateral* regulation where management implements direct participation with little or no involvement of workers' representatives of any kind; (2) *bilateral or multilateral* regulation between management and workforce representatives, and (3) *legal* regulation where direct participation is based on state legislation. These different types of regulation touch upon differences in national industrial relations systems which have to be considered when investigating the implementation of organisational innovation. When we look at such practices on the basis of empirical research, we focus on the problem of how far management complies to established rules or tries to by-pass them.

Our data suggest one general conclusion which should be outlined at the outset: *in countries with a system of works councils or elected representatives at the establishment level, employee representatives are generally not by-passed by management.* Where such systems are legally bound, in most cases, the involvement of workforce representatives has developed beyond information. For instance, management literature on how to introduce quality circles and Total Quality Management in Germany advises managers to draw employee representatives into the process: "When introducing quality circles, it is self-evident that the early involvement of union representatives [meaning: works councils] is inevitable" (Oess 1991-D:295). Accordingly, in Germany, almost all forms of direct participation are regulated by written agreements ('Betriebsvereinbarung') between works councils and management (Ackermann 1989-D; Kunzmann 1991-D; Greifenstein, Jansen and Kißler 1993-D for the German car industry; Scheinecker (1988-A) for Austria). Yet it would be too easy to interpret such consistent results as the automatic outcome of legal regulation. As workplace reorganisation is not covered by the German Works Council Constitution Act, such results are the outcome of prolonged bargaining processes between works councils and management. Needless to say, the inclusion of works councils is often motivated by management's 'enlightened self-interest'. For Belgium, Baisier and Albertijn (1992) report that management knows direct participation to be a sensitive topic for unions and that unions and works councillors are always informed about quality circle introduction to avoid employee representative resistance (for Germany: Oess 1991-D:300-301).

Management's inclusion of employee representatives in the implementation of direct participation is, of course, influenced by general union presence in companies and by industrial relations traditions. With a union density that ranges between 81% and 91% in Finland, Denmark and Sweden in 1985 (Western 1993-US:267), unions quite naturally play a strong part on the national scene as well as in companies. Bypassing unions is therefore not feasible. In addition, Scandinavian industrial relations is noted for its co-operative stance, and research evidence testifies to a very pro-active role of workforce representatives in matters of direct participation and organisational change. This pro-activity is so pervasive that Swedish trade unions tended to see the EPOC approach to direct participation as a managerial, a top-down policy, as somewhat outdated and "too conditioned by a Tayloristic background, where the issues of 'control' "... were crucial, while the topics of 'autonomy' and 'bottom-up' influence on work organisations should be given greater emphasis" (Regalia 1995-I:35).

Regarding the motives of Scandinavian management, we rely on the knowledge that the general atmosphere of industrial relations is one of co-operation, given the paucity of our empirical data on how such co-operation works in the realm of new management strategies. The only piece of research which shows this positive management commitment comes from Denmark. In two Danish clothing companies both sides evaluated the results of semi-autonomous work groups positively, and concluded that "... the way in which things work today makes us both believe that this type of work organisation is the road for survival of the sector" (Banke 1991:52). Such a co-operative climate takes time to develop, as can be seen from older Danish research (DTI 1978-DK) regarding the introduction of job development projects in ten companies. These were initiated by management, and trade unions were sceptical at the beginning. The example warns us of being too idealistic in depicting Scandinavian processes of organisational change to be smooth and problem-free. That problems do exist is shown indirectly in a Swedish engineering company which introduced CNC-technology: "Initially, the union did not take any offensive against management regarding the way in which the machines should be introduced. It lacked any well-considered approach.

Nor did the central union have any ready-made strategy or other help to offer" (Sandberg 1992:167-168). For Denmark, also, we find instances of management's' attempts not to involve unions, as they tend to "politicise discussions" (Clausen and Lorentzen 1986-DK). These descriptions do not suggest a management strategy of early and co-operative inclusion of the unions.

We find more examples of such managerial styles and 'traditional' management neglect of unions in other countries. For instance, in Butera's (1988-I) investigation of 14 Italian manufacturing companies which had introduced measures of job enlargement, job enrichment, job rotation and group work, management had by-passed the unions to a large extent in most cases. For Spain, we learn that measures of direct participation rarely seem to be negotiated with unions (Castillo, Jimenez and Santos 1991-E). In the Barcelona region, direct participation measures were negotiated only in large companies (Miguelez et al. 1993-E). For Belgium, Baisier and Albertijn (1992-B) found that while management does not see the unions as a partner in regard to measures of direct participation, it does not obstruct union and works councillors' participation. According to the information given by 198 union representatives, each representing a separate establishment in Belgian metal sector, workforce representative inclusion was rather poor: in 50% of the cases where polyvalent skills or teamwork was introduced in firms, the representatives were not even informed by management (Dielen and Janssens 1994-B).

However, such examples only tell us half the story, and we find evidence of co-operative implementation processes of direct participation implementation in countries not identified with co-operation. For France, there is an unexpected spread of various types of direct participation in addition to the (stagnating) 'expression groups' (Coutrot and Parraire 1994-F). Although the study does not give detailed figures, we learn indirectly that employee representatives must have been drawn into this process, as the most 'communicative' firms seem to be those with employee representatives, and where organisational measures have been introduced. Further, we know that quality circle introduction with Peugeot in France was negotiated between management and the unions (Greifenstein, Jansen and Kißler 1993). For Italy, Carpo (1994) indicates that in 10 companies of the industrial and service sector the unions were always informed about TQM introduction. Survey evidence supports the case study finding: In 77% of Italian cases of quality circle introduction, employee representatives were involved, and in only 18% of cases were they by-passed (ANCQUI 1987-I). Teixeira (1984-P) reports a job enrichment measure in a large Portuguese firm where the workers' commission had an 'extremely positive position' and was fully involved in the measure including training. The Opel car factory in Antwerp included workforce representatives from the very beginning of the introduction of group work and other measures (Vanbuylen 1993-B). As a whole, our sources are not conclusive about management strategies which could be labelled as 'avoiding' or 'accepting' workforce representations. We find instances for both types of strategies in all countries, with acceptance occurring more frequently in Northern and Central Europe, whereas for Southern Europe we cited a number of sources that might point more towards an avoidance strategy.

But in the end, we cannot fully substantiate such a labelling. There are several reasons for the equivocal and unsatisfying picture. First of all, we had to rely on social research, and such research might represent specific research interests at the expense of others. Such concentration might express discussion strongholds that misses newer developments, and factual change might not have come into research focus yet. The surprise about the advanced stage of organisational change in France that was illustrated by a recent survey (Coutrot and Parraire 1994-F) - the first of its kind - is a case in point. In this instance, management strategy is not a one-way road, but also depends on partners and their strategy. Despite consistency of industrial relations systems and cultural traditions, we are likely to find instances of union avoidance and union acceptance at company or establishment level. These instances depend on former experiences of trust or mistrust, of long grown co-operation or antagonist conflicts. Yet, from our scattered pieces of evidence we are inclined to draw one conclusion about institutional influences supporting a union-acceptance managerial strategy: regulations which tie workforce representatives into company affairs on a legally regulated basis seem to guarantee inclusion of workforce representatives in the process of organisational change. Other research supports this view (Kochan and Weinstein 1994).

6.2 The Attitude of Employee Representatives Towards Direct Participation at Establishment Level

How were direct participation measures perceived by unions and employee representatives at establishment level? The most general result of our literature review is that there are no consistent patterns in regard to initial reactions and actions of workforce representatives. In the same countries and the same systems and traditions of industrial relations, we find instances of initial suspicion that did not change in the course of time; of suspicion followed by careful monitoring of management actions without opposing it;

of initial suspicion followed by disinterest once employee representatives were convinced that measures of direct participation did not negatively affect their role and their members' interests. We also have instances where initial suspicion turned in active support in the end, and there are cases where representatives actively promoted, even initiated direct participation. As previously noted, such instances occur in most countries. If we generalise and point to patterns at establishment level, we arrive at a common sense conclusion: where workforce representatives are consciously by-passed or fought against by management, direct participation is resisted; where employee representatives are not informed, suspicion prevails; then, after some experience with direct participation over a longer time, such measures are accepted or even actively supported.

For Spain, Martin Hernandez (1993a-E) indicates that the unions were not very enthusiastic about participation, fearing a loss of importance through direct co-operation between management and employees. But this attitude obviously did not negatively affect practical policy: in a survey carried out in the Barcelona region (Miguelez et al. 1993), management reported that the various kinds of direct participation met with the approval of the majority of employee representatives. In some cases they noted a lack of interest, but they never encountered opposition. On the basis of these attitudes, management respondents interpreted that no importance was given to the changes or that the scope of changes was unknown or underestimated. Belgian managers of four larger establishments which operated with consultation groups (Baisier and Albertijn 1992) did not regard unions as important partners as they did not show great interest in the topic. They explain union abstention as a result of a lack of knowledge of possible effects of direct participation and indicate that union members and works councillors in the plant are not adequately supported by their organisations which do not grasp the importance of the topic. In the same study, interviews with union members and works councillors revealed that they did not see a serious problem in regard to task participation and indicated that their traditional role and influence remained unaffected. Yet, they voiced some uncertainties about the long-term effects of employee participation regarding the information monopoly of unions and works councils: the new communications networks developing between management and employees might threaten their monopoly on information.

Other sources give another perspective, showing Belgian workforce representatives and unionist to be rather alarmed: interviews with 198 representatives (Dielen and Janssens 1994-B) reveal that almost two thirds of them (64%) believe that the new management strategy aims at weakening the union position. Union researchers share this view and talk of 'union evasion' through a 'divide and rule' strategy and through concepts of company culture, at least as a side effect (Ramioul 1989-B). Horman (1991-B) found out that such attitudes cannot be generalised, as they depend on the particular union, with attitudes ranging from destruction to co-operation. For the Cockerill-Sambre steel plant in Wallonia, Hormon reports that the unions initially regarded quality circles as some kind of management fad, destined for oblivion. When they realised that about 20% of the workforce participated and obviously liked them, some years had passed and they found themselves outside the new communication nets and circle activities. Although the union delegates were split in their assessment of the situation, they tended to accept management's invitation to join into the programme and to become a partner in the end. After six years experience, union delegates were most concerned over the time needed to cope with the new demands and over their loss of information monopoly to the workforce. At Caterpillar, also located in Wallonia, union delegates had similar apprehensions when the company introduced quality circles and group work: they warned of 'hidden agenda' aiming to undermine worker solidarity, of new communication channels, parallel to collective bargaining. It is reported that this topic continued to fuel discussion within the unions, thus binding them to formulate a clear policy approach. A similar case of excessive discussion within unions is reported for Portugal (Freire et al. 1994-P). In a scarce piece of Greek social research on direct participation, Raftis and Stavroulakis (1991-G) found twelve Greek private firms experimenting and applying participation techniques. According to the authors, union representatives opposed direct involvement in decision-making at the shop floor level, but strongly supported participation of union officials on company boards because of its constitutional power and the prestige of its members.

For Italy, Butera (1988-I) characterises unions' overall reactions towards direct participation as favourable, but not enthusiastic. A study on 1,600 Italian industrial establishments which experimented with quality circles in 1985 (Nicoletti 1986-I) showed that half of the employee representatives were favourable towards the circle idea, 42% were neutral, whereas 7% were hostile. A survey carried out by the Italian National Quality Circle Association (ANCQUI 1987-I) stated a deep change of union attitudes towards quality circles insofar as initial suspicion and opposition was followed by support within a few years. In 1987, one third of all employee representatives fully supported them, 28% were tepid supporters, 32% did not feel concerned, whereas only 7% were against quality circles. Regalia and Rossella (1989:24-I) support this positive picture for Italy: they point to a positive correlation between quality circle introduction and union involvement. According to the authors, circle introduction did not create conflict with unions and did not effect works councils in the firms. For five Italian companies of the food industry (Citarella and Vitale 1988-I), union reaction to quality circle introduction was mixed, depending on the general industrial relations climate in the firms. Some initial union resistance was reported, but when unionists participated, initial suspicion finally disappeared (similar for Spain: Martin Hernandez 1993a-E; UK: for the UK: Wilkinson et al. 1992-UK; for the U.S.: Thomas 1989-US). Turnbull (1986-UK) presents the case of a large British company, where shop stewards rejected team structures on the shop floor for various reasons. They finally lost out to management and had to accept the new organisation scheme. Management continued to negotiate with the unions, but now on a much stronger basis.

Our limited data on France seem to depict a situation of unionists to be very apprehensive about new management approaches: The encompassing representative establishment survey, where almost 2,000 employee re-presentatives were interviewed (Coutrot and Parraire 1994-F), indicates an obvious deep rift between management and unionists. Whereas management evaluate their experience with these new forms of task participation very positively and indicate that the workforces assess the situation similarly positive, the workforce representatives are reported to have a rather negative attitude: for them, employees get involved mainly due to a fear of job loss, irrespective of the level of communication or direct participation in the firm (no further details given). Bernoux et al. (1985-F) report in their study of expression groups that unions consciously did not engage in them as they did not want to be drawn into workplace problems. According to a study on the training of low-skilled workers at Renault to work in semi-autonomous groups (Fixari, Moisdon and Weil (1991-F), the CGT unionists kept out of this scheme in order not to support workforce integration "in the Japanese way", in particular if the job classifications were not revised to account for the workers' new skills.

So far, we have primarily reported research evidence on union and workforce representative attitudes and actions that vary between refusal and acceptance of direct participation measures. Yet, this passive acceptance had a re-active stance. But there are other, pro-active examples with unions and works councillors even taking the initiative and the lead: Cerruti and Rieser (1991-I) report for Fiat in Italy, that the unions were very supportive in establishing teamwork as they expected to find a new and central role for the future. They promoted the new organisational structure and influenced ambivalent workers in accepting the new ways of working. In an Italian food processing plant (Zoccatelli and Umberto 1992-I), the Total Quality programme formed the basis on which both unions and management developed "high estimation" for each other, and the unions experienced that co-operation did not endanger their status as collective actors. Also for Italy, Regini and Sabel (1989) found establishments where unions suggested direct participation measures which were accepted by both management and employees. In the U.S. (Accordino 1989:349), unions are very proactive in regard to QWL programmes: "Participating unions viewed QWL as a way to improve working conditions and to build a more cohesive union. " But such policies were rather easy to pursue as management did not really enter into these programmes. From a management point of view, the topics were only peripheral, and management easily tolerated them: "Its direct and visible costs are negligible. Since unions and workers like it, QWL is at least a potential bargaining chip, and it makes no serious threat to management authority" (ibid.: 354-355). In a UK plant with co-operative industrial relations (Bradley and Hill 1983-UK), unions welcomed a quality circle programme, believing that it enhanced the intra-company communication flow and allowed employees to find out more about management's behaviour and objectives. Through its active involvement, the union's position was not undermined, as some feared, but its power and influence was said to have strengthened in the process (similarly Clark 1993-UK).

In Germany and Scandinavia, we find examples of very proactive union and works councils' in regard to organisational change through direct participation. After protracted internal discussion, and after it was discovered that quality circles did not destroy worker solidarity, the German metal workers union IGM officially decided in 1989 to pursue a 'participative establishment policy' ('beteiligungsorientierte Betriebspolitik'). It is aimed at promoting workplace co-determination, particularly via the small-group concept. This means, at establishment level, that works councillors actively engage themselves, putting forward ideas and seeking their realisation. A survey of 33 works councillors of all German car companies and their most important suppliers (Howaldt 1994-D) revealed a very positive assessment of organisational change in their companies, with only 18% negative answers. The majority of respondents reported active contributions in these processes (similar for a medium sized German company Haindl 1987-D).

We find a similar learning process in regard to organisational change in Scandinavia: "The attitude of Swedish unions has changed over time from resistance to support for change, in part because co-determination rights were enacted in law. The metalworkers union in particular has in recent years developed proactive policies for work reorganisation" (Turner and Auer 1994-D). In a Swedish dairy factory (Sandberg 1992-S), the unions had made advance-plans on how to organise work after the introduction of new technology. In reorganising a department of ABB, the union is said to have been an active promoter of task delegation (Steen 1991-S). Other examples for the proactive role of workforce representatives in Scandinavia are given by Banke (1991-DK), Gustafsson, Carlsson and Hendrikson (1991-S) and Berggren (1992-S).

For Swedish and German unions, the considerable length of time taken in deciding to actively co-operate with organisational change, was due, among other reasons, to various misgivings on the part of the actors involved regarding the future functioning of the works councils: unionists feared that works councils would lose their status as the first intra-establishment address for workplace problems; that a new, parallel communication structure would be established in which unions would not be involved and that they could easily be by-passed by management; that close management-employee co-operation might result in very quick solutions to problem, thereby making works councillors look incompetent; that a new, critical workforce would develop through direct participation which might make higher demands to works councillors (Beisheim, v. Eckardstein and Müller 1994-D). In five German case studies, Bundesmann-Jansen and Frerichs (1995-D) present various examples of problems and chances works councillors have when actively engaging in the new measures of organisational change. For many works councillors, the legal basis for their activities seems limiting, and they ask for new binding rules for conflict management which relieves them of some of their daily duties. They often refer to their new engagement openly as 'co-management'. This new role requires new skills as co-ordinators and moderators are needed, and these skills are difficult to acquire, due to their other duties. As co-managers some works councillors are sometime "torn apart" between their traditional and new self-image (ibid.:70). On the positive side, many works councillors discovered that information flowed much easier, coming from various employee groups that they traditionally had no access to. Some found that the new situation allowed even more discretion to conduct their traditional role and enabled them to devise long-range programmes that they could not envisage under the 'old', traditional works councils regime. Others found out that too much formal regulation of direct participation is not always functional, particularly in high-trust organisations. Other research in three companies came up with very similar results regarding the problems and chances of works councillors involved in organisational change (Beisheim, v. Eckardstein and Müller 1994-D).

Our literature reviews tell us very little about the attitude of Japanese unions towards measures of direct participation. Koumura's (1986-JP) quantitative survey of 173 manufacturing firms, reports that unions are rarely concerned with quality circle activities: In 63% of these companies, unions are not involved in quality circles. According to managers, about one third of unions have a positive attitude towards quality circles, whereas another third opposes them. According to Maemura (1990-JP), the attitude of unions towards quality circles is "generally friendly".

6.3 Direct Participation as a Potential Source of Conflict Between Workforce Representatives

Management is not the only actor that unions and employee representatives might have problems with. In countries with a dual representational structure of unions and works councils or elected representatives at establishment level, conflicts can arise between both representational institutions. This source of conflict continues to be seen as an old topic for unionists. The new management strategy of organisational change through direct participation has heightened the importance of this issue: unions fear that the active engagement of enterprise-based workforce representatives in company matters might lead to their losing sight of overriding union problems and that unions might lose their influence in defining general workforce interests. In this context, works councillors might then co-operate too closely with management. The term 'co-management' might indicate a situation where workers representatives identify too strongly with their firm at the expense of their union. With regard to this issue, we can only present limited evidence.

We can cite a German example of conflict between the union and the works council on the issue of direct participation (Bundesmann-Jansen and Pekruhl 1992-D): the Bertelsmann company ranks among the biggest media-groups in the world and is known for its highly developed system of direct participation. There is a written code for management how to operate (the 'Ten Commandments of Management'), and a whole set of strategies aimed at improving communication between management and the workforce. Regular surveys and talks with employees about the company and their work and career chances take place, and working in teams is strongly supported. In addition, the company has a highly developed system of profit sharing. The comparatively far-reaching legal rights of the works councils are voluntarily enhanced by top management: works councillors take part in the planning and execution of organisational strategies and in devising employee questionnaires.

Although Bertelsmann is not a member of the German Employers' Federation and, thus, is not obliged to deal with the unions, it communicates with the German Media Union (*IG Medien*): wages, working hours and other problems are regulated in a collective agreement. This agreement is particularly remarkable as the degree of unionisation of the workforce in the company is unusually low, and union members do not dominate the works councils in any way, which is generally the case in large German companies. Top management tries to keep the works councils 'union free' to assure the smooth functioning of daily, workplace related matters. On the other hand, the works councils are not considered to be the proper body for general and durable agreements. Therefore, more general problems are regulated with the union.

The works councillors are somewhat critical about the gap between the management concept and its practical application. But their overall attitude is characterised by high acceptance of this policy and by strong identification with the idea of partnership. It is precisely this sharing of the company's culture that creates continuous dissent and conflict with the media union. According to the union, these direct participation measures only deal with peripheral topics and do not provide real co-determination. Moreover, problems emerge through special agreements between management and the works council which undermine general wage agreements and the unions' general policy on wages and working hours. Both works councillors and employees reject the union's stance, and consequently, the union has lost influence and members. In view of the study's results, the authors advise the union to give up its opposition and to be supportive to the company's policy in what they call "Konfliktpartnerschaft" (partnership in conflict). Otherwise it will lose out completely.

Also for Germany, Bundesmann-Jansen and Frerichs (1995-D), in a survey of 202 union and workforce representatives on the problems and chances of new 'participative union policy in companies', report considerable differences in perception between both groups in regard to the latter's proximity towards the union: according to the unionists, works councillors moved too far away from union principles, a reproach that works councillors distinctly reject. It is said that works councillors did gain considerable self-confidence in their new roles. They expect the unions to develop more strongly towards a service organisation to help them carry out their new tasks in the establishments (ibid.:113-114).

Another conflict between workforce representatives is reported in the U.S. (Ellinger and Nissen 1987): this analysis is based on a case study of an extensive quality of work life (QWL) project at a large manufacturing facility whose workers are represented by a large union. Approximately 10,000 union members are employed in this facility. The study approaches the issue of worker participation from the standpoint of its effects on union locals. In the case examined, the QWL programme initially received enthusiastic support from both management and labour, yet it failed after several years of operation. The authors describe several problems that emerged in how the structures of collective bargaining clashed with those of the QWL programme. For instance, the QWL shop floor committees were set up such that a grievance representative either sat on the committees or chose someone else to do so. However, "... if they sat on the panels, they were continuously off the shop floor, unable to respond adequately to the needs of those they represented. If they appointed someone else, they could be by-passed, as QWL teams instantly solved problems which the grievance representatives had been attempting to solve for months" (ibid.:204). The authors report that in either case, grievance representatives often felt that the QWL programme interfered with their jobs.

In addition, the problem of the QWL committees encroaching on contract issues became very serious. The authors explain: "First, the minutes of the QWL steering committee and of some of the QWL panels at the departmental level show that requests were made repeatedly to implement proposals that would have violated the union contract. For this reason, such requests were being turned down. Second, the critics allege that both management and union QWL activists wanted so badly to make the programme work that they actively encouraged workers to transfer their loyalty and efforts from the union to the QWL programme" (ibid.:204). The authors emphasise that the political problems within the local union caused by the QWL programme were instrumental in the ultimate failure of the programme: "'Union politics' was the one thing that all respondents and all interviewees could agree had been a major problem. Differing assessments were made of these problems, but all agreed that they had been key in the demise of the program" (ibid.:212).

In countries where different groups of workers (white-collar, blue-collar) have their own representative bodies operating in the same company and at the workplaces, other problems can arise. In a study of the Swedish car industry, Berggren (1992) points to the importance of the large proportion of white-collar employees being union members: "The unusual extent of white-collar organisation in Sweden has contributed to producing a friendly climate for unions and favourable legislation as well. In the matter of workplace reforms, however, the effect of white-collar organisation has sometimes been ambiguous. Vertical organisational changes, involving a transfer of work tasks, prerogatives, and responsibility from the office to the shop floor, have been complicated by the fact that white-collar employees and foremen have had abundant opportunities through their separate union organisations to stand guard over existing organisational structures" (ibid.:76). In the workplace, these attitudes collide with blue-collar workers' wish to gain a higher degree of direct influence on their own work which is supported by their representative bodies. Conflicts between the two bodies are a natural consequence. In an Austrian greenfield car plant precisely the same problem arose between the white-collar and the blue-collar works council (Scheinecker 1988).

6.4 Does Direct Participation Endanger Representative Participation?

A very urgent problem of unions and employee representatives is the question of whether employees task participation endangers their propensity towards unions, union representatives and works councils, and whether direct participation makes employees lose sight of the necessity to have representative institutions and bodies to defend their interests. As to this critical problem, our general answer is: Direct participation does not endanger indirect participation. In making this statement we are on rather safe ground as all our research evidence testifies to this point. Our general explanation for this conclusion is that employees have a 'division of labour attitude' according to which they feel able to deal with concrete work task problems themselves, while preferring to delegate more general problems to institutions like works councils and unions. Hodson et al. (1993-US:401) state that "... workers usually prefer to participate directly only in decisions affecting their immediate work..., and to leave more general concerns to representative bodies like unions and work councils". The following research evidence testifies to this.

Initial, indirect support for our conclusions comes from the extensive inter-cultural study on Industrial Democracy in Europe (IDE 1981). A group of 25 social scientists interviewed 7,832 employees in all positions within companies, in both the service and the manufacturing sectors of 12 European countries (including the former Yugoslavia and Israel). The authors found, *inter alia*, that employees, in the first instance, wanted to be informed and to be able to voice their own opinion in work related matters. At the same time, most workers, foremen and middle managers prefer highly formalised systems of participation. These results did not vary along national, cultural or geographical lines.

At case study level, our proposition is supported by various sources. In Germany, Greifenstein, Jansen and Kißler (1991-D) studied three metal processing firms of different size which had introduced new technology based on micro-electronics, and which applied various forms of direct participation. The interviews with employees show that they first wanted to voice their opinion (71%), to make suggestions (54%), and to have decision-making power regarding their immediate work tasks (52%). Based on these and other results, the authors conclude that employees first of all want to be consulted and listened to. They want to deal with task problems independently. In medium sized and large companies, employees have a delegative attitude and prefer a model of work division: unions and works councils are expected to deal with more general topics, and they are addressed only if employees' means of coping with problems seem insufficient.

In Sweden, Gardell and Svensson (1981-S) investigated a mechanical engineering firm which had introduced 'autonomous work groups' in some departments. Together with the metal workers union, which was very strong in this company, they attempted to find out "the relation of autonomy to, and the consequences of, the work for the unions". Using an action-research approach which was supplemented by closed interviews, the authors identified that in the 'autonomous departments', employees wanted to exercise influence in: premises, choice of machines and tools, quantity of daily production, planning and supply of material (with percentages between 84 to 72). Employees in non-autonomous departments had the same priorities, but to a much lower extent. When asked which issues should be influenced by the union board, respondents from the autonomous departments stated: external recruitment, economy and investments, choice of nearest manager and choice of higher manager (between 84 and 51%). Again, the comparison group in the non-autonomous departments had a similar priority list, yet on a lower level. These results indicate that all employees of that company preferred to control problems closely related to their own tasks, while corporate issues are turned over to the union.

The Gardill and Svensson findings contradict other research that found a "... surprisingly strong negative relationship between de facto participation in low-level decisions ... and desire for influence over high-level decisions..., suggesting that workers who are provided with substantive influence over task-related matters and little influence over managerial decisions in fact become less desirous of influence at the higher level. It appears that by involving workers in relatively mundane matters, management is simultaneously able to satisfy demands for involvement and to divert employee attention away from strategic issues" (Drago and Wooden 1991:193). These findings which are based on a survey of over 900 private-sector employees in Australia and New Zealand, are sometimes cited to point to the dangers of direct participation. The authors wanted to test the hypothesis that "... low level participation programmes [like quality circles and similar involvement initiatives] are designed to deflect worker loyalties from the unions to the firm... " (ibid.:178).

As so often in research, findings are a matter of definition and measurement, in this case of "high-level decisions". Drago and Wooden operationalise them as decisions in (1) "health and safety and physical working conditions", (2) "the introduction of new processes and technology", and (3) "the purchase of new equipment" (ibid.:184). Here, the question arises as to whether these topics can be called "high-level matters" and whether employees place them that high. In the context of the Gardil and Svensson findings, one can clearly deny the Drago and Wooden view: Employees wanted to exercise influence in: premises, choice of machines and tools, quantity of daily production, planning and supply of material - action fields that Drago and Wooden had defined as high-level topics. In addition, Swedish employees with high work autonomy opted for influence more strongly than employees with less autonomy. Swedish employees defined the 'high level issues' quite differently from Drago and Wooden, namely: external recruitment, economy and investments, choice of nearest manager and choice of higher manager, and they wanted these issues to be taken care of by unions and works councils. In the light of these Swedish research results, the findings of Drago and Wooden are very questionable.

The pattern of direct participation in task related problems and of delegative participation in regard to general problems is indicated by Kern and Schumann (1984-D) as well. This pattern applies even to union members: as union members, skilled blue-collar workers first try to solve their immediate work problems with their superiors, addressing works councillors only when direct intervention failed. The union is considered the last resort in very basic questions: going on strike is the last means of threatening employers, mainly regarding wage increases and job security. The same pattern of graded interest delegation is found among white-collar employees in the German metal, electrical and electronics industry (Fröhlich, Kindler and Sombetzki 1996-D): interviews with highly skilled employees, members of the German metal union (IG Metall), most of whom had union functions, reveal that they try to solve their work problems with their superiors in the first instance, "as a matter of trust and correctness". Works councils are only rarely addressed in matters where they have real responsibility. In such cases, and contrary to blue-collar workers who tend to delegate their problems, works councillors are only asked for advice, whereas problem solution remains an individual task for them. They were waiting for management to venture into extended direct participation programmes and criticised the union for its reluctance to pursue a similar policy in the union organisation. At the same time, the interviewees were staunch union supporters who wanted a strong union for matters of "overriding importance".

In his study on the Swedish car industry, Berggren (1992-S) found out that "... in areas where workers enjoyed high levels of direct influence, there was, for rather obvious reasons, low interest in union intervention. Generally, workers wanted to take care of group-level matters themselves; these were not considered a union concern. A (small) majority favoured the direct handling section-level questions as well. Here, however, the proportion emphasising the importance of union influence rose markedly. Finally, in management-level issues such as the pace and design of production, the majority favoured union influence rather than direct influence. This was especially distinct regarding the pace of production: three quarters of the workers thought it important that the union have influence in this area" (ibid.:228). There was no direct connection between actual direct influence and the desire for union influence at the level of each individual car plant. But taking the workforce responses of all five plants together, "... negative correlations appear between actual direct influence and the wish for union influence. No such connections, either positive or negative, appear, however, in the case of management-level issues... *The latter probably occupies another dimension*" (ibid.:229; emphasis by DF and UP). Or worded differently: Increases in real direct influence did not affect the distinct desire for union influence over management-level questions.

On a different data base (survey interviews with union representatives in 191 Italian companies), Negrelli (1990-I) comes to the similar conclusion that direct participation seems to be a complementary, but not an alternative model of employee involvement. The notion of two dimensions that do not interact is supported in an Austrian study of 14 data processing establishments as well (Aichholzer, Flecker and Schienstock 1991-A). Baisier and Albertijn (1992-B) concluded that in five larger Belgian establishments the topics discussed in consultation groups ('werk overleg') and in quality circles did not interfere at all with union and works councils' topics. The traditional agenda of bodies of indirect participation was left untouched. On the base of the Industrial Democracy in Europe data, Lammers, Meurs and Mijs (1987-NL) did not find any evidence that shop floor participation and co-determination via works councils are interdependent.

In the U.S., Fenwick and Olson (1986-US) examined, *inter alia*, the role of unions in promoting or discouraging worker support for participation. The data were obtained from the 1977 Quality of Employment Survey, which involved 1,114 wage and salaried employees, 341 of which were union members. The study found that participation had a broader appeal among union members. The authors argue that autonomy is perceived differently in union and non-union workplaces and attribute this difference to union influence: "... union workers likely perceive their autonomy as resulting from collective, rather than individual, efforts, and therefore view collective efforts in the form of participation as a way of extending their control" (ibid.:519). In non-union workplaces, workers perceive autonomy as a function of individual resources and performance. From their results the authors challenge the scepticism about the role of unions in encouraging support for participation. They argue that this study reveals the significant indirect role unions play in increasing such support among employees of all skill-levels.

As to the relationship between direct participation and both member commitment to the union and satisfaction with the union, the study of Eaton, Gordon and Keefe (1992-US) is a case in point. The authors investigated the union concern that Quality of Work Life (QWL) programmes in unionised workplaces might erode such commitment and satisfaction. The data came from interviews with 364 workers within three different bargaining units in the same local union representing both technicians and clerical workers. The QWL activities consisted of meetings of local work force committees made up of employees and management "to solve problems and develop new opportunities at work" (ibid.:596). The purpose of the QWL activities "... was to promote greater employee participation in establishing working conditions so that the jobs are made more satisfying and organisational performance and service quality are improved" (ibid.:569). The study was primarily concerned with the attitudes of union members who work in settings in which participation practices are being implemented, whether or not they were participants in the programmes themselves.

The authors emphasise that their study provides no evidence that QWL committees result in less favourable attitudes toward unions. As they point out, "QWL participation apparently does not influence members' sense of responsibility to the union or satisfaction with the union, and it is associated with higher levels of union loyalty" (ibid.:599). The base for this positive result is an effective union with a functioning grievance system. The authors conclude that unions may be able to play both an adversarial and co-operative role regarding workplace matters, i. e., they can benefit from co-operating in QWL programmes but also from devoting resources to a properly functioning grievance system (similar for quality circle application in one UK and US company: Bradley and Hill 1983-UK; for an Irish company: Faughnan 1991-IRL).

These results do not support fears sometimes expressed by unions that direct participation estranges unionised workforces from established industrial relation attitudes. We take these findings as further evidence that direct and indirect participation touch different dimensions: workforces see a difference between work problems they want and can deal with themselves, and other problem areas where they like to delegate power to institutions which are considered more expert and powerful.

6.5   The New Workplaces: Improved or Deteriorated?

With very few exceptions, there is surprisingly little consistent concern among unions and workforce representatives about the quality of future workplaces in transformed organisations. Attempting to explain this fact, we have to remember that 'direct participation' aims at enhancing employees' work roles, either as individuals or in groups. Workforce information and consultation as well as job rotation, enlargement, enrichment and group work were long-standing policy goals of most Western unions which were extremely difficult to reach in most countries. When management, then, invited employees to embark on such working schemes, unions mainly wondered about management's change of mind. But most schemes were rarely questioned as such.

Apart from scarcity of research findings (and explicitly developed union standpoints) in regard to the hazards and chances of future workplaces, we face an additional problem: When unionists and employee representatives refer to the merits and demerits of direct participation, they do so in a general way. We have learned that 'direct participation' has various types with different consequences. A general focus on direct participation makes analysis difficult, if not impossible. We therefore have to be very general by necessity. Then, there is a great diversity of assessments regarding the workplace repercussions of direct participation. What Horman (1991-B) expressed in regard to the assessment of quality circles in a Belgian steel plant might serve as a *motto* to describe the general problem: "There seemed to be as many positions ... as were union delegates. "

General Assessment of Direct Participation

Judging from the lack of explicit information on the chances and hazards of new workplaces, we must assume that unions and employee representatives do not expect critical developments. Distinctly positive or negative overall evaluations are rarely found. The Scandinavian representatives have the least problems with the new trend for direct participation as this is in line with established union goals and union practice. Their organising principle is the 'good work' which prioritises wide discretion at work and which is equally highly valued by Swedish employees. To quote Berggren (1992-S:226) on this point: "A high degree of influence over one's work is a good in itself. " The Amalgamated Engineering and Electrical Union (AEEU) in Great Britain expressed a very positive attitude towards direct participation on the grounds that the new developments put higher value on employment and work than traditional mass production systems. 'Quality' was a leading principle of craft production, and the new quest for quality production is seen as the revitalisation of this positive principle (Geary, Rees and Sisson 1995-UK:112).

Quite an opposite position is maintained by the French unions Force Ouvriere (FO) and the Confédération Général du Travail (CGT). Both unions substantiate their rejection of direct participation strategies by pointing to considerable hazards for the quality of working life. They refer to the results of a survey which was conducted by the French Ministry of Labour in 1991. According to this survey, working conditions have deteriorated since 1987, work stress has increased, and employees themselves have rejected the idea of direct participation. Also from 1987 on, work accidents are said to have increased distinctly. These negative developments are attributed to organisational change through direct participation (Tchobanian 1995-F:15). A similarly negative assessment of direct participation is given by French employee representatives in a later survey of a similar kind: according to these findings workforce commitment to participation schemes mainly comes from employees' "fear of job loss", even in highly communicative firms (Coutrot and Parraire 1994-F).

Assessments of Group Work

These Swedish, British and French examples mark the extremes of general evaluations of the benefits and hazards of direct participation for the workforce. As to assessments of working conditions under the impact of particular types of direct participation, we find the most frequent positions in regard to group work or team work. They are not always compatible: The largest Belgian union, ABVV-FGTB, with about 50% of Belgian unionists, organised a campaign under the heading 'teamwork - c'est nous', propagating group work while imposing a rigid number of restrictions on its functioning (Albertijn 1995-B:38). A similar position is taken by the German IG Metall (Roth 1992-D). Both positions favour the Scandinavian type of group work ('Volvoism') or at least a modified version that permits productivity gains while always keeping the Quality of Working Life aspects in perspective. As to Scandinavian type group work, unions' assessment of working conditions are generally very positive.

Other unionists point to various hazards of group work: A very general concern relates to the voluntary nature of group work. Turnbull (1986-UK) quotes shop stewards at Lucas Electrical in Great Britain as saying that employees had been 'blackmailed' into accepting 'module production' or 'cellular manufacturing', combined with JIT schemes. The largest Dutch union FNV indicates the danger that teams might chose the more highly skilled employees as their members, in case they have the right for self-recruitment. They further point to clique building within work groups, when 'in-group' members reserve the best tasks for themselves and less interesting work is turned to 'out-groups' (van der Meché et al. 1995-NL:219). Austrian unions see peer pressure as a problem (Flecker 1994-A:3). The Finnish metal workers union fears that team work and task versatility might erode the status of the skilled, both in terms of skills and remuneration (Mikkola-Lahnalammi and Alasoini 1995-FIN:92). The Irish Congress of Trade Unions ICTU is concerned about the problem of 'workplace equality': Teams and teamworking are considered as ongoing schemes of work organisation. This reduces the reintegration chances for women leaving the firm for a while (O'Kelly 1995-IRL:162).

Table 9: Evaluation of Teamwork by Union Representatives*

rather positive	19%
positive and negative feelings	67%
rather negative	14%

positive aspects of teamwork:

more interesting and diverse work	50%
improves qualifications and job security	26%
improves wages and offers promotion opportunities	15%
improves labour conditions	9%

negative aspects of teamwork:

increased production pressure and stress	43%
cheap way to make better use of labour	21%
strict separation between core workers and periphery employees	16%
conflicts between employees; workers envy each other	12%
position of individual employees is weakened	8%

*based on companies with teamwork

Source: Dielen 1994-B

This array of various group work hazards might best be summarised with an evaluation of group work by 200 Belgian unionists of the metal sector (cf. table 9). The figures show a very ambivalent assessment of groups working conditions. Two thirds have positive and negative feelings at the same time. On the positive side, the increased challenge and diversity of work, improved qualifications and safer workplaces are highlighted. These positive aspects are accompanied by increased production pressures and stress, and the feeling that management uses group work as a cheap means of work intensification.

Additional Merits and Demerits

In many cases, the chances of employees to become polyvalent through additional vocational training are positively evaluated. Where such training is missing or unsystematically applied, unionists vote for its intensification. 'Safer jobs' are sometimes put forward as a result of organisational change through direct participation. But this effect is not uncontested: For the Danish unions, job security is the main issue (Lund 1995-DK:66).

Austrian unions fear the self-exploitation of employees, indicating that the new workplaces will be so attractive to the workforce that they might over-identify with their jobs and their company and display a work behaviour similar to that of the highly motivated self-employed. But this view is not uncontested: In a British engineering firm employees had to be lured into TQM procedures by pay increases, as a *quid pro quo* for accepting such work (Wilkinson et al. 1992-UK). And if we accept the French union view of a general employee aversion towards direct participation, such self-exploitation should not develop.

In the limited literature, the pay problem stands out as an urgent one. There is a general trend that polyvalence of workers and increased employee productivity should lead to higher remuneration. Italian unions press for pay increases to account for higher employee flexibility (Regalia and Rossella 1989-I). Wages should be increased "in order to avoid the feeling that (employees) are doing more work for the same pay - thus the Dutch FNV (van der Meché et al. 1995-NL:217). The Irish ICTU maintains that payment should be based on skill and knowledge, including schemes of gainsharing, share ownership, individual merit pay and rewards for team performance (O'Kelly 1995-IRL:163). But pay schemes for group work seem to be highly controversial among employees themselves. Palmroth, Hanki and Kirjonen (1993-FIN) report considerable conflicts in Finnish work groups: some group member wanted individual piecework pay, others objected the idea. A bonus system ran into difficulties because of problems over how to allocate dividends between groups and group members.

Italian unions fear that TQM strategies might result in using employees' intelligence and knowledge without granting them autonomy and career development (Regalia 1994-I:25-26). The Irish ICTU is worried about promotion chances in lean production schemes, as the 'flattening of hierarchies' curtails upward mobility in firms (O'Kelly 1995-IRL:162).

Finally, there are Belgian voices which question the present focus on work groups: Baisier and Albertijn (1992-B) quote employee representatives as saying that with this strong focus on group work, the individual employee might be overlooked. The same representatives then warn of enhanced competition among employees in direct participation schemes. The Dutch FNV is afraid that "task enrichment for some employees can mean task impoverishment for other employees" (van der Meché et al. 1995-NL:213).

Our short overview of union and employee representative assessments of the impact of direct participation on the workplaces and on the quality of working life is very patchy, to say the least. We do not want to explain this bleak impression to poor reviewing of research, but assume a systematic trend. In this assessment we are supported by the results of the EPOC Social Partner Study (Regalia 1995-I) showing that the European unions are, on average, rather relaxed about the workplace repercussions of direct participation, provided certain provisions are regarded. The unions do see problems, but most tend to rate them as not too alarming. We already indicated that such a rather positive evaluation might be due to the positive connotation that 'direct participation' carries for unionists, having asked for 'task participation' since long.

Another handicap for properly assessing consequences of task participation' on employees might be a general lack of knowledge about different types of participation, their preconditions and consequences. Much older research, particularly in the QWL phase which still guides our perceptions, was carried out under particular socio-economic conditions, often government funded. This research tended to look for the 'bright side' of different types of workforce involvement and produced positive results. That employees experience considerable problems of various kinds when dealing with task participation, particularly of the group type, was elaborated in parts of the preceding text.

Finally, we do think that certain problems of direct participation are systematically under-represented, not only among the unions, but among all actors involved, social researchers included. They centre around the labour market effects of new work schemes: the problem of job loss in 'lean' approaches, the intra-firm core-periphery problem of workforces, and the future work situation of certain employee groups, such as women, older workers, the unskilled - but the skilled as well.

160

Summary

When management systematically promoted organisational change through various forms of direct workforce participation, many unions were alarmed and questioned management's motives: Are direct participation policies really pursued for their 'intrinsic' benefits, to make the organisation more effective in economic terms? Or does management have afterthoughts and conceives direct participation as a means toward other ends, namely to weaken unions? Whatever the answer to this problem might be, additional questions arose: How should unions and other representative bodies react to management policies? Where are the dangers for their constituency, for their own organisations, and for the idea of representative participation? And how might workforce attitudes towards unions be affected by direct participation?

Although we have gathered and analysed a considerable amount of empirical research from different countries, most answers to these questions are still tentative: As far as we can see, in continental Europe, direct participation was fostered by management for competitive and productivity reasons. We did not encounter a single piece of research which has made management's motives to damage works councils and unions the focus of investigation. This lack of research alone might be taken as a strong indicator that 'union busting' is not a continental topic. But various studies show that this does not apply to the Anglo-Saxon countries. Particularly in the USA, industrial relations are sensitive and conflictual, and management's motives have been subject to research. Yet, the results are not conclusive: we find research evidence for and against a conscious anti-union stance in management's motives. At the same time, it must be pointed out that in the US and in the UK, management strategies for organisational change through direct participation gained momentum in a situation of serious economic crisis, just like in all other countries, and this indicates a strong economic motive in the new management strategy.

At union level, direct participation measures, beginning with quality circle introduction in the 1980s, met with some suspicion and prompted extended discussions about how to react. In some countries, like Ireland, Germany and Sweden, these discussions ended in conscious decisions to actively engage in the new trends for organisational change, but to guard own interests carefully. Empirical evidence tells us that at establishment level, measures of direct participation, as a rule, met with much suspicion from employee representatives at the beginning. But we rarely found outright opposition. Sometimes suspicion turned into disinterest, having learned that direct employee involvement did not touch upon the vital interests of representative bodies and their constituency. But we found more instances of learning processes where employee representatives developed an attitude of co-operation and support, sometimes even distinct pro-activity. Such instances cut across the various cultural, national and industrial relations lines, and direct participation policies at establishment level are obviously confounded with situational specifics which we do not know and which vary at random. It is difficult to detect *patterns* of action and reaction, except the common sense insight, that unfriendly management policies create suspicion, but that a longer acquaintance of direct participation policies results in support in the end. As a trend, workforce representative involvement in organisational change seems to be most intense and pro-active under conditions of legally regulated works councils and with elected representatives at shop-floor level in high-trust companies.

Whether direct participation has the capacity to create tensions between different bodies of employee representation or role conflicts within such bodies depends to a large degree on particularities of national representative systems. In the case of a dual structure, with unions and independent works councils at establishment level, rifts between both parties can appear when works councillors see the benefits of direct participation for the company and its employees, whereas unions sometimes oppose such co-operation for more general policy reasons. From what we learned through empirical evidence, union opposition to direct participation which contradicts works councils policies is likely to have negative repercussions for these unions: for various reasons, direct participation is often very attractive to employees, and works councils will support their constituency at company or establishment level. In case of conflict between both representative bodies, employees will side with their councils at the expense of the unions. Such possibilities point to severe changes in the self-concept and the roles workforce representatives are facing. We already provided evidence of such re-orientation problems for works councillors, with repercussions for unions which have to find a partially new role as well.

As to the important union problem, the question of whether direct participation endangers the idea and functioning of representative participation, we can safely conclude that direct and indirect participation are not competing concepts. There is ample research evidence that employees have clear preferences for dealing with task related problems on their own. This is, of course, variable: the higher skilled see more potential action areas for themselves than lower skilled employees. But both skill groups are aware that there are problems and topics which should be handled by other mechanisms and by particular institutions. Employees feel that unions' and works councils' tasks tap another dimension of working life problems, and they are ready to delegate power to 'professionals' to solve problems they cannot solve individually. From this perspective, direct and indirect participation are not contradicting, but rather complementary concepts. If this is the case, union apprehensions that their future role and functions are endangered by employee task participation are unjustified.

These findings might seem to be overly optimistic in regard to union problems in present organisational change. But this assessment somewhat parallels the results of the EPOC Social Partner study which revealed a surprisingly 'relaxed' overall view on direct participation on the European union side.

In regard to workplace repercussions through 'task participation', unions and employee representatives are not very alarmed. Few unions have an outright positive attitude towards these new developments, stressing the potential of enriched work for employees. A few others presume that 'task participation' is basically forced upon the workforce and, thus, must be a burden for employees. The majority of unionists point to hazards such as increased stress, increased competition between individuals and groups, to problems within groups, to possibly disadvantaged workforce groups (females, older workers, skilled and unskilled) and to vocational training needs. But our sources do not indicate that direct participation is perceived to pose very urgent threats. Sometimes the hazards envisaged are contradictory. There seems to be a systematic blank regarding information and evaluation as to the adverse labour market effects of the new management strategies, both in the economy and within companies and establishments.

7 An Overview Of Direct Participation in Europe, Japan and the USA

So far, we have analysed direct participation cross-nationally in terms of its separate types, distinct topics and problems of management and employees, and in regard to middle management and unions, investigating the relationship of direct and indirect, representative participation. This chapter will present survey results on direct participation. Separate findings for each nation included in our literature review are included.

Ideally, this chapter would quantify the extent to which different types of direct participation are applied in the countries under study: how far advanced are individual countries in re-shaping their organisations, and: do we find preferences for certain types of direct participation in the particular countries? However, international comparisons on the basis of existing research are problematic as *the national data do not permit international comparisons*.

An initial problem is: *did we identify all relevant research*? On the basis of the EPOC concept of direct participation, our foreign correspondents were explicitly asked to supply us with representative, quantitative research results on direct participation in their countries, as a matter of priority. Accordingly, if there is no research reported for a certain country we have to conclude that such information is missing as to mid-1994.

As will be shown, we encountered *very diverse research universes*: organisations, companies and management are by far the prime sources of research. But one could as well - and sometimes did - concentrate on the majority of organisations' members, on the workforces, and analyse organisational change from their experience and point of view. Accordingly, we find many differently defined 'objects' of survey research.

Such 'objects', then, have been *operationalised differently*: definitions of specific types of direct participation vary considerably, and the indicators chosen to measure them are equally diverse. Making strict comparisons is therefore impossible. In addition, determining whether sample selection is representative, both in regard to questionnaires / interview response rates and in regard to national, regional and/or sectoral coverage is problematic. These are further factors which limit country comparisons.

As a result, *we do not attempt to compare nations* on the basis of 'hard' indicators such as the spread of certain types of participation or the degree of organisational change. The reader interested in *true comparative data* will find some information on the spread of suggestion schemes, workforce surveys and quality circles in European countries in the last section of this chapter.

7.1   The Separate Countries

Austria

The case of Austria illustrates the problems involved in undertaking international comparisons of direct participation. As of the end of 1994, representative research concentrating on organisations and companies was not available in Austria. Only two representative studies with the working population as research universe are reported. These only give subjective, 'perceptual' assessments of some working life traits from an employee point of view.

The slightly earlier results (ÖSTAT 1987-A) are based on a micro-census of the Austrian dependently employed working population. It is not very informative about types of direct participation in that it only asks about 'discretion in work' in general. The findings show that 38% have no discretionary work content, 29% have some, and 29% have large discretion at work. These shares vary considerably with the skill level and the duration of the working life of the respondents: the higher the skill level and longer employees have been active, the higher their discretion at work (further details missing).

More informative is a representative survey of the dependently employed working population (Grausgruber-Berner and Grausgruber 1990-A) in the tradition of Quality of Working Life surveys and Social Indicators research. Work discretion - whether employees could decide for themselves about the amount of daily work to do, what and when they would do it during the day, and in which speed - was measured. The positive answers are:

Table 10: Dimensions of Work Discretion of the Austrian Labour Force

own decision about work speed	73%
own decision on daily work load	53%
own decision on when to do	49%
own decision on what to do	39%

Source: Grausgruber-Berner and Grausgruber 1990-A

Again, these average figures vary considerably in regard to skill levels and formal education. For instance, 62% of employees with secondary education and/or a university degree can decide when to carry out a task, whereas this percentage is down to 40% among those with only primary education. The choice of kind of daily work (what to do) is particularly restricted to employees with primary education only: here, 67% of male employees and 79% of female employees have no discretion. On the other hand, discretion of this sort is particularly high for people with secondary education and university degrees.

All in all, 39% consider their work variable and challenging, while for 26% it is boring. Apart from the fact that work challenge, again, heavily depends on position and skill levels, it influences attitudes towards work: the wish to work less increases with lower chances to self-actualise in work. At the same time, a distinct need towards higher discretion in work became apparent: whereas 17% of the lower qualified expect their superiors to grant more discretion, 48% of the high skilled employees voice this expectation.

The obvious dependence of positive or negative work circumstances on skills and positions is rather common knowledge. Yet, the overall results of these two studies do strengthen older theoretical assumptions that participation chances, defined by the level of general and professional education, result in even higher work engagement and the wish for more task participation. Unfortunately, these two studies do not permit assessment of how far different types of direct participation have gained ground in the scope of our definition, namely as a new managerial strategy to modernise organisations.

Belgium

For Belgium, we have a representative overview of the spread of Total Quality Management (TQM) practices (PRACQ 1990-B). 1,400 companies with more than 20 employees were interviewed with a mailed questionnaire of which 42% were returned. Two questions related to practices of direct participation: the types of teamwork the company applied systematically and the percentage of employees affected by these initiatives. A very large portion of Belgian companies (two out of three) indicated that they pursue a TQM policy. The authors of the study themselves are doubtful about this very positive result and question its representativeness, hinting that the questionnaires were mainly returned by very enthusiastic TQM supporters. The authors observed that quality circles seem to be the inroad to TQM and more teamwork in the firms. The amount of teamwork reported is impressive, though somewhat vague in substance: 60% of all TQM companies indicate that they have 'Employee Involvement (EI) groups' which were defined as "forms of teamwork with no clear content outlined". In addition, 40% had TQM-project teams and 21% quality circles. Even if these figures are overly positive, they nevertheless indicate considerable activity in the re-shaping of Belgian organisations.

Unlike most other quantitative studies, this one tried to measure the number of employees drawn into teamwork as well. Again, the figures are very positive: 65% of the TQM-companies had drawn in up to 20% of their workforce, in 24% of the companies 20-50% of employees were affected by teamwork, and more than half of the workforce were "teamworkers" in 11% of companies. In regard to firm size, a greater than 50% coverage of employees was particularly frequent (21%) in small companies with up to 50 employees (8% in medium and large firms). There were no significant regional differences between Flanders and Wallonia in regard to frequency of teamwork and employee coverage.

As a means of cross-checking these results, it is helpful to consider the results of a survey of 198 union representatives (Dielen 1994-B), representing metal processing companies in Flanders (employing 61% of the workforce in this sector). According to the unionists, 65% of their companies apply TQM policies, 92% foster polyvalent skills and/or team work, 75% operate with Just-In-Time techniques, 63% follow a distinct Human Resource Management strategy, and 51% practice employee participation (unspecified). The reviewer of this study is a little apprehensive of the "rosy picture of the metal sector buzzing with new forms of management". But both studies taken together do point to substantial dynamism in regard to organisational change in Belgium.

Denmark

For Denmark, we face the same problem that we encountered in the case of Austria: the absence of quantitative data pertaining to companies and their organisational strategies. As in Austria, Danish research follows the post-war tradition of viewing the problem of direct participation in Quality of Working Life terms and from a workforce perspective. Accordingly, quantitative evidence of employee involvement in Denmark was gathered via two representative surveys with employees about Quality of Working Life.

To identify current occupational environment problems, the Danish Work Environment Fund (Nord-Larsen et al. 1992-DK) conducted a telephone survey with 5,940 employees aged between 19 - 59 years. Work participation (as one research topic among several) was measured by an "index of influence" that contained the degree to which employees are meant to be able to influence work pace, work process, and work tasks - individual delegative participation in conceptual terms. The results show familiar patterns: employees with extended vocational training and senior salaried employees enjoy the highest degree of influence possibilities (ranging between 75 - 60%) whereas influence potential decreases towards about 20% among unskilled workers and apprentices/trainees. In 1992, the Danish Social Partners and the Government agreed that in the year 2000 work characterised by factors such as little self-determination and influence should be halved. To validate this goal, a follow-up survey is planned.

A similar survey was conducted by the Danish Federation of Trade Unions (Joergensen et al. 1992-DK) to analyse members' changed position in society as well as their new demands and wishes for occupational and political initiatives. From its approx. 1.4 million members about 5,300 were randomly chosen and interviewed. The seven indicators used to measure employee participation centred around the discretionary content of jobs in the tradition of the Quality of Working Life research.

The survey shows that a very large number of members (41%) had experience of new ways of organising work whereas 29% positively denied such experience. These types of new work organisation were most widely used within the public sector (53%) as opposed to 17% in the private sector. Here, new forms of work organisation are most common in commerce, restaurant and hotel businesses (39%) and within manufacturing (36%). Close co-operation with colleagues seems to be widespread, as 50% of all employees report that they plan and organise work together with colleagues always or most of the time. Again, this is more frequent among public employees than in case of privately employed workforces. But we must be very cautious not to confuse such co-operative work as 'group work' in the narrow sense developed earlier, as cross-functional teams responsibly working on a rounded task. Workplace co-operation can assume a variety of forms, many (or most?) of which just stand for everyday proceedings in organisations, without any reference to conscious and elaborate schemes. We must therefore treat the Danish data with caution.

At the time of research, 37% of the interviewees were employed in companies where management plans to change the work organisation: 14% expect autonomous groups, 11% job rotation, and 23% an expansion of work tasks (multiple responses). Again, more publicly employed persons (47%) than private employees (31%) report such planned changes. In parallel with the first survey reviewed above, the information about management's plans decreases with skill level, indicating that the better educated employees are likely to get the benefits of such new practices.

Although evidence gained from employee perceptions cannot be compared with results from company studies, the data seem to indicate that working within new types of organisation is common among the Danish workforce, that this trend is ongoing, and that the public sector is leading this development.

Finland

According to two large-scale workforce surveys concerning changes in working life, Finnish employees believe that opportunities to influence their work and working conditions have grown continuously. The Finnish workforce indicates that its task contents have also become more demanding. From a Quality of Working Life survey (N=4,109), carried out by the Statistical Office in 1990, we learn that Finnish employees have considerable discretion at work.

Table 11: Dimensions of Work Discretion of the Finnish Labour Force

69 %	can influence their work schedule
65 %	can influence their working methods
57 %	can participate in planning their own work procedures
43 %	can influence much or quite a lot of their work duties
32 %	can influence much or quite a lot regarding work assignment among employees

Source: Statistics Finland, 1990-FIN

The Working Life Barometer (N=1,209), carried out by the Finnish Ministry of Labour in 1994, tried to identify current changes in some of these workplace traits and investigated newer developments that increasingly arise with regard to company reorganisation.

In regard to personal influence on one's job there have been significant net improvements ('improved' minus 'decreased') in respect to various workplace facets.

**Table 12: Improvements of Workplace Facets
of the Finnish Labour Force**

influence on:	
daily duties improved	28 %
work pace improved	5 %
task assignment between employees improved	12 %
learning of new skills improved	15 %

Source: Ministry of Labour, 1994-FIN

Other data indicate considerable changes in business life within one year: 12% of the workforce report downsizing strategies of their companies. Another 13% indicate company mergers. According to 14% of the interviewees, their companies have begun to pay efficiency bonuses to their employees, and almost half of the workforce (46%) indicate that performance based remuneration schemes are gaining ground in their firms. The latter development is said to have followed from new management systems introduced since the early 1990s when Finland gained more independence from the Russian (Soviet) market. Altogether, Finnish workplaces are characterised by large workforce discretion, while Finnish companies and labour relations are experiencing far-reaching changes in the 1990s.

France

Until very recently, there was very little information about measures of direct participation and organisational change in France. Few figures existed about the development and functioning of expression groups (*groupes d'expression*) which were introduced by legislation in 1982 to reinforce direct worker participation on topics of health and safety, work organisation, work content and work environment. The formation of expression groups in French firms was very successful initially in quantitative terms, but their numbers staggered at around 10,000 by the end of the 1980s, and they are said not to have been really filled with life (Pinaud 1994-F, Heidenreich 1994-D). At the beginning of the 1980s, quality circles were very strongly advocated by French management, making France the leading country in regard to this type of consultative group participation in Europe (with an estimated number of 4,000 circles in 1988; Krieger and Lange 1992-D). As to more elaborate schemes of workforce involvement, observers had to rely on case studies from which they concluded that in France, the 'Japanization' of company organisation was largely fended off by traditional, bureaucratic patterns of work and organisation which are anchored in the specific French system of industrial relations and traditional patterns of social inequality (Heidenreich 1994-D:67).

A new, and obviously the first representative company survey (Coutrot and Parraire 1994-F) clarifies the French situation. In 1993, the French Ministry of Labour, Employment and Vocational Training conducted a survey among 3,000 French establishments (with more than 50 employees) with an almost 100% response rate. 200 researchers visited the companies and had the questionnaire filled out in their presence. This was done with management and (with a partially different questionnaire) with employee representatives, particularly where unions were represented in a firm (1,915 respondents).

As yet, only preliminary data are available and results are fairly surprising. They tend to show that direct participation measures are more widespread than French observers thought. Moreover, these measures are continuing to make headway. In 1990, 70% of all establishments had workshop meetings under management supervision; 33% operated with quality circles; expression groups existed in 30% of the firms, and 26% drew up a company plan (projet d'entreprise). These figures show an upward trend, with the single exception of expression groups, which meet very infrequently (fewer than four meetings for the whole workforce in 50% of the cases). Quality circles, which are said to have declined after 1988, seem to have been experiencing a revival since 1990, and are particularly widespread in the manufacturing industry. Regular workshops, office or department meetings, which are very widespread and frequently a recent innovation, are held at least seven times a year in half of the establishments concerned.

The organisational changes that encourage direct participation involving the delegation of responsibility are less widespread than consultation groups. 20% of the establishments claim to operate a just-in-time system. One third uses 'multi-disciplinary work groups' or 'project groups', which bring together members of different departments in order to plan or implement a project. One third claim to have embarked upon the introduction of total quality management, and 11% say that between 1990 and 1992 they introduced 'self-regulating work groups' made up of multi-skilled workers who organise their work on a collective basis.

Although these data must be interpreted with caution (e.g. no information on the share of employees affected is given), the survey shows that, in particular, consultational measures have been adopted on a large scale and are increasingly used, with delegative participation also increasing. The data show a cumulative effect, in that about 60% of the companies have introduced at least two types of organisational change. Here, participation based on consultation and direct participation based on delegation seem to go hand in hand. A final result: the most 'communicative' establishments seem to be those that have employee representatives and in which organisational changes have been introduced.

Germany

Looking at the widespread scientific and public debate on new production concepts, group work, lean production etc., one would think that direct participation should be a well investigated topic in Germany. Surprisingly, there is comparably little information about the dissemination of participation practices in German enterprises.

Zöller and Ziegler (1992-D) investigated the place value and the degree of dissemination of Total Quality Management in Germany. 204 companies responded to a postal survey (no information on the gross sample given). The authors state that very large companies operating internationally are distinctly over-represented. Of the 204 responding firms, about 50% are already engaged in TQM activities, and another 10% are ready to introduce it in the very near future. In TQM firms, programmes for the active involvement of employees and the introduction of new work organisation like group work and quality circles are reported by 53% of these firms (no further detailed information given). As active employee participation also requires employee training, the scarce data on training measures qualify the positive figures: "In most cases only 1-10% of different employee groups were drawn into training measures" (ibid.:25). Some discrepancies between officially stated employee orientation and related measures become apparent in the rather low percentage (16%) of firms that carry out regular employee surveys. Accordingly, the authors summarise their findings rather negatively: "Characteristic indicators for TQM organisations are neither reached in regard to customer orientation nor in regard to employee orientation" (ibid.:34).

Another study investigated the existence and effects of 'problem solving groups' in the Fortune-100-companies in Germany (Antoni, Bungard and Lehnert 1992-D). Here, managers of the largest 100 German companies (measured by annual turnover) were reached by phone interviews. Problem solving groups were defined as "groups of employees belonging to the lower hierarchical layers, who regularly and voluntarily meet in order to discuss and solve problems directly concerning their proper work". Actually, the authors wanted to gather information about the dissemination of quality circles. But as this term was not used in all companies, they finally subsumed all kind of groups under the label of quality circles. Half of all enterprises applied these circles, and three quarters of them applied them in their manufacturing departments. The number of circles appears to have been almost constant since 1986, when a similar survey was carried out. As about another 11% of companies stated their intention to introduce quality circles in the future, the authors concluded that their diffusion is widespread and will even increase in the future.

In regard to group work, the only representative study was carried out by Kleinschmidt and Pekruhl (1994-D) with the German *working population as the universe*. Fifteen percent of employees stated that the form of work they are employed in is labelled 'group work' by management. But singling out employees whose work structure was, in fact, not co-operative, and others who claimed to be individually responsible for their own work, the authors concluded that 7% of the employed workforce actually work in groups. But this figure must not be mistakenly assumed to denote group work in the scope of our definition, as groups with delegated rights and responsibilities. Further checks proved that the term 'group work' covered very diverse forms.

According to the authors, only the first type, the semi-autonomous groups, qualify for desirable group work, and only 2.2% of the working population work under such circumstances. Even if we include the 'high responsibility, high outside control' type of group as representing a Japanese group solution, both types taken together only amount to 3.9%.

Table 13: Types of Group Work in the German Working Population

semi-autonomous groups	2.2 %
high group responsibility for results plus outside control	1.5 %
no group responsibility for results plus outside control	1.4 %
task-dictated traditional cooperation	1.9 %

Source: Kleinschmidt and Pekruhl 1994-D

Either viewed separately or together, the percentage(s) is (are) surprisingly low and difficult to validate. But they somewhat fit other, more limited research findings that concentrate on companies in specific economic sectors.

Mechanical engineering is the most important and most highly export-oriented branch of the German production sector. A detailed study on all 5,500 mainly small and medium sized companies (Sauerwein 1993-D) identified only 2.6% of the firms operated with semi-autonomous groups. According to a representative sample of 572 companies in the production sector (Hirsch-Kreinsen et al. 1990-D) group work was applied in 4% of mechanical engineering companies and in 9% of all other investment goods producing enterprises. Although we cannot compare data from employees with information about enterprises, both sources of information suggest surprisingly low shares of direct participation of the group work type.

Both the methodologically weak figures on quality circles and TQM approaches as well as the obviously small shares of group work seem to indicate that in Germany there is more talk about organisational dynamics than actual change.

Greece

Although the Greek reviewer of the study has some doubts about its methodological quality, the only study which gives us some information about the dissemination of DP in Greece shall briefly be referred to (Greek Centre of Productivity 1990-GR). The study is based on postal interviews with 346 managers in Greek enterprises with more than 10 employees. The major topics in this study are questions about labour-management-relations which are considered to have an impact on the firm's productivity. The study is relevant for the topic of direct participation because it tried to measure the number of quality circles. According to the results quality circles were an absolutely minor issue in Greek enterprises: only 10 respondents (less than 2% of the companies) indicated the existence of quality circles. There is no more information about the manner or the extent to which QCs are applied in these companies. Further evidence of the minor significance of direct participation practices in Greece is managers attitude towards group work: only 3 respondents considered group work as a measure that might increase a firm's productivity. All in all, our knowledge about the dissemination of direct participation in Greece is very poor, and we are unable to say whether the 1990 figures depict the Greek situation correctly.

Ireland

Similar to Greece, the Irish situation can hardly be assessed as no recent research evidence exists. At present, we only know about one study carried out in 1984 by the Irish Industrial Development Authority (IDA). The study concentrates on the Irish private sector manufacturing industry (Murray 1984-IRL). The study's main objectives were to provide information regarding industrial relations reform and to make recommendations on national manpower policy. New work organisation practices were not a particular concern.

A postal questionnaire was mailed to 228 randomly chosen companies with more than 50 employees from which 141 responses were suitable for analysis (62% of sample). Given the particular research interests, information on direct participation measures is scarce and limited to communication and 'consultative' participation. As only 21% of all companies conferred substantial autonomy on their supervisors, and as 70% of all manufacturing processes were categorised as routine or semi-skilled work, we can expect that in the vast majority of the companies decision making was still highly centralised.

In the area of employee participation the results of the study indicate that the majority of firms relied on rather formalised communication mechanisms like regular weekly or monthly meetings and written methods such as notice boards. In relation to upward communication, roughly half of the companies had departmental consultative meetings, employee opinion groups and employee suggestion schemes. Quality Circles as a practice were only investigated as to their effectiveness from a management point of view, without reference to their existence and spread throughout the companies. The early date of research and the specific research interest of the study do not permit any assessment of direct participation in Ireland at present.

Italy

To characterise the Italian situation we have to rely on sources that investigated the spread and functioning of quality circles. The Italian National Quality Circle Association (ANCQUI 1987-I) repeated a national postal survey that was first carried out in 1985. Supplemented with additional information, the second survey found that in 1987, about 300 Italian firms worked or experimented with this type of consultative group participation and operated with a total of 802 circles. The survey was then updated two years later (Galgano 1990-I) in the 200 largest companies, 24% out of which had active quality circles. In the 1990 survey a total of 1,900 circles were counted - an average of 42 per company. This high average indicates that Italian employers obviously took the quality circle idea seriously and that more than just a few employees seem to have been affected: The 1985 survey showed that one quarter of employees in the companies under review participated in circles (Regalia and Rossella 1992-I). The same authors estimate the number of active quality circle companies at the beginning of the 1990s to be around 400-500.

Regalia and Rossella explain this great interest in quality circles in the 1990s as something of a 'late-comer effect', "a solution which was imported into Italy from outside with a certain delay" (ibid.:12). Recently it seems that quality circles have lost popularity as an isolated measure of direct participation, and interest has shifted more strongly to Total Quality Management, for which quantitative findings were missing up to 1992. The authors point out that various (as yet unquantifiable) additional measures like information schemes and training in social skills became popular in Italian companies around the turn of the decade (ibid.:16). These scattered pieces of information do not enable us to make any conclusions about where Italian companies stand in regard to organisational change. In any case, we have to consider that the changes reported took place in larger companies (70% in companies with more than 1,000 employees) in the Northern and Middle Italy.

Netherlands

A series of three successive representative company surveys permit a better overview of the general climate of direct participation in the Netherlands (Loontechnische Dienst 1979-NL, 1987-NL, 1993-NL). These studies focus on the special Dutch institution called *work consultation* (werkoverleg), which is described as "regularly held, more or less structured mutual communication between the leadership (of a working unit) and the employees as a group, about work and the work situation". In this definition, it resembles quality circles and is similar to consultative participation at group level. But as will be shown, this definition of work consultation as a consultative tool is too narrow, as it also has delegative traits. Our review of the Dutch situation will be based mainly on the 1993 survey, with occasional references to the earlier studies. The information is drawn from a representative sample of 1,578 organisations with at least 10 employees. The personal, closed interviews with management were carried out in the second half of 1992. According to the survey, work consultation is carried out in 41% of the Dutch firms. It is positively related to firm size in that its spread increases from 28% in very small companies to 74% in firms with more than 500 employees. It is relatively popular in both private and public services (65%), and least common in transport, construction and 'other manufacturing' sectors (26-29%). In about half of cases, there are 5 - 12 work consultation meetings a year, the other half of cases have more meetings than this. In the majority of cases an agenda is used and minutes are taken. 84% of meetings are chaired by the direct manager. This organisation of work consultation is very strongly reminiscent of quality circle procedures, and the obvious lack of quality circles in Dutch firms might be attributed to competition from work consultation. While the 1993 survey did not touch upon quality circles, the 1987 study found a ratio of work consultation to quality circles of about 11 to 1 in Dutch firms. Fifty nine per cent of all employees were engaged in work consultation at that time, engagement in quality circles affected only 2-3% of the employees.

Table 11, based on management information, shows a considerable degree of employee involvement in decision-making. This is particularly evident in task related matters such as work procedures, work support devices, health and safety (around 53%). Even in general organisational topics and questions of the technical development of the firm, about one quarter of group participants are said to be involved in decision-making. Thus, Dutch work consultation can be characterised as a mixture of consultative and delegative direct participation on a group basis. It seems to have gained in importance during the last decade: in 1977, only 21% of the Dutch firms worked with it, whereas in 1993 this share had almost doubled to 41%. Organisations which do not apply this participation measure, pointed, by way of explanation, to their small size which makes such a rather formal approach ineffective.

Table 14: Work Consultation in the Netherlands:
Employee Involvement in Decision-Making

Topic	Employees are involved in decisions
Work assignments	55 %
Work scheduling	34 %
Days off	42 %
Purchase of supporting devices	57 %
Working procedures	59 %
Schooling and training	42 %
New employees	14 %
Personnel affairs	22 %
Safety	56 %
Health	54 %
Well-being	57 %
Primary labour conditions	7 %
Secondary labour conditions	14 %
Organization as whole	24 %
Technical developments	32 %

Source: Loontechnische Dienst 1993-NL

Portugal

"Only 2,7% [of Portuguese managers] think that innovation is the replacement of men by machines". This statement from a recent study, which had been carried out as a representative company survey (with 1,000 companies of which 120 responded; Kovacs, Cerdeira and Moniz 1992-P) indicates a rather "modern" way of thinking in Portuguese private and public enterprises. But further results and the low rate of questionnaire returns correct that image: in 52% of companies the implementation of new technological equipment was said to be the main factor for innovation, and in only 12% of all cases was the emphasis put on improving enterprise efficiency.

But we should not, however, underestimate the relevance of work organisation as a basis for innovation. 62% of all enterprises introduced polyvalent teams, and 30% maintain that semi-autonomous group work is applied in their companies. Even if the authors of the study doubt that all these semi-autonomous groups are meeting the requirements of semi-autonomy, particularly with regard to the question of decision power, the figures are still very high. In addition to the introduction of various forms of group work, about 50% of the companies stated that they introduced new forms of work organisation such as job rotation.

Another interesting result concerns the dissemination of quality circles. 12% of all companies are using this instrument of consultative participation. Compared with a previous survey in 1986, however, the total number of companies using quality circles had decreased, whereas the figures for group work and other means of work organisation were higher than in the 1986 study. This can, with some caution, be taken to indicate a shift away from consultative forms of direct participation towards more delegative patterns which are directly related to the production process.

Considering that industrialisation in Portugal is still in its infancy, the quoted figures are quite significant, and one might assume that the Portuguese situation enjoys the advantage of a 'late-comer' to industrialisation, avoiding certain phases of industrial development and taking short-cuts to more modern structures. However, the survey is said to be of questionable value, with a response rate of only 12%. There is a well-founded suspicion that only highly motivated companies took part in the survey thus distorting the overall picture which may be much less positive in reality.

Spain

Prieto (1991-E) informs us that Spain is a country of small firms: in 1988, 98% of all enterprises employed less than 50 workers and 86% employed less than 10 workers. As there is no room for elaborate direct participation schemes in such small firms, or as direct participation is often a daily routine here by necessity, we cannot expect much direct participation. Common sense expectations are supported by facts: in 1987, a Spanish Quality Circle Association census registered a total of 548 circles in 34 'active' enterprises and in 13 firms which had since given up circle activities. A year later the same institution registered 687 quality circles in an unknown number of companies (Martin Hernandez 1993a-E). The author informs us that this management tool is mainly confined to multinational companies. Here, quality circles are fairly widespread, whereas in the few Spanish firms applying them, scarcely 10% of the staff are involved. The author estimates that about 1,000 circles with less than 10,000 participants exist in 1991. He further points to a weak trend to incorporate quality circles into more encompassing management strategies such as Total Quality Management. The majority of circles operate as isolated groups, and are not integrated into wider participative programmes.

No further nation-wide information on direct participation is available. Two case studies, based in the Barcelona and Catalonia regions, document considerable new developments. Although their regional approach limits generalisations, the studies should at least be briefly summarised as they seem to indicate substantial organisational change in the modern sections of Spanish business life.

The study of the Barcelona metropolitan region (Miguélez et al. 1993-E) investigated structural change in the wake of preparations for the Olympic games. The main emphasis of the representative establishment survey was on labour market issues, but also contains some information on organisational change: about 25% of the companies of the Barcelona region were found to be operating with quality circles and (unspecified) team work; 9% reported a reduction of hierarchical layers; 16% had programmes to broaden tasks, and 13% operated Just-In-Time practices. The earlier study (Miguélez et al. 1991) which concentrated on the whole of Catalonia, adopted a different approach in that it addressed a representative sample of works councillors in larger establishments in the metal, chemical, food and textile industry: 40% of them reported work rotation schemes in their firms, 32% indicated the existence of work teams (no specification given), and 29% pointed to work islands. These impressive figures must be taken with some caution: the authors found considerable inconsistencies in the data which cast some doubts on the overall results.

Although these results are limited in terms of methodology or application, they seem to indicate sizeable organisational dynamism in certain Spanish regions.

Sweden

Since the early 1970s, Sweden gained a worldwide reputation for humanised working conditions with large employee discretion at workplace level. Scandinavian type autonomous work groups became, to some extent, a trademark for Swedish working conditions.

Telephone interviews with 1,986 management representatives in companies of all sizes in 1991 (Edling and Sandberg 1993-S) revealed that quality circles are used very often: in 62% of public sites and in 53% of the private sector (there was no reference to the proportion of employees affected within the companies). 'Development talks' where future career development is discussed between supervisors and employees, were taken as another indicator of employee involvement. In the private sector such talks are carried out almost entirely with higher white-collar workers (95%) and with 65% of blue-collar workers. This pattern is largely repeated in the public sector with blue-collar involvement being only 5% less.

With these positive results in mind, the authors develop seven additional measures for workforce involvement, ranging from on-the-job training to several ways in which employees can use independent judgement as to which tasks should be performed and how they should be performed. An additive index ranging from 0 - 9 points was used to categorise work organisation in sites, with 9 points representing the most advanced organisations. 2.2% of the Swedish firms fall into this pattern. Firms in different sectors show considerable differences in regard to new organisational patterns: almost one third of firms in the private sector comply with seven and eight items, whereas in the public sector the corresponding figure amounts to 20%. A breakdown along particular business lines sometimes reveals very low percentages (e.g. 7% in engineering).

In the Scandinavian tradition of caring about the Quality of Working Life, an employee survey was conducted with roughly 2,000 respondents in 249 Swedish companies (Leion, ed., 1992-S). From a workforce point of view, 72% of all employees indicated that within three years their work had become enriched with more responsibility, it had become more qualified (63%), more difficult and less monotonous. Among non-managerial employees, white-collar workers reported greater overall gains (52%) compared to blue-collar workers (40%). More revealing in the context of new work organisation is a breakdown of *changes* in responsibility in work by several dimensions (cf. table 15).

Table 15: Net Gains in Different Dimensions of Responsibility

	white-collar (%)	blue-collar (%)
choice of work method	20	18
own planning of daily work	21	18
own quality control	17	18
maintenance of machines and equipment	8	14
instruction or training	12	15
recruitment of new co-workers	6	8

Source: Leion (ed.) 1992-S

According to these figures, Swedish employees seem to have gained considerable discretion in work in the short time of three years, white-collar and blue-collar workers alike. Even if we consider the strong subjective element in this type of information, the figures indicate a distinct and consistent trend towards a kind of work organisation that can be characterised as direct participation. This positive result is not quite in line with the Swedish study reported earlier. But different research designs, operationalisation of direct participation and methods of analysis make a comparison of both studies impossible. However, organisational restructuring in Sweden is probably not as undeveloped as some Swedish researchers identified to their surprise, although it might be somewhat less exemplary than many people believed.

United Kingdom

The Workplace Industrial Relations Surveys (WIRS) which are carried out regularly in the UK are a valuable source which permit the analysis of developments over time. Like the earlier ones, the 1990 WIRS (Millward et al. 1992-UK) is a representative national survey of over 2,000 establishments with more than 25 employees in all economic sectors, with an 83% response rate. Although the survey did not focus explicitly on new work organisation, some insight into this topic can be gained. Analysis shows that different types of information and communication schemes seem to be the preferred tools in management-employee relations.

By far the most frequently mentioned method of communication was a systematic use of the management chain. This was reported by 60% of all managers with little variation between sectors. The next most common means were regular meetings between junior managers and direct supervisors, and their employees (48%). Both regular meetings between senior managers and all sections of the workforce and regular newsletters distributed to all levels of employees were reported by 41% of managers. Regular meetings of work-groups was mentioned in 23% of workplaces in the private manufacturing sector but was recorded nearly twice as often (45%) in the public sector and in a third of private services workplaces. Such information initiatives are increasingly used by management in a simultaneous way: the mean number of combined measures increased from 2. 0 to 2. 4 from 1984 to 1990.

'Has management here made any changes in the last three years with the aim of increasing employees' involvement in the operation of the establishment?' The survey reports that 45% of establishments had taken such initiatives. This represents an increase of 10 percentage points compared to 1984. This growth was primarily a private services and public sector phenomenon. In private manufacturing there was no increase in the proportion of managers reporting the introduction of such initiatives. As to the nature of the initiatives themselves, by far the most significant mechanism adopted was two-way-communication.

Quality circles and semi-autonomous work groups are rarely applied in UK businesses: Quality circles remain confined to 2% of establishments, although their incidence had increased from a low of less than 0.5% in 1984 to 5% of manufacturing workplaces in 1990. Equally low is the rate of semi-autonomous work groups: only 2% of workplaces applied these new 'delegative' practices in 1990, a similar proportion to that reported in the 1984 study.

The 1990 WIRS conveys the message that within six years the UK managers had made considerable progress in involving employees. However, this increased involvement was confined to more elaborate two-way-communication only. According to this survey, quality circles as well as semi-autonomous workgroups do not seem to represent practices for UK managers.

This picture changes somewhat in large establishments (of multi-establishment enterprises only; Marginson et al. 1988-UK). One-way communication is still the preferred type of human resource management, followed by meetings between direct supervisors and employees. One third of these establishments operate with suggestion schemes, and less than one fifth had a distinct policy on quality circles. For the researchers, the comparatively large share of quality circles was an unexpected result. Given the significant role of large establishments in British manufacturing and services where more than half of Britain's labour force worked in companies with over 1,000 employees in 1984, such group suggestion schemes seem to reach more employees than a strictly representative survey would reveal.

USA

The particularly intensive debate in the 1980s about work organisation, flexible work systems and Internal Labour Markets (ILM) was concerned about US industrial performance and international competitiveness. This discussion contrasted US conditions with realistic or idealistic views of German and Japanese firms, using numerous 'anecdotal' evidence to suggest a serious lag in modern organisational structures and procedures. In recent years three nationwide company surveys tried to produce clearer evidence about the US situation in quantitative terms.

The mail survey carried out by Lawler, Mohrman and Ledford (1992-USA) targeted 987 organisations on the 1990 FORTUNE-1000 list, and yielded a response rate of 32%. Hence, all the companies in the sample are among the largest corporations in the US with the median size of firms between 9,000 and 10,000 employees. In addition to the results of the 1990 survey, the study also refers to the results of a 1987 survey conducted by the Government Accounting Office (GAO). As several of the authors were involved in both surveys, there are strong parallels in survey design and content which make the findings somewhat comparable.

In the 1990 study, the authors relied on a concept of employee involvement that emphasised broad diffusion of information, knowledge, and power throughout the organisation. In this context, *information sharing* means: sharing company performance results, unit operating results, information on new technologies, information on company goals, etc. - indicators in the scope of the Human Resource Management approach. *Increasing knowledge* means: training and skill development, group problem-solving skills, team building skills, job skills and others. *Power sharing practices* were operationalised as quality circles and related participation groups, self-managing work teams, job enrichment and others.

Information sharing was a widespread measure of employee involvement and reached, on average, more then 60% of all employees in the firms under study. This information refers, first of all, to the company's overall business results, followed by the operating results of the employees unit, and to business plans and goals (ranging from 76% to 47%). There is no overall change in information provisions between 1987 and 1990. As to skill development, the study indicates "a tremendous void in the training of American workers" (p. 18). In summary, about half of the firms were doing limited training in interpersonal skills and technical/analytical skills. Only in the case of job skills training, did 35% of firms provide training for most of their employees.

The authors found that the companies in the sample, in the first instance, prefer power-sharing practices that do not require fundamental changes in the organisation of the company. Accordingly, quality circles, which mean a parallel organisational structure, are the most preferred practices and are applied by 66% of companies. These circles affect, on average, short of half of employees. Self-managing teams which require more fundamental changes in the organisation were used less frequently, but were still used by 47% of companies. 37% use them with about 20% of their employees; the remaining 10% of companies involve more than 20% of their employees in group work of this kind.

Viewing employee involvement in a temporal perspective, the authors see distinct increases (planned and factual) in different direct participation measures, and suggest that such programmes are becoming increasingly popular in the US. The greatest planned increases were reported for employee participation groups like quality circles, self-managing work teams and job enrichment. Two of these practices - job enrichment and participation groups - already have a high adoption rate which suggests that high numbers of employees would eventually be covered in the firms that already use them. Also, self-managing work teams, though they were not adopted on a very broad basis, were more popular in 1990 than in 1987.

More recent representative study of US firms was carried out by Osterman (1994-USA). 694 representatively selected non-agricultural establish-means with 50 or more employees were interviewed by phone, of which 451 establishments completed the interview (65.5% response rate). Using the general frame of reference of 'flexible work systems', Osterman attempts to establish the extent to which workplace innovations have diffused throughout American businesses and in what combination of practices. Further, he examines the determinants of adoption: what explains which firms implement these practices and which do not? The notion of 'flexible work system' is operationalised as:

* Self-directed work teams: employees supervise their own work; workers make their own decisions about pace and flow and occasionally the best way to get the work done.

* Job rotation is operationalised as changes between sections or departments of a firm.

* Problem solving groups and quality circles are defined as quality programmes where employees are involved in problem solving.

* Total Quality Management (TQM) means a quality control approach that emphasises the importance of communication, feedback, and teamwork.

Detailed information on these new facets of work organisation was obtained only for 'core' employees. The notion of a core job was developed because collecting data on all job families in a firm was considered impractical. A *core group* was defined as "the largest group of non-supervisory, non-managerial workers at this location who are directly involved in making the product or in providing the service at the location".

Table 16: Types of Flexible Work Organization in U.S. Establishments

	Percent of all establishments regardless of the level of penetration	Establishments with a 50% level of penetration
Teams	55%	41%
Job Rotation	43%	27%
Quality Circle	41%	27%
TQM	34%	25%
Nothing	22%	36%

Source: Osterman 1994-US

The first outcome of the study is that flexible work organisation appears to be widespread among US businesses if one just considers whether the practice is used at all: Over half of the establishments (55%) use teams, 43% operate job rotation, 41% have quality circles, and one third (34%) apply TQM schemes. If the degree of penetration is taken into account, i.e. if we only look at establishments where at least 50% of core employees are involved in a practice, the data trend is the same, but frequencies fall off by roughly 15 percentage points. Teams are still the most widespread practice with 41% of establishments applying them. The other three practices are applied in roughly one quarter of these establishments, with integrated TQM approaches being the least widespread, found in 25% of businesses.

There seems to be some evidence of an 'anchoring' practice in non-manufacturing establishments where core employees are not blue collar: 71.7% of those that engaged in at least one practice had self-managed teams. However, there is no evidence of an anchoring practice among blue-collar core employees in manufacturing. Further, all of the practices are more common in manufacturing with the exception of self-directed teams which is a specific feature of white collar work in transformed establishments.

The author notes that the quantitative results describing the dissemination of flexible work practices are much higher than estimates commonly cited in the literature: 36.6% of the entire sample, 43% of non-manufacturing, and 35.9% of manufacturing establishments can be characterised as 'transformed' which means that these establishments employ at least two practices with 50% or more of the core employees involved in each. Obviously, direct participation practices are much more prevalent in the USA than has been commonly thought.

Both the FORTUNE 1000 study and Osterman's research display considerable overlap in two ways: they both use quality circles and self-managed work teams as important target variables indicating and measuring new organisational structures. They also reach similar conclusions about the spread of these new practices throughout US businesses: The FORTUNE 1000 study of 1990 already showed that these new practices had spread remarkably, and Osterman's research reveals even higher percentages of 'transformed' US establishments. Differences in the two studies may be due to the fact that they were both undertaken at different times and in different research universes.

Japan

Japan has been the epitome of direct participation characterised by group work. A recent study by Okubayashi et al. (1994-JP) strongly supports this popular. The data were gathered from a representative sample of 1,394 large Japanese firms with more than 1,000 employees, of which 786 belonged to the manufacturing sector and 609 to the service sector. Data from 183 manufacturing and 110 non-manufacturing firms were collected, giving a response rate of 21% for the questionnaire. Details about survey administered sample distortions from non-responses are not given. The purpose of the study was to investigate the influence of new technology on work structure (both operational and managerial), job content and the firm's labour management system.

Table 17: Teamwork in Large Japanese Companies

	Manufacturing	Non-Manufacturing
independent teams with equal tasks	7%	6%
independent teams, based on task similarity	31%	28%
cooperating teams with member rotation between teams with similar tasks	55%	49%
individual work assignments, no job rotation	7%	17%
N=	183	110

Source: Okubayshi et al. 1994-JP

Of central importance is the fact that in manufacturing, 93% of firms indicate that their operational personnel work in groups. Group work is the norm for 83% of employees in non-manufacturing firms as well. In both sectors, about half of the teams have a homogeneous task structure, and team members rotate between similar tasks, with close co-operation between such teams. Another 30% of operators work in a similar manner, although the teams operate independently from each other. In addition to the regular procedures of working in groups, formalised small group activities in quality circles are very prominent (93% in manufacturing and 70% in non-manufacturing). These additional quality circle activities have definitely gained ground during the last five years in both types of firms.

Okubayashi (1988-JP) reports the findings of another representative study of large firms in Japan which had introduced micro-electronics. The study which was confined to manufacturing, was carried out in 1985. For this sector he summarises the changes in work organisation and of managerial organisation in the first half of the 1980s. Under the influence of micro-electronics, job content was distinctly simplified, the discretionary content of work remained unaltered and mutual help at the work place was increased.

This points to the development of simpler jobs in a group set-up. On the managerial side, delegation of authority and co-operation between individual sections of the firm definitely increased, while the hierarchical ladder was shortened and the functions of finance, planning and personnel management became more strongly concentrated in headquarters The surveys are somewhat comparable for large Japanese manufacturing firms. Such a comparison (cf. Okubayashi et al. 1994-JP, Okubayashi 1995-JP) reveals an ongoing tendency for Japanese firms to move towards the flattening of hierarchies and towards group work in the way we tried to elaborate the concept above: with multi-skilled workers who operate and rotate between similar tasks. Okubayashi interprets this as a definite development towards a "loosely structured" organisation. In summary, the outstanding information emerging from recent Japanese research is that in the larger companies, almost all employees work in groups.

7.2   The Countries in Comparative Perspective

For all countries we presented various survey results which report on how widely different types of direct participation are applied. Based on this information it would be very interesting to compare the countries in various respects: Where do individual countries stand in regard to initiating workplace innovation and organisational change to become flexible and competitive? Do businesses and organisations pursue identical or similar strategies in all countries or do we find regional or other distinct types of direct participation and organisational change, and how might these be explained? How profound is change in companies? What proportions of national workforces are affected by these new developments?

Unfortunately, we cannot answer these questions on the basis of available material. Assuming that we are truly informed about quantitative research on direct participation measures up to the middle or the end of 1994, the research itself is characterised by extreme diversity: in the problems investigated, methods applied and the depth of measurement, and analysis. In some countries, like Austria, Denmark and Finland, only workforces were interviewed. In other countries like Greece, Italy and Spain, we learned something about the spread of quality circles, without much reference to other types of workforce involvement. For Germany, we have to rely on management consultancy research of poor methodological value, on a workforce survey and on the spread of group work in mechanical engineering. For Belgium, France, the Netherlands, Portugal, Sweden, UK, the USA and Japan we have more general surveys. But they, again, tap different dimensions of task participation and organisation change which make comparison difficult. Thus, if we don't find quality circles or other forms of direct participation mentioned in one country, this does not necessarily mean that they do not or did not exist. It may simply mean that they were not investigated.

To somewhat repair this unsatisfactory situation, we revert to the Price Waterhouse Cranfield project, a truly European comparative study. This project is planned as regular surveys on the situation and development of strategic human resource management in the whole of Europe. The first survey, sampling all organisations with more than 200 employees in all economic sectors, has been carried out in 15 European countries. For ten EU countries we have comparative data on the spread of suggestion schemes, workforce surveys and quality circles in companies.

Suggestion schemes are a rather traditional and 'low-impact' type of individual direct participation (cf. chapter 2). Against a European average of 28%, German, Swedish and Finnish firms stand out as using suggestion schemes most frequently (between 47% and 45% of firms). In contrast, companies in the Latin countries of France, Portugal and Spain make distinctly less use of the chance to ask their employees for workplace and process improvements (between 10% and 14% of firms). Rates of application in Denmark, Ireland, the Netherlands and the UK are somewhere in between these two extremes.

Figure 1: The Spread of Suggestion Schemes
in European Companies in 1992

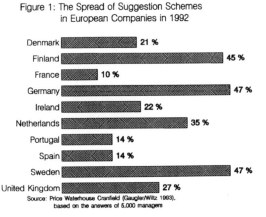

Source: Price Waterhouse Cranfield (Gaugler/Wiltz 1993).
based on the answers of 5,000 managers

Workforce surveys are another 'low-impact' type of consultative participation at the individual level. They received heightened public attention in the 'Company Culture Movement' of the 1980s. In 1992, they were applied in about 23% of European companies, but wide variations exist: they are particularly popular in the two Nordic countries, Finland and Sweden being applied in 50% and 43% of all companies. At the other extreme is the Netherlands (6%), with other countries somewhere in the middle.

Considering the positive management-workforce relationship and the generally relaxed industrial relations climate in the Netherlands, companies' disinterest in workforce surveys is surprising and not easy to explain. It might well be that the indigenous Dutch institution of 'work consultation' (werkoverleg) implicitly fulfils the functions of workforce surveys. At the other extreme, management's great interest in both suggestion schemes and workforce surveys in Sweden and Finland might reflect the paramount importance given to employees in the Nordic countries. This was already apparent when the national survey results were presented earlier: In both countries, surveys were carried out in the Quality of Working Life tradition, with the workforce as a target group. Companies in the remaining countries' workforce surveys attach medium importance to consultative participation (between 14% and 30%). This group includes very diverse countries, a fact that cannot easily be explained.

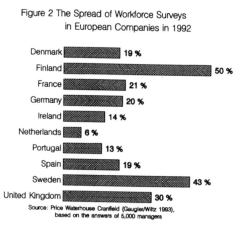

Figure 2 The Spread of Workforce Surveys
in European Companies in 1992

Source: Price Waterhouse Cranfield (Gaugler/Wiltz 1993),
based on the answers of 5,000 managers

From what we now know, European type quality circles are a third rather 'low-impact' type of direct participation. One could define quality circles as group based suggestion schemes. As was suggested in chapter three, quality circles had already reached their peak in the late 1980s. Our 1992 figures are very likely to represent a decline. In that year, an average of 15% of all European companies applied these group suggestion schemes. Finland, France, Germany, Spain and the UK are above this average, with shares ranging between 17 and 20%. With quality circles in only 9% to 11% of

Danish, Irish, Portuguese and Swedish firms, these countries mark the extreme of low-users.

The Price Waterhouse Cranfield comparative data leave many questions open. Their greatest limitation stems from the study's concentration on low-impact types of direct participation, and neglect of high-impact issues of group work and integrated approaches like Total Quality Management and Lean Production schemes. But the project is a step in the right direction: if we are interested to know where Europe stands today and how the European countries relate to each other in regard to organisational transformation, we need a cross-national research approach, using similar methods to investigate the same topics and types of direct participation. At present, we have to treat information from different countries as a snapshot of different participation measures which, at best, gives an impression of national developments.

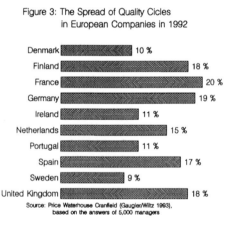

Figure 3: The Spread of Quality Cicles
in European Companies in 1992

Source: Price Waterhouse Cranfield (Gaugier/Wiltz 1993),
based on the answers of 5,000 managers

Widening our view beyond Europe and looking at the USA and Japan as Europe's economic competitors, we gain valuable insights. The best information to emerge from the literature search relates to the USA, both in regard to content and methodology. According to these results, US organisations seem to be undergoing dynamic organisational change, much more so that even US observers expected. Although the research cited for this country is open to much criticism, comparable studies have not been done in other countries, and so comparisons with the European and Japanese world of business and organisations is not possible.

About Japan we learned that almost all larger companies operate group work, complemented by quality control circles. This applies to the production sector and the service sector alike, and results seem to confirm 'conventional wisdom' that group work might be the secret behind Japan's economic success. But a closer look at the functioning of Japanese type group work told us that such simple explanations must be qualified (cf. chapter 4.1). We, further, should be very cautious about interpreting Japanese concepts in a 'European' way. 'Groups' for instance, are understood quite differently from European-American 'groups'. They represent parts of the normal organisational structure of companies and resemble our sections in departments. Even without knowing the exact implications of such information, we should be cautious about reaching sudden conclusions about 'productivity secrets' or the 'one-best type of work organisation'.

8   Conclusions

This report is an attempt to inform the reader of the current state of knowledge on direct participation, its diverse forms, the reasons for its introduction, its success or failure and its effects on traditional patterns of employee relations and industrial relations practice. The report also points to knowledge gaps which need to be filled in order to assess the merits or failings of direct participation. In our conclusions we concentrate on the problems of organisational change from a management perspective, on the relationship between profitability and work humanisation, on union concerns, and on various research gaps.

Results and Problems from a Management Perspective

Direct participation as it was discussed here has a double function: its various forms constitute what has been termed *high performance work systems* or *transformed organisations*. At the same time, direct participation can act as a change agent leading to such work systems. High performance work systems differ from traditional organisations which apply bureaucratic principles: bureaucratic structures rely on hierarchical control of the workforce and award compliance with fixed rules and punish deviance from such rules. Such rule adherence makes them increasingly inflexible and slow to respond to changed product market conditions and customer demands. The new type of organisation which is able to respond to new competitive pressures flexibly relies on employees's skills and initiative, and the core idea of employee initiated 'continous improvement' is the opposite of rule adherence, in principle. The new, 'transformed organisation' is, to a certain degree, the negation of bureaucratic principles.

Before management ventures into new organisational solutions they need to be sufficiently assured of their future success, that direct participation 'pays' in the end, that 'high performance work systems' really 'perform' and in what way. In our research overview we presented various examples of effects of direct participation in regard to productivity, efficiency and rentablility. Such effects are difficult to measure in quantitative terms as the isolation of multiple causes and effects is no easy task. But accepting less stringent measurements and relying on overall management assessments, the evaluation of the effects of direct participation is very positive, particularly regarding the outcome of delegative types of direct participation. Yet to substantiate such a statement solidly we would need additional information on companies that tried to 'transform' their organisation but failed in their effort and gave up in the end. Unfortunately, such information is not available.

Our research has shown that a transformed organisation is not easy to achieve. It is not sufficient to apply isolated measures of direct participation and confine them to a few departments or sections of employees. The key to success seems to be the determination of senior management to take a fresh look at the organisation and to make the new systems work in an integrated way. The efforts of time and money should not be underestimated: to see the development of such high performance work systems, management must facilitate the decentralisation of decision-making processes to employees, help and train employees to accept these new responsibilities, develop new roles for the 'displaced' managers, and adopt personnel practices to support this new direction in work organisation structures.

The process of organisational change is a very difficult tasks, and this is one reason that many companies, particularly multinational firms which venture into new countries, try to avoid the change problem by devising completely new organisations, popularly called 'greenfield sites'. Here, management have the advantage of being able to start from a clean sheet and do not need to 'transform' their workplaces like their counterparts in in established firms, in 'brownfield sites'. They are also able to implement sophisticated selection techniques to identify suitable employees.

But in the majority of cases we are dealing with established organisations which have their grown traditions, values and internal power structures were organisational change is not welcome and difficult to achieve. Here the second function of direct participation might come into play: direct participation is not only an indicator for high performance work systems; it is also a means to arrive at new organisational structures; it can function as a 'change agent'. It is established knowledge of organisation research that early workforce participation in change programmes is a suitable way to overcome resistance to change and to make new schemes function. Particularly in regard to high performance work systems the necessity of a high trust relationship between all actors is often voiced. In this context, our literature review has shown that even consultative types of direct participation, which are considered 'low profile' in the concept of 'transformed organisations', can greatly contribute to create a high trust atmosphere. The quality circles are a case in point: they had their most positive effect not in quality improvements but in stimulating intra-organisational discussion, communication and cooperation. There is agreement that quality circles are a suitable means to prepare the ground for more encompassing organisational change through forms of delegative participation. The quality cirlce survival in Total Quality Management testifies to this capacity.

Direct Participation: Between Profitabilty and Work Humanization

There are hopes that the new managerial schemes might reconcile the two hitherto opposing aims of company efficiency and the Quality of Working Life. But the effects on employees' working lives are somewhat ambiguous. They depend on the type of direct participation and on the type of employees. Quality circles, for instance, have proven their worth particularly in creating a more communicative and cooperative atmosphere. We also know that the majority of employees looks forward to enlarged work discretion and more rights and responsibilities. On average, such enlarged jobs are more stressful, but we found convincing evidence that stress increase is accepted as the necessary price for more workplace discretion.

Workers' reactions to group work is more ambivalent. Not everybody likes 'cooperative' tasks on an ongoing, everyday basis or is capable of carrying them out. The various screening procedures for manning work groups testify to this problem. As we showed in detail, there are different types of group work, ranging from very wide group discretion in 'Scandinavian' groups to very limited discretion in lean production groups. Whereas working in Scandinavian type groups had many benefits for employees, their productivity effects are far from clear. Where management adopted lean production systems, productivity does not seem to be a problem, but workforces have many reservations. The fact that lean production systems are typically applied in greenfield sites seems to underline the problematic features of such work: these establishments are mostly located in structurally weak regions of Europe and the USA which offer only few employment alternatives. Our research has shown that even Japanese workers are not greatly in favour of working under lean production regimes. Clearly, there is a need to develop some hybrid form of group work which optimises the strength of both group applications, minimising their undesired effects. Such hybrid forms are still in the experimentation stage, and their outcome is uncertain.

One of the big concerns of employees with the introduction of direct participation is its effects on skill structures and job boundaries. These concerns are particularly pronounced among skilled groupings who fear loss of income, status, skills and qualifications. Such problems become particularly urgent in countries were labour relations rely on 'job demarcations' and in countries with a highly developed vocational training system, resulting in narrowly defined 'professions'. On the other hand, unskilled and semi-skilled workers often welcome the opportunity to expand their skills' portfolio and the opportunity to acquire more discretion and autonomy.

One of the main preoccupations of employees with the introduction of team working has been with pay. This has often proved to be one of the main stumbling blocks and demotivators for employees who otherwise might have reacted very positively to direct participation.

Union Concerns

Initially, European unions had a very sceptical attitude towards the idea of direct workforce participation that was advocated by management. One of their greatest concern, perhaps the most crucial issue, was the suspicion that management may be using direct participation to win over employees' hearts and minds and, as a consequence, employees will be less committed to their union. The review of the literature, however, would suggest that this has not been management's motive; performance reasons have been paramount in management's thinking to introduce direct participation. In most European countries employers have actively sought trade union and works council involvement in the introduction of direct participation. In the US, too, management's motives for introducing direct participation have been similar to employers in Europe, but the evidence of management's intentions in regard of unions is more ambiguous. Some research has shown that management are using direct participation to marginalise trade unions, but this has not been a common management strategy. In most European countries, and after expressing some initial reservations and apprehensions, unions at a local level have usually co-operated with the introduction of direct participation. Indeed in some instances, unions have been very pro-active in their co-operation with, and support for, direct participation. This was particularly the case in countries that had a long history of experimenting with direct participation.

Workforce behaviour has helped to disperse union concerns about possible alienating effects of direct participation. The majority of employees wants enlarged tasks, and we observed a 'Matthew effect' meaning that employees already enjoying large discretion at work strive for and get more rights and responsibilities at the workplace. But as union members they see clear limits of their workplace influence and continue to delegate certain issues to the more influential institutions of union representation. In labour relations with a works councils system, such delegation of important tasks towards the works councils is practiced even by non-members. It is perhaps this experience of a continuing integrity of the representational system that dispersed the initial concerns of European trade unions and which led European trade unionists "... to view the crucial and controversial issue of the impact of direct on indirect or representational participation with a quite relaxed attitude" (Regalia 1995:102).

Then, there is the concern among some trade unionists that the introduction of direct participation may create some tensions between the union and works councils where they exist, or in their absence shop stewards. As management generally included the works councils in their direct participation policies, influence and status of works councils is often enhanced with their co-operation with management, and such active works councils mostly enjoy employees' confidence. There is some evidence that divisions between both parties have appeared when works councillors/shop stewards have given precedence to the benefits which direct participation may bring for employees and their firms without regard for national union policy. There are instances that unions try to losen control of works councils and attempt to find a somewhat changed role in their relationship to works councils: from a directive towards a coaching and service function. Thus, organisational change seems not only to affect management and employees, but employee representational systems as well.

With the exception of working in lean production systems trade unionist are not overly alarmed about a general deterioration of working conditions. Where such concerns were put forward they sometimes contradict each other. Very often, there are expectations of higher quality work and workplaces. Pariculary high hopes are attached to a modified Scandinavian group work concept. This outright positive view of group work tends to overlook the problematic aspects of working in groups, even of the Scandinavian type.

Finally, and perhaps one of the more immediate challenges to trade unions is the threatened loss of employment and members which may follow the adoption of direct participation and particularly in its lean production form.

Research Gaps

While this research review has brought together some very rich material and has considerably improved our knowledge of direct participation, there are serious gaps in our understanding. Among the most serious are: first, we know relatively little of the employment effects of the introduction of direct participation. One would imagine that where it is introduced alongside lean production principles that the job losses may be significant. Certainly the MIT study referred to earlier argues that this is a likely outcome.

Second, who are the 'winners' and 'losers'? Are we to assume that skilled and professional categories of employees have more to gain or to lose than employees in less skilled occupations? What about older employees, female employees and employees from racial minorities? How do such practices affect part-time and temporary employees?

Third, while our knowledge of direct participation as it affects manufacturing is far from complete we know considerably less of its impact in public and private services. The latter must be examined in more detail if only because an increasing proportion of European employment is concentrated in this sector. Public services, too, are encountering significant changes and one would imagine that there is, at least, some experimentation with direct participation principles.

Fourth, our investigation of direct participation and quality of working life issues raised a number of inconsistencies. Much of this is as a consequence of poor theorisation: 'humanised work' is basically a normative concept. To make it operational for research and, thus, amenable for scientific and public debate, we need to develop better theory on human work motivation and 'humane work'. So far, such theories have concentrated on individual's work and basically presumed an interest in the 'task itself', at the expense of 'secondary' interests such as income, promotion, and efficacy in work. Yet our literature review brought forward many instances indicating the importance of such 'secondary' motives, sometimes at the expense of the presumed 'primary' work interests. Further with regard to group work, theories based on individual work behaviour are often simply extended to group work situations, overlooking the fact that the social structure of such work relations is significantly different. More attention needs to be given to the development of theory in this broad area.

Fifth, political actors, scientists and public commentators should be cautious about attributing the 'secrets' of Japanese organisational and production successes only to direct participation. The MIT study of lean production, for example, claims that the use of team working was crucial to Japanese competitive success. More recently, however, commentators have pointed to other elements of the Japanese employment model which were not given adequate consideration by the study's authors, for example, management of supplier relations, longer working hours, product design and selection of personnel. When such factors are taken into account differences in levels of employee productivity may not be as great as was once thought.

Finally, the introduction of direct participation in Japan and the US is probably more advanced than it is in Europe, particularly when it comes to delegative participation. While we can be clear on this, there are problems in making clear and precise comparisons between practices in a variety of countries because of the different concepts and methodologies employed. Such difficulties also exist when we compare experience within Europe. The EPOC establishment survey of direct participation should correct many of these shortcomings and will be the first detailed examination of direct participation in Europe. Such data is essential for understanding why companies do and do not chose to introduce direct participation and for identifying the key conditions which promote the successful implementation of such practices.

References

Accordino, J., 1989: *Quality-of Working-Life Systems in Large Cities: An Assessment,* in: Public Productivity Review, Vol. 12, No. 4, pp. 345-360.

Ackermann, M. P., 1989: Quality Circles in der Bundesrepublik Deutschland. Hemmende und fördernde Faktoren einer erfolgreichen Realisierung *(Quality Circles in the Federal Republic of Germany. Hindering and Supporting Factors for Success),* Frankfurt/Main: Peter Lang.

Adler, P. S., 1991: *Workers and Flexible Manufacturing Systems: Three Installations Compared,* in: Journal of Organizational Behavior, Vol. 12, pp. 447-460.

Aichholzer G., J. Flecker and G. Schienstock 1991: Betriebliche Innovationsprozesse im Angestelltenbereich *(Innovation Processes Among White Collar Employees),* in: Bundesministerium für Arbeit und Soziales (ed.): Einführung neuer Technologien als sozialer Prozeß. Forschungsberichte aus der Sozial- und Arbeitsmarktpolitik, No. 40, pp. 35-179.

Alasoini, T., 1990: Tuotannolliset rationalisoinnit ja teollisuuden työvoiman käyttötapojen muutos. Tutkimus viidestä modernista suomalaisesta konepaja-teollisuuden, kevyen sahköteknisen teollisuuden ja paperiteollisudden yksiköstä *(Production Rationalisation and Changed Ways of Using Industrial Manpower. A Study of Five Modern Finnish Units in the Engineering, Light Electrical and Paper Industries),* Helsinki: Työpoliittinen tutkimus 5.

Alasoini, T., 1992: Organisaatioinnovaatiot Suomen kevyessä sähköteknisessä teollisuudessa *(Organisational Innovations in the Finnish Light Electrical Industry),* Helsinki: Työpoliittinen tutkimus 23.

Albertijn, M., 1995: *Belgium: The Beginnings of Direct Participation,* in: I. Regalia and C. Gill (eds.) 1995, pp. 29-47.

Altmann, N., 1995: *Japanese Work Policy: Opportunity, Challenge or Threat?* in: Å. Sandberg (ed.): Enriching Production. Aldershot, Brookfield USA, Hong Kong: Avebury, pp. 329-365.

Ambrosini, M., 1989: Non solo automi. Risorse umane e relazioni di lavoro nell' impresache cambia *(Not Only Automations. Human Resources and Work Relations in a Changing Enterprise)*, Milano: Angeli.

ANCQUI (National Quality Circle Association) 1987: Lo sviluppo dei Circoli di Qualità in Italia *(The Development of Quality Circles in Italy)*, in: Rapporto di ricerca ciclostilato, pp. 1-43.

Antoni, C., W. Bungard and E. Lehnert 1992: Qualitätszirkel und ähnliche Formen der Gruppenarbeit in der Bundesrepublik Deutschland: Eine Bestandsaufnahme der Problemlösungsgruppen-Konzepte bei den 100 umsatzgrößten Industrieunternehmen *(Quality Cirles and Similar Forms of Group Work in the FRG: An Inventory of Concepts of Problem-Solving Groups in the 100 Companies With Largest Turnover)*, in: W. Bungard (ed.): Qualitätszirkel in der Arbeitswelt. Beiträge zur Organisationspsychologie No. 7, Göttingen, Stuttgart: Verlag für Angewandte Psychologie, pp. 109-138.

Applebaum, E., and R. Batt 1994: *The New American Workplace. Transforming Work Systems in the United States*, Ithaca, N. Y.: ILR Press.

Argyris, C., 1957: *Personality and Organization*, New York: Harper.

Asendorf, et al. 1988 (Asendorf, I., M. von Behr, C. Köhler, B. Lutz, C. Nuber, and H. Schultz-Wild): Sozialwissenschaftliche Begleitforschung *(Evaluation Research)*, in: P. Knaur (ed.): Wandel der Arbeitsbedingungen durch ein flexibles Ferti-gungssystem mit modularem Aufbau. Sozialwissenschaftliche Begleit-forschung. *(Change of Working Conditions Through a Flexible Manu-facturing System With a Modular Structure. Evaluation From a Social Science Point of View)*, Karlsruhe: Projektträger Fertigungstechnik.

Baisier, L., and M. Albertijn 1992: Werken in kringen, kwaliteit in overleg. Werkoverleg en kwaliteitskringen in Vlaanderen *(Working in Circles, Quality in Consultation. Work Consultatin and Quality Circles in Flanders)*, Brussels: Stichting Technologie Vlaanderern.

Balog, A., 1991: Informationstechnologie im Spannungsfeld betrieblicher Akteure. Fallstudie in einem Produktionsbetrieb *(Information Technology in the Arena of Organizational Actors. Case Study of a Production Firm)*, in: Bundesministerium für Arbeit und Soziales (ed.): Einführung neuer

202

Technologien als sozialer Prozeß. Forschungsberichte aus der Sozial- und Arbeitsmarktpolitik, No. 40, pp. 185-286.

Banke, P., 1991a: Gruppeorganisering. Fleksibel produktion og jobkvalitet i den syende industri *(Group Organization. Flexible Production and Job Quality in the Clothing Industry)*, Danish Technological Institute.

Banke, P., 1991b: Forsøg med gruppeorganisering. Kvalifikationsprojektet inden for textil- og beklædningsindustrien. Baggrundsrapport, *(Testing Group Organization. Qualification Project Within the Textile and Clothing Industry. Background Report)*, Danish Technological Institute, Human Resources Development.

Barker, J. R., 1993: *Tightening the Iron Cage: Concertive Control in Self-Managing Teams,* in: Administrative Science Quarterly, Vol. 38, pp. 408-437.

Beck, F., and I. Stone 1992: *New Inward Investment and the Northern Region Labour Market*, Employment Department, Research Series No. 6, London.

Bednarek E., 1985: Veränderungen der Arbeitsmotivation durch Qualitätszirkel und Lernstatt *(Change of Work Motivation Through Quality Circles and Learning Schemes)*, University of Munich, Ph.D. Dissertation.

Beisheim, M., D. von Eckardstein and M. Müller 1991: Partizipative Organisationsformen und industrielle Beziehungen *(Participative Forms of Organi-zation and Industrial Relations)*, in: W. Müller-Jentsch (ed.): Konfliktpartnerschaft, München and Mering: Rainer Hampp, pp. 123-138.

Berggren, Ch., 1992: *Alternatives to Lean Production. Work Organization in the Swedish Auto Industry*, Ithaca, NY: Cornell University, ILR Press.

Beriger, P., 1987: Quality Circles und Kreativität *(Quality Circles and Creativity)*, Schriftenreihe des Instituts für betriebswirtschaftliche Forschung an der Universität Zürich, Bd. 53, Bern and Stuttgart: Haupt.

Bernoux, Ph. et al. 1985: De l'expression à négociation. Les groupes d'expression directe dans 6 entreprises de la région Rhône-Alpes *(From Expression to Negotiation. Direct Expression Groups in 6 Firms in the Rhône-Alpes Region)*, GLYSI, Lyon.

Blauner, R., 1964: *Alienation and Freedom. The Factory Worker and His Industry,* Chicago and London.

Bonazzi, G., 1993: Il tubo di cristallo. Modello giapponese e Fabbrica Integrata alla Fiat Auto *(The Crystal Pipe. Japanese Model and Integrated Factory at Fiat Auto),* Bologna: il Mulino.

Bottrup, P., and B. Clematide 1992: Lad operatørerne brede sig - det betaler sig! Uddannelse og jobudvikling i plastindustrien *(Let the Operators Diversify - It Pays! Training and Job Development in the Plastics Industry),* Danish Technological Institute.

Bouche, G., et al. 1991: Réussir une organisation en juste à temps. L'exemple d'un atelier de méchanique chez Renault *(Make Success of an Organization Through 'Just in Time'. An Example of a Mechanics Workshop at Renault),* Montrouge: ANACT Editions.

Bradley, K., and S. Hill 1983: *After Japan: The Quality Circle Transplant and Productive Efficiency,* in: British Journal of Industrial Relations, Vol. 21, pp. 291-311.

Bradley, K., and S. Hill 1987: *Quality Circles and Managerial Interests,* in: Industrial Relations, Vol. 26, pp. 68-82.

Brady, T., et al. 1993: *Teams in Action - A Report on Teamworking in Leading Irish Companies,* in: Irish Business and Employers Confederation; Dublin.

Brater, M., and U. Büchele 1993: Entwicklungsschritte zur Gruppenarbeit in der Mengensachbearbeitung *(Steps Towards Group Work in Mass-Records Processing),* Gesellschaft für Ausbildungsforschung und Berufsentwicklung e.V. München, München and Mering: Rainer Hampp.

Bratton, J., 1991: *Japanization at Work: The Case of Engineering Plants in Leeds,* in: Work, Employment and Society. Vol. 5, pp. 377-395.

Bravermann, H., 1974: *Labor and Monopoly Capital,* New York: Monthly Review Press.

204

Brödner, P., 1985: Fabrik 2000. Alternative Entwicklungspfade in die Zukunft der Fabrik *(Factory 2000. Alternative Paths of Development Into the Future of the Factory)*, Berlin.

Brödner, P., and U. Pekruhl 1991: Rückkehr der Arbeit in die Fabrik *(The Return of Work Into the Factory)*, Institut Arbeit und Technik: Gelsenkirchen.

Bundesmann-Jansen, J., and U. Pekruhl 1992: Der Medienkonzern Bertelsmann. Neues Management und gewerkschaftliche Betriebspolitik *(The Media Trust Bertelsmann. New Management and Union Company Policy)*, Köln: Bund-Verlag.

Bundesmann-Jansen, J., and J. Frerichs 1995: Betriebspolitik und Organisations-wandel *(Company Policy and Organizational Change)*, Münster: Westfälisches Dampfboot.

Burawoy, M., 1979: *Manufacturing Consent. Changes in the Labour Process under Monopoly Capitalism,* Chicago and London.

Butera, F., 1988: L'orologio e l'organismo. Il cambiamento organizzativo nella grande impresa in Italia *(The Clock and the Organism. The Organizational Change in the Large Manufacturing Companies in Italy),* Milano: Angeli.

Carpo, S., 1994: La cultura della qualità: prodotto, processo, risorse umane. Uno spaccato di dieci realtà aziendali *(The Culture of Quality: Product, Process, Human Resources. A Study on Ten Companies),* working paper.

Carrasquer, P., X. Coller and F. Miguelez 1993: Polítiques de regulació de la mà d'obra a l'Europa dels noranta. El cas de Catalunya *(Managerial Policies of Labour Regulation in the Europe of the 90s. The Case of Catalonia),* in: Grup d'Estudis Sociológics sobre la Vida Quotidiana i el Treball (QUIT), Working Paper No. 1, Bellaterra, Departament de Sociologia, Universidad Autónoma de Barcelona.

Castillo, J. J., V. Jimenez and M. Santos 1991: Nuevas formas de organiza-ción del trabajo y la implicación directa en España, *(New Modalities of Work Organization Methods and Direct Participation in Spain),* in: REIS (Revista Española de Sociología), No. 56, October-December, pp. 115-137.

Cerruti, G., and V. Rieser 1991: Fiat: qualità totale e fabbrica integrata *(Fiat: Total Quality and Integrated Factory)*, Roma: Ediesse.

CIRC (Current Information Research Committee) 1987: Joho-ka jidai jinnzai ikusei *(Making Good Manpower in the Information Age)*, Sogo Rodo Kenkyu-syo.

Citarella, F., and I. Vitale 1988: L'esperienza dei circoli di qualità nella industria alimentare *(The Quality Circle Experience in the Food Industry)*, in: Quaderni ISRIL; Vol. 3-27.

Clark, J., 1993: *Full Flexibility and Self-Supervision in an Automated Factory in Human Resource Management and Technical Change,* London: Sage.

Clausen, C., and B. Lorentzen 1986: Deltagelse i beslutninger om ny teknologi *(Participation in Decisions Regarding New Technology),* Danish Technological Institute.

COB/SER 1990: Zelfstanding samenwerken in taakgroepen; Praktijkervaringen in industrie en dienstverlening *(Cooperating Independently in Taskgroups; Practical Experiences in Manufacturing and Service Industries),* The Hague: COB/SER.

Collard, R., and B. Dale 1989: *Quality Circles,* in: K. Sisson (ed.): Personnel Management in Britain, Oxford: Blackwell.

Cooke, W. N., 1992: *Product Quality Improvement Through Employee Participation: The Effects of Unionization and Joint Union-Management Administration,* in: Industrial and Labor Relations Review, Vol. 46, No. 1, pp. 199-234.

Cotton, J, L., 1993: *Employee Involvement. Methods for Improving Performance and Work Attitudes;* Newbury Park, London, New Delhi: SAGE Publications.

Coutrot, Th., and J. L. Parraire 1994: Le développement récent des politiques de motivation des salaries *(Recent Development in Employee Motivation Policies),* in: Premières synthèses DARES, Ministry of Labour, Employment and Vocational Training, Paris, No. 47.

Cristóvam, M. L., A. C. Efertz and J. R. Jorge 1993: O factor Humano e Qualidade *(The Human Factor and Quality)*, PEDIP.

Crozier, M., and E. Friedberg (1979): Macht und Organization. Die Zwänge kollektiven Handelns *(Power and Organization. The Constraints of Collective Action)*, Königstein/Ts.

Daniels, W. W., 1987: *Workplace Industrial Relations and Technical Change,* Shaftesbury: Blackmore Press.

Danish Technological Institute (DTI) 1978: Jobudvikling i praksis (Job Development in Practice), Kopenhagen.

Dawson, P., and J. Webb 1989: *New Production Arrangements: The Total Flexible Cage?* In: Work, Employment and Society, Vol. 3, pp. 221-238.

Deal, T., and A. Kennedy 1982: *Corporate Cultures - The Rites and Rituals of Corporate Life,* Addison-Wesley.

Deming, W., 1986: *Out of the Crisis,* Cambridge: Cambridge University Press.

Dielen, I., 1994: Resultaten enquete 'nieuwe vormen arbeidsorganisatie' *(Results from the 'Survey on New Forms of Work Organization'),* Christelijke Centrale van Metaalbewerkers van Belgie (CCMB), Brussels.

Dielen, I., and F. Janssens 1994: Fabriek 2000. Vandaag reeds doorgelicht *(Investigating the Company 2000),* in: Metaal (Belgium), No. 3, pp. 6-9.

Drago, R., and M. Wooden 1991: *The Determinants of Participatory Management,* in: British Journal of Industrial Relations, Vol. 29, No. 2, pp. 177-204.

Eaton, A., and P. Voos 1992: *Unions and Contemporary Innovations in Work Organization, Compensation, and Employee Participation,* in: L. Mishel and P. Voos (eds.): Unions and Economic Competitiveness, Armonk, NY: M.E. Sharpe.

Eaton, A., M. Gordon, and J. Keefe 1992: *The Impact of Quality of Work Life Programs and Grievance System Effectiveness on Union Commitment,* in: Industrial and Labor Relations Review, Vol. 45, No. 3, pp. 591-604.

Edling, Ch., and Å. Sandberg 1993: Är Taylor död och pyramiderna rivna? Nya former för företagsledning och arbetsorganisation *(Is Taylor Dead and the Pyramids Torn Down? New Forms of Management and Organization of Work)*, in: NUTEK: Att organisera för produktivitet? En jämförelse av elektronikproduktion i Sverige och Tyskland *(To Organize for Productivity? A Comparison of Electronics Manufacturing in Sweden and Germany)*, B 1993:5, pp 139-173.

Ellinger, Ch., and B. Nissen 1987: *A Case Study of a Failed QWL Program,* in: Labor Studies Journal, Vol. 11, No. 3, pp. 195-219.

Etlinger, H., P. Gruber and M. Scheinecker 1989: Entwickeln - Effizienz steigern - Mitbestimmen. Erfahrungen aus betrieblichen Beteiligungs-projekten *(Development - Efficiency Increase - Codetermination. Experience from Participation Programs in Companies)*, Katholische Sozialakademie Österreichs (ed.), Vienna.

Elorriaga Achutegui, A., 1991: La gestión de la calidad en las experiencias financieras. Experiencia del Banco Bilbao Vizcaya *(Quality Managament in Financial Companies. The Experience of Bilbao-Vizcaya Bank)*, in: Boletín de Estudios Económicos, No. 143, August, pp. 278-293.

Emery, F. E. 1980: *Designing Socio-technical Systems for 'Greenfield' Sites,* in: Journal of Occupational Behavior. Vol. 1, pp. 19-27.

Emery, F. E., and E. Thorsrud 1982: Industrielle Demokratie *(Industrial Democracy)*, Bern: Huber.

Eyer, E., 1994: Entlohnung in teilautonomen Arbeitsgruppen *(Pay in Semi-Autonomous Groups)*, in: C. H. Antoni (ed.): Gruppenarbeit in Unternehmen, Weinheim: Beltz, pp. 100-115.

Faughnan, P., 1991: *The Dynamics of Work Group Operation in Bord Na Mona;* Social Science Research Centre, University College Dublin; December 1991.

Faust, M., P. Jauch, K. Brünnecke und Ch. Deutschmann 1993: Dezen-tralisierung von Unternehmen. Bürokratie- und Hierarchieabbau und die Rolle betrieblicher Arbeitspolitik *(Decentralization of Enterprises. Reduction of Bureaucracy and Hierarchy and the Role of Work Policy in*

Companies), Forschungsinstitut für Arbeit, Technik und Kultur e. V., Tübingen.

Fenwick, R., and J. Olson 1986: *Support for Worker Participation: Attitudes Among Union and Non-Union Workers,* in: American Sociological Review, Vol. 51, pp. 505-522.

Fixari, D., J. C. Moisdon and B. Weil 1991: La requalification d'ouvriers de faible niveau. Le cas d'une usine automobile du groupe Renauld à Mauberge (MCA) *(Requalification of Poorly Qualified Workers. The Case of an Automobile Establishment of Renault at Mauberge),* Montrouge: ANACT Editions.

Flecker, J., 1994): *Austria: The Position of the Social Partners on Direct Participation in Europe;* Working Paper for the European Foundation for the Improvement of Living and Working Conditions, Dublin (unpublished).

Freiman, J. M., and B. O. Saxberg 1989: *Impact of Quality Circles on Productivity and Quality: Research Limitations of a Field Experiment,* in: IEEE Transactions on Engineering Management, Vol. 36, No. 2, pp. 114-118.

Freire, J., M. de Lurdes Rodrigues and V. Tena Ferreira 1994: A funcao da chefia directa na industria *(Line Management in the Industry),* IEFP, Serie Estudos.

French, W. L., and C. H. Bell 1977: Organizationsentwicklung *(Organizational Development),* Bern: Haupt.

Frese, M., and D. Zapf 1987: Die Einführung von neuen Techniken verändert Qualifikationsanforderungen, Handlungsspielraum und Stressfaktoren kaum *(The Introduction of new Technologies Does Hardly Change Needed Qualifications, Work Discretion and Stress Factors),* in: Zeitschrift für Arbeitswissenschaft, Vol. 41, pp. 7-14.

Fröhlich, D., 1983: Machtprobleme in teil-autonomen Gruppen *(Power Problems in Semi-Autonomous Groups),* in: F. Neidhard (ed.): Gruppensoziologie; Sonderheft 25/1983 der Kölner Zeitschrift für Soziologie und Sozialpsychologie, pp. 532-551.

Fröhlich, D., C. Gill and H. Krieger 1992: Quantitative Beschäftigungs-wirkungen neuer Informationstechnologien in Anwenderbetrieben der Europäischen Gemeinschaft *(Quantitative Employment Effects of New Information Technology in the Companies of the European Community)*, in: Mitteilungen aus der Arbeitsmarkt- und Berufsforschung, vol. 25, pp. 192-200.

Fröhlich, D., C. Gill and H. Krieger 1993: *Workplace Involvement in Technological Innovation in the European Community. Volume I: Roads to Participation;* Luxembourg: Office for Official Publications of the European Community.

Fröhlich, D., and P. Hild 1991: Arbeiten mit neuer Technik. Weiterbildungserfolg und Arbeitsbedingungen am Beispiel der CNC-Technik *(Working with New Technology. Training and Working Conditions in CNC Applications),* Frankfurt and New York: Campus.

Fröhlich, D., B. Kindler and M. Sombetzki 1996: Drahtseilakt. Die angestelltenpolitische Initiative der IG Metall zwischen Organisationsreform und Mitgliederwerbung *(Walking a Tightrope. The White-Collar Initiative of the Metal Workers Union Between Organizational Reform and Recruitment of New Members),* München and Mering: Rainer Hampp (1996).

Gardell, B., and L. Svensson 1981: Medbestämmande och självstyre. En lokal facklig stragegi för demokratisering av arbetsplatsen *(Co-determination and Autonomy. A Local Union Strategy for Democratisation of the Workplace),* Malmö: Prisma, Infotryck AB.

Garrahan, P., and P. Steward 1992-UK: *Work Organisation in Transition: The Human Resource Management Implications of the 'Nissan Way',* in: Human Resource Management Journal, Vol. 2, No. 2, pp. 46-62.

Gaugler, E., and S. Wiltz 1993: Personalwesen im europäischen Vergleich *(Personnel Management in a European Perspective): The Price Waterhouse Cranfield Project,* Mannheim (working paper).

Geary, J. F., 1993: *New Forms of Work Organization and Employee Involvement in Two American Electronics Plants: Plural, Mixed and Protean,* in: Economic and Industrial Democracy, Vol. 14, No. 4, 511-534.

Geary, J., and K. Sisson 1994: *Conceptualising Direct Participation in Organisational Change - The EPOC Project,* Luxembourg: Office for Official Publications of the European Community.

Geary, J., C. Rees and K. Sisson (1995): *Great Britain: Direct Participation as a Management Strategy,* in: I. Regalia and C. Gill (eds.) 1995, pp. 103-135.

Gerst et al. 1994 (D. Gerst, Th. Hardwig, M. Kuhlmann and M. Schumann): Gruppenarbeit in der betrieblichen Erprobung *(Experimenting With Group Work in Production),* in: Angewandte Arbeitswissenschaft, No. 142, S. 5-30.

Gill et al. 1993 (C. Gill, Th. Beaupain, D. Fröhlich and H. Krieger): *Workplace Involvement in Technological Innovation in the European Community.* Vol. II: *Issues of Participation,* Luxembourg: Office for Official Publications of the European Community.

Gottschall, D., 1994: Sand im Betriebe (*A Spanner in the Works*), in: Manager Magazin No.12/1994, pp. 234-247.

Grausgruber-Berner, R., and A. Grausgruber 1990: Humankapital. Fördern oder Vergeuden? *(Human Capital - Supported or Squandered?)* Vienna: Signum Verlag.

Greek Centre of Productivity 1990: *Labour Relations, Work Enviroment and Productivity* (in Greek), Athens.

Greifenstein, R., P. Jansen and L. Kißler 1991: Neue Techniken und Mitbestimmung am Arbeitsplatz *(New Technology and Co-determination at the Workplace),* Sozialverträgliche Technikgestaltung, Bd. 21, Opladen: Westdeutscher Verlag.

Greifenstein, R., P. Jansen and L. Kißler 1993: Gemanagte Partizipation. Qualitätszirkel in der deutschen und in der französischen Autoindustrie *(Managing Participation. Quality Circles in the German and French Automobile Industry),* München and Mering: Rainer Hampp.

Grenier, G. J., 1988: *Inhuman Relations: Quality Circles and Anti-Unionism in American Industry,* Philadelphia, PA: Temple University Press.

Griffin, R. W., 1988: *Consequences of Quality Circles in an Industrial Setting: A Longitudinal Assessment,* in: Academy of Management Journal, Vol. 31, No. 2, pp. 338-358.

Grob, R., 1994: Erfahrungen mit teilautonomen Arbeitsgruppen in der Siemens AG. Eine empirische Studie *(Experience With Semi-Autonomous Work Groups at the Siemens Corporation),* in: C. H. Antoni (ed.): Gruppenarbeit in Unternehmen. Weinheim: Beltz, pp. 249-267.

Grönning, T., 1995: *Recent Developments at Toyota Motor Co,* in: Å. Sandberg (ed.): Enriching Production. Aldershot, Brookfield USA, Hong Kong: Avebury, pp. 665-382.

Groth, U., A. Kammel and Y. Tsumura 1994: Das japanische Personalmanagement zwischen Tradition und westlicher Wertorientierung *(Japanese Personnel Management Between Tradition and Western Culture),* in: Zeitschrift für Personalforschung, Vol. 8, No. 3, pp. 317-336.

Gustafsson, R. Å., A. Carlsson and J. Henriksson 1991: Kan vården demokratiseras? *(Can the Health Care be Democratised?),* Arbetslivscentrum, Stockholm.

Hackman, J.R., 1975: *Is Job Enrichment Just a Fad?* in: Harvard Business Review, Vol. 53, pp. 129-238.

Hackman, J. R., and G. R. Oldham 1976: *Motivation through the Design of Work: Test of a Theory,* in: Organizational Behavior and Human Performance, Vol. 16, pp. 250-279.

Hackman, J. R., and G. R. Oldham 1980: *Work Redesign,* Reading, MA: Addison-Wesley.

Haindl, G., 1987: Erfahrungen eines mittelständischen Unternehmens bei Konzeption und Einführung von Quality Circles *(Conceptionalizing and Introducing Quality Circles in a Medium Sized Company),* in: Zeitschrift für Betriebswirtschaftliche Forschung, No. 5, pp. 391-404.

Harfield, T., 1995: *The Rover Experience.* Paper presented at the First European Round Table on Direct Participation in Organisational Change, Dublin, 14-15 Feb. 1995.

Heidenreich, M., 1994: Gruppenarbeit zwischen Taylorismus und Humanisierung. Eine international vergleichende Perspektive *(Group Work Between Taylorism and Humanization. An International Comparative Perspective),* in: Soziale Welt, Vol. 45, No. 1, pp. 60-83.

Henniges, H. von, 1987: Auswirkungen moderner Technologien auf Arbeitsbedingungen *(Effects of Modern Technology on Working Conditions),* in: BIBB/IAB (eds.): Neue Technologien: Verbreitungsgrad, Qualifikation und Arbeitsbedingungen (New Technologies: Diffusion, Qualification and Working Conditions), Nuremberg.

Herbst, P.G., 1962: *Autonomous Group Functioning,* London: Tavistock.

Herzberg, F., 1966: *Work and the Nature of Man,* New York.

Herzberg, F., B. Mausner and B. B. Snyderman 1959: *The Motivation to Work,* New York, London, Sydney.

Hildebrandt, E., and R. Seltz 1989: Wandel betrieblicher Sozialverfassung durch systemische Kontrolle? *(Change of the Company Social System Through Systemic Control?),* Berlin: Edition sigma.

Hill, S., 1991a: *How do you Manage a Flexible Firm? The Total Quality Model,* in: Work, Employment and Society, Vol. 5, No. 3, pp. 397-416.

Hill, S., 1991b: *Why Quality Circles Failed but Total Quality Management Might Succeed,* in: British Journal of Industrial Relations, Vol. 29, pp. 541-568.

Hirsch-Kreinsen et al. 1990 (H. Hirsch-Kreinsen, R. Schulz-Wild, Ch. Köhler and M. v. Behr): Einstieg in die rechnerintegrierte Produktion. Alternative Entwicklungspfade der in der Industriearbeit im Maschinenbau *(Getting Into Computer Integrated Production. Alternative Paths of Developing Industrial Work in Mechanical Engineering)* Frankfurt/New York: Campus.

Hodson et al. 1993 (R. Hodson, C. Sorenson Jamison, S. Rieble, S. Welsh and S. Creighton): *Is Worker Solidarity Undermined by Autonomy and Participation?* in: American Sociological Review, Vol. 58, pp. 398-416.

Horman, D., 1991: Syndicalisme et Management Participatif *(Unionism and Participative Management),* in: Courier Hebdomadaire CRISP (Centre de

Recherche et d'Information Socio-Politiques), Belgium, No. 1342-1343; pp. 1-47.

Howaldt, J., 1994: KVP-Aktivitäten in Deutschland ('Continous Improvement' Activities in Germany), in: Arbeit, Vol. 3, No. 4, pp. 320-330.

Hvenegaard, H., and J. Hassing Pedersen 1994: Direct Participation in Denmark, Danish Technological Institute (unpublished).

Hyman, J., and B. Mason 1995: Managing Employee Involvement and Participation, London: Sage.

Income Data Services 1992: Teamworking, IDS Study No. 516, London: IDS.

IDE 1981: Industrial Democracy in Europe (International Research Group), Oxford: Clarendon Press.

IDE 1993: Industrial Democracy in Europe - Revisited (International Research Group), New York: Oxford University Press.

Inglehart, R., 1989: Cultural Change, Princeton: Princeton University Press.

Ishikawa, K., 1985: What is Total Quality Control? The Japanese Way, Englewood Cliffs, N.J.: Prentice-Hall.

Ito, M. 1988: Gijyutsu Kakushin to Human Network gata Soshiki. (Technological Innovation and Human Network Organization), Nihon Rodo Kyokai.

Jørgensen et al. 1992 (H. Jørgensen, M. Lassen, J. Lind and M. Madsen): Medlemmer og meninger - rapport over en spørgeskemaundersøgelse blandt medlemmer af LO-forbundene (Members and Opinions - Report on a Questionnaire Enquiry Among Members of the Danish Federation of Trade Unions), The Danish Federation of Trade Unions and the Centre for Labour Market Research at Aalborg University Centre, Aalborg.

Jones, D. T., 1991: 'Mager' ist beautiful - Japaner auf Erfolgskurs ('Lean' is Beautiful - The Japanese on the Road to Success), in: Technische Rundschau, No. 38, 1991, pp. 40-50.

Juran, J., 1988: Juran on Planning for Quality. New York: Free Press.

214

Kalliola et al. 1994 (S. Kalliola, A. Kasvio, A. Kuula, R. Nakari, I. Pesonen, H. Rajakaltio and S. Syvänen): Kunnallisten palveluorganizaatioiden tulkosellisuuden ja työelämän laadun tutkimusohjelman loppuraportti 12.1.1994. *(Final Report on the Research Program Into Productivity of Municipal Service Organizations and the Quality of Working Life)*, Tampere University, Social Science Research Institute, Working Life Research Centre, Tampere (unpublished).

Kauppinen, T., and T. Alasoini 1985: Työtaistelut telakoilla. *(Labour Disputes at the Dockyards)*, in: Consultative Committee on Working Life Relations 1/1985, Helsinki.

Kawakita, T., 1985: Kodo-jidoka-kojou ni Okeru Untenkou to Hozenkou *(Operators and Maintenance Workers in Highly Automated Factories)*, in: Tokyo Gaidai Ronsyu (Bulletin on Tokyo Factories), Vol. 35.

Kelly, J.E., 1978: *A Reappraisal of Socio-technical Systems Theory*, in: Human Relations, Vol. 12, pp. 1069-1099.

Kelly, J., and C. Kelly 1991: *'Them and Us'. Social Psychology and 'The New Industrial Relations'*, in: British Journal of Industrial Relations, Vol. 29, No. 1, pp. 25-48.

Kern, H., and M. Schumann 1984: Das Ende der Arbeitsteilung? Rationalisierung in der industriellen Produktion *(The End of Labour Division? Rationalization in Industrial Production)*, Munich: Beck.

Klein, J. A., 1991: *A Reexamination of Autonomy in Light of New Manufacturing Practices,* in: Human Relations, Vol. 44, No. 1, pp. 21-38.

Kleinschmidt, M., and U. Pekruhl 1994: Kooperation, Partizipation und Autonomie: Gruppenarbeit in deutschen Betrieben *(Cooperation, Participation and Autonomy: Group Work in German Companies)*, in: Arbeit - Zeitschrift für Arbeitsforschung, No. 2/1994, pp. 150-172.

Kling, J., 1995: *High Performance Work Systems and Firm Performance*, in: Monthly Labor Review, vol. 118, no. 5, pp. 29-36.

Knauer, P., 1988: Wandel der Arbeitsbedingungen durch ein flexibles Fertigungssystem mit modularem Aufbau. *(Change of Working Conditions*

Through a Flexible Manufacturing System with a Modular Structure), Karlsruhe: BMFT-Projekttr äger Fertigungstechnik.

Ko, M. 1989: Kyodai Tekko-kigyo ni Okeru Konpyuta no Tenkai to Shokuin-so no Rodo to Kanri: Kobe Seiko-syo no Jirei no Kanto wo Chushin to Site *(Computerization in Large Companies and Work and Management of White-Collar Workers: An Assessment of the Kobe Steel Corporation)*, in: Oita University: Keizai-ronsyu (Economic Review), Vol. 40, No. 6.

Kochan, T., and M. Weinstein 1994: *Recent Developments in US Industrial Relations,* in: British Journal of Industrial Relations, Vol. 32, No. 4, pp. 483-504.

Kochan, T. A., R. B. McKersie and J. Chalykoff 1986: *The Effects of Corporate Strategy and Workplace Innovations on Union Representation,* in: Industrial and Labour Relations Review, Vol. 39, No. 4, pp. 487-501.

Koumura, S. 1986: QC-sakuru no Jittai to Rodokanri: Syogai-yoin Jittai-chosa wo Tsujite *(The Reality of QC-Circle and Labour Management: An Empirical Research on its Disturbing Factors in the Manufacturing Industry)*, Romu kenkyu, Vol. 39, No. 3 and No. 4.

Kovacs, I., C. Cerdeira and A. Brandao Moniz 1992: *Technological and Work Organizational Change in the Portuguese Industry,* Lisbon: D.G.I., G.G.T. p. e Ceso I&D, Program PEDIP.

Kovacs, I., 1990: Concepcao e Implementacao de um modelo flexível de organizacao *(Conception and Implementation of an Flexible Model of Organization),* in: Organizacoes e Trabalho, No. 3/4, 1990.

Krieger, H., und R. Lange 1992: Der 'New Deal' für die 90er Jahre. Die Verzahnung repräsentativer und direkter Arbeitnehmerbeteiligung in Europa *(The 'New Deal' for the 1990s. Combining Representative and Direct Employee Participation in Europe)*, in: WSI-Mitteilungen, 1992/12, pp. 788-799.

Kubicek, H., and G. Welter 1985: Messung der Organisationsstruktur *(Measuring the Structure of Organizations)*, Stuttgart: Enke.

216

Kunzmann, E. M., 1991: Zirkelarbeit. Evaluation von Kleingruppen in der Praxis *(Circle Work. Evaluation of Small Groups in Operation)*, München and Mering: Rainer Hampp.

Lammers, C. J., P. L. Meurs and T. A. Mijs 1987: *Direct and Indirect Participation in Dutch Firms and Hospitals*, in: Organization Studies, Vol. 8, No.1, pp. 25-38.

Lavikka, R. 1992: Ryhmätyö tulee vaateteollisuuteen *(Group Work Comes to the Clothing Industry)*, Tampere University, Social Science Research Institute, Working Life Research Centre, Work Report No. 29/1992.

Laville, J. L., et al. 1988: L'évaluation des pratiques participatives dans les PME et les coopératives *(The Evaluation of Participative Management Practices in Small to Medium-sized Firms and Cooperatives)*, Luxembourg: Office for Official Publications of the European Community.

Lawler, E.E., 1973: *Motivation in Work Organizations,* Monterrey, CA: Brooks/Cole.

Lawler, E. E., G. D. Jenkins and G. E. Herline 1974: *Initial Data Feedback at General Foods, Topeka Pet Food Plants: Selected Survey Items*, Unpublished Manuscript, Institute for Social Research, Ann Arbor, MI.

Lawler, E. E., and S. A. Mohrman 1985: *Quality Circles After the Fad*, in: Harvard Business Review, Vol. 85, No.1, pp. 64-71.

Lawler, E. E., S. A. Mohrman and G. E. Ledford 1992: *Employee Involvement and Total Quality Management: Practices and Results in Fortune 1000 Companies*, San Francisco: Jossey-Bass Publishers.

Leion, A., (ed.) 1992: Den nyttiga kompetensen *(The Useful Competence)*, Ystad: AB Timbro, Ystads Centraltryckeri.

Likert, R., 1961: *New Patterns of Management,* New York: McGraw-Hill.

Lillrank, P., and N. Kano 1989: *Continuous Improvement - Quality Control Circles in Japanese Industry,* Michigan University Center for Japanese Studies Publications, Ann Arbor.

Loontechnische Dienst 1979: Werkoverleg en werkstructurering in Nederland in 1978 *(Work Consultation and Work Structuring in the Netherlands in 1978)*, Ministerie van Sociale Zaken en Werkgelegenheid, The Hague.

Loontechnische Dienst 1987: Werkoverleg en werkstructurering in Nederland in 1985 *(Work Consultation and Work Structuring in the Netherlands in 1985)*, Ministerie van Sociale Zaken en Werkgelegenheid, The Hague.

Loontechnische Dienst 1993: Werkoverleg in het Nederlandse bedrijfsleven in 1992 *(Work Consultation in Dutch Companies in 1992)*, Ministerie van Sociale Zaken en Werkgelegenheid, The Hague.

Lope Peña, A. 1993: Innovación tecnológica: gestión de la mano de obra y cambios organizativos en las empresas *(Technological Innovation: Management of the Labour Force and Organizational Change of the Enterprise)*, Grup d Estudis Sociológics sobre la Vida Quotidiana i el Treball (QUIT), Departamento de Sociología, Universidad Autónoma de Barcelona, unpublished.

Lund, R., 1995: Denmark: *The Primacy of Collective Agreements,* in: I. Regalia and C. Gill (eds.) 1995, pp. 53-79.

Maemura, M., 1990: Nihon ni Okeru Sho-syudan Katsudo no Jittai *(The State of Small Group Activities in Japan)*, in: Roudou-toukei-chousa (Statistical Labour Research), Vol. 42, No. 9.

Marginson et al. 1988 (P. M. Marginson, P. K. Edwards, R. Martin, J. Purcell and K. Sisson): *Beyond the Workplace: Managing Industrial Relations in the Multi-Establishment Enterprise,* Oxford: Blackwell.

Marks et al. 1986 (M. L. Marks, E. J. Hackett, P. H. Mirvis and J. F. Grady, Jr.): *Employee Participation in a Quality Circle Program: Impact on Quality of Work Life, Productivity, and Absenteeism,* in: Journal of Applied Psychology, Vol. 71, No. 1, pp. 61-69.

Martin Hernandez, A., 1993a: Los Circulos de calidad como forma de participación directa en el trabajo. Evolución y perspectivas en España *(Quality Circles as a Way of Direct Participation at Work. Evolution and Perspectives in Spain)*, Universidad de Cantabria: Ph. D. Thesis.

Martin Hernandez, A., 1993b: La experiencia empresarial española de los grupos de trabajo *(Spanish Management Experience With Work Groups)*, in: Capital Humano, No. 57, June, pp 14-20.

Maslow, A. H., 1954: *Motivation and Personality*, New York: Harper.

McGregor, D., 1957: *The Human Side of Enterprise*, in: Management Review, Vol. 46, No. 22, pp. 88-92.

Membrado Martinez, J., 1991: La participación de los empleados en la mejora de la calidad. La experiencia de la Fábrica de IBM en España *(Worker Participation in Quality Improvement. The Experience of the IBM Company in Spain)*, in: Boletín de Estudios Económicos, No. 143, August, pp 295-308.

Merli, G., 1986: I circoli della qualità. Filosofia, organizzazione, gestione ed esperienze italiane *(Quality Circles. Philosophy, Organization, Management and Italian Experiences)*, Roma: Edizioni Lavoro.

Metz, E. J., 1981: *Caution: Quality Circles Ahead*, in: Training and Development Journal, Vol. 35, No. 8, pp. 71-76.

Miguelez, F., et al. (1993): El impacto económico, social y laboral de los Juegos Olímpicos de 1992 en Barcelona ciudad y su entorno *(Economic, Social and Labour Impact of the 1992 Olympic Games in Barcelona City and Surroundings)*, Grup de Estudis sobre la Vida Quotidiana i el Treball (QUIT), Bellaterra, Departamento de sociología, Universidad Autónoma de Barcelona.

Mikola-Lahnalammi, T., and T. Aloisini 1995: Finland: *Direct Participation in a Centralised Industrial Relations System*, in: I. Regalia and C. Gill (eds.) 1995, pp. 79-102.

Millward et al. 1992 (N. Millward, M. Stevens, D. Smart and W. Hawes): *Workplace Industrial Relations in Transition. The ED/ESRC/PSI/ACAS Surveys*, Aldershot: Dartmouth.

Minssen, H., 1994: Risiken von Gruppenarbeit in der Fertigung *(Risks of Group Work in Production)*, in: Angewandte Arbeitswissenschaft, No. 142, pp. 31-53.

Mortimer, J. T., and J. Lorence 1989: *Satisfaction and Involvement: Disentangling a Deceptively Simple Relationship,* in: Social Psychology Quarterly, Vol. 52, No. 4, pp. 249-265.

Muffels, R., T. Heinen and G. van Mil 1982: Werkoverleg en werkstructurering en de subsidieregeling arbeidsplaatsverbetering: En onderzoek bij bedrijven met meer dan 100 personeelsleden *(Work Consultation and Work Structuring and the Subsidization Rule 'Improvement of Work Places'),* IVA: Tilburg.

Murray, S., 1984: *Survey of Employee/Industrial Relations in Irish Private Sector Manufacturing Industry Carried Out for the Industrial Development Authority,* Industrial Development Authority, Dublin, Autumn 1984.

Negrelli, S., 1990: Relazioni industriali e relazioni interne nelle piccole, medie e grandi imprese *(Industrial Relations and Internal Relations in Small, Medium-sized and Large Enterprises),* C.N.R. Research Report.

Nicoletti, B., 1986: I circoli di qualità. Concetti base ed esperienze italiane *(Quality Circles),* Milano: Angeli.

Nielsen et al 1991 (K. Nielsen, K. J. Møller, C. Koch, M. Nørby, A. Richter and N. Toft): JIPS. Japansk Inspirerede Produktionssystemer og arbejdsforhold *(JIPS. Japanese Inspired Production Systems and Working Conditions),* Danish Technological Institute.

Nitta, M., 1988: Nippon no Rodosya Sanka *(Workers' Participation in Japan),* Tokyo University Press.

Nørby, M., 1992: Just-In-Time. Visioner og erfaringer *(Just-in-time. Visions and experiences),* Samfundslitteratur, Copenhagen.

Nord-Larsen et al. 1990 (M. Nord-Larsen, E. Ørhede, J. Nielsen and H. Burr): Lønmodtagernes arbejdsmilj 1990 - bind 1 og 2 *(The Working Environment of Employees 1990 - Volumes 1 and 2),* The Danish Work Environment Fund, Copenhagen.

NUTEK 1993: Att organisera för produktivitet? En jämförelse av elektronik-produktion i Sverige och Tyskland *(To Organize for Productivity? A Comparison of Electronics Manufacturing in Sweden and Germany),* B 1993:5.

O'Connell Davidson, J., 1990: *The Road to Functional Flexibility: White Collar Work and Employment Relations in a Privatized Public Utility,* in: The Sociological Review, Vol. 38, No. 4, pp. 689-711.

O'Hehir, J., and F. O'Mahony 1993: *New Forms of Work Organization: Options for Unions,* Irish Congress of Trade Unions, Dublin, 1993.

O'Kelly, K., 1995: *Ireland: A Joint Approach to Direct Participation,* in: I. Regalia and C. Gill (eds.) 1995, pp. 135-175.

Oess, A., 1991: *Total Quality Management,* Wiesbaden: Gabler.

Okubayashi, K., (ed.) 1988: Me Gijyutsu Kakushin-Ka no Nihon-teki Keiei *(Japanese Management System under Microelectronic Technology),* Chuoukeizaisha.

Okubayashi, K., et al. 1994: Jyukozo soshiki paradaimu jyosetsu *(An Introduction of the 'Flexibly Structured Organization' Paradigm),* Bunshindo.

Okubayashi, K., 1993: *Japanese Style of Management,* in: The Annals of the School of Business Administration, Kobe University, No. 37, pp. 87-114.

Okubayashi, K., 1995: *Japanese Effects of New Technology on Organzation and Work,* Discussion Paper No. 9508, School of Business Administration, Kobe University.

Oliver, N., and B. Wilkinson 1989: *Japanese Manufacturing Techniques and Personnel and Industrial Relations Practice in Britain: Evidence and Implications,* in: British Journal of Industrial Relations, Vol. 27, No. 1, pp. 73-91.

Olsen, B., 1988: Hjemmehjælpens organizering og dens betydning for hjemmehjælpernes arbejdsmiljø *(The Organization of Home Help and Its Significance for the Working Environment of Home-help Personnel),* University of Copenhagen.

Olsen, K. B., 1993: En virksomhed under forandring. Om forsøg med selvstyrende grupper i en tayloristisk organiseret produktion. Rapport Nr. 1 *(An Enterprise in Transition. About the Testing of Autonomous Groups in Taylorist Organized Production. Report No 1),* Institut for Arbejdsmiljø

(Institute for Working Environment), The Technical University of Denmark.

Osterman, P., 1994: *How Common is Workplace Transformation and How Can We Explain Who Adopts It? Results from a National Survey,* in: Industrial and Labor Relations Review, Jan. 1994, pp. 173-188.

Österreichisches Statistisches Zentralamt (ÖSTAT) 1987: Arbeitsbedingungen. Ergebnisse des Mikrozensus September 1985 *(Working Conditions. Micro Census Results September 1985),* in: Beiträge zur Österreichischen Statistik, No. 858, Vienna 1987.

Palmroth, A., M. Hanki and J. Kirjonen 1993: Tuikkaan saumaan - ompelijat teollisuuden muutoksissa *(Into a Tight Seam - Sewers in Industrial Change),* Jyvöskylä: Publications of the Working Life Research Unit at Jyvöskylä University.

Peters, T., and R. H. Waterman 1982: *In Search of Excellence,* Harper and Row.

Petmesidou, M., and L. Tsoulouvis 1990: *Planning Technological Change and Economic Development in Greece: High Technology and the Microelectrics Industry,* in: Progress in Planning, Vol. 33, No. 3, pp. 175-262.

Pinaud, H., 1994: *The Role of the Social Actors in the Development of Worker Participation in 10 West European Countries,* in: G. Kester and H. Pinaud (eds.): Trade Unions and Democratic Participation, Scenario 21, Vol. 1: Politics and Strategies, pp. 21-35.

Piore, M. J., and C. F. Sabel 1984: *The Second Industrial Divide,* New York: Basic Books.

Poole, M., 1992: *Industrial Democracy,* in: G. Szèll (ed.): Concise Encyclopedia of Participation and Co-Management, Berlin/New York.

Popitz et al. 1957 (H. Popitz, H. P. Bahrdt, E. A. Jüres and H. Kesting): Das Gesellschaftsbild des Arbeiters. Soziologische Untersuchungen in der Hüttenindustrie *(Workers' Image of Society. Sociological Research in the Steel Industry),* Tübingen.

PRAQC 1990: Enquete sur la recherche de la Qualité Totale dans les entreprises Belges *(Survey on Total Quality Management in the Belgian Enterprises)*, PRACQ, Bruxelles.

Price Waterhouse-ESADE 1992: Tres años de investigación internacional en gestión de recursos humanos *(Three Years of International Investigation in Strategic Human Resource Management)*, Barcelona: ESADE.

Prieto, C., 1991: Las prácticas empresariales de gestión de la fuerza de trabajo *(Management Practices and the Workforce)*, in: F. Miguelez and C. Prieto (eds.): Las relaciones laborales en España *(Labour Relations in Spain)*, Madrid: Siglo Veintiuno de España Editores, pp. 185-210.

Raffaeli, A., 1985: *Quality Circles and Employee Attitudes*, in: Personnel Psychology, Vol. 38, No.5, pp. 603-615.

Raftis, A. C., and D. G. Stavroulakis 1991: *Attitudes Towards Worker's Participation in Greek Industry: A Field Study* (in Greek), in: Spoudai, Vol. 41, pp. 290-315.

Ramioul, M., 1989: Personeelsbeleid en Vakbondsontwijking *(Personnel Policy and Trade Union Evasion)*, in: De Gids op Maatschappelijk Gebied (Belgium), No. 11, pp. 1013-1021.

Regalia, I., 1994: *New Forms of Organization and Direct Involvement of the Workers in Italy*, European Foundation for the Improvement of Living and Working Conditions, Working Paper No.: WP/92/11/EN.

Regalia, I., 1995: *Direct Participation: The Position of the Social Partners. A Comparative Study in Fifteen European Countries*, Luxembourg: Office for Official Publications of the European Community.

Regalia, I., and C. Gill 1995 (eds.): *The Position of the Social Partners in Europe on Direct Participation. Country Studies:* Vol. 1; European Foundation for the Improvement of Living and Working Conditions, Working Paper No.: WP/95/35/EN.

Regalia, I., and R. Rossella 1989: Le relazioni industriali nelle imprese lombarde *(Industrial Relations in the Lombard Enterprises, Annual Survey)*, Istituto di Ricerche Economiche e Sociali (I.R.E.S.), Report No. 20.

Regalia, I., and R. Rossella 1992: Le relazioni industriali nelle imprese lombarde *(Industrial Relations in the Lombard Enterprises, Annual Survey)*, Istituto di Ricerche Economiche e Sociali (I.R.E.S.), Report No. 34.

Regini, M., and C. F. Sabel (eds.) 1989: Strategie di riaggiustamento industriale *(Strategies of Industrial Re-adjustment)*, Bologna: Il Mulino.

Roethlisberger, F., and W. Dickson 1939: *Management and the Worker,* Cambridge, MA: Harvard University Press.

Roth, S., 1992: Japanisierung oder eigener Weg? *(Japanization or Own Way?)*, in: IG Metall (ed.): Zukunft der Automobilzulieferer, Stuttgart.

Sandberg, Å., et. al. 1992: *Technological Change and Co-Determination in Sweden,* Philadelphia: Temple University Press.

Sandberg, Å., 1995: *The Uddevalla Experience in Perspective,* in: Å. Sandberg (ed.): *Enriching Production,* Aldershot, Brookfield USA, Hong Kong: Avebury, pp. 1-37.

Saurwein, R. G., 1993: Gruppenarbeit im westdeutschen Maschinenbau: Diffusion und Merkmale - Ergebnisse des NIFA-Panels 1991 und 1992 *(Group Work in West German Mechanical Engineering: Diffusion and Indicators - Results from the NIFA Panel)*, Sonderforschungsbereich 187 der Ruhr-Universität Bochum, Arbeitspapier Z2-1/93, Bochum.

Scheinecker, M., 1988: Neue Organizationskonzepte in der Automobilindustrie: Entwicklungstendenzen am Beispiel General Motors Austria *(New Organi-zational Concepts in the Automobilie Industry: Trends at General Motors Austria)*, in: B. Dankbaar, U. Jürgens and Th. Malsch (eds.): Die Zukunft der Automobilindustrie *(The Future of the Automobile Industry)*, WZB - Forschungsschwerpunkt Technik, Arbeit, Umwelt, Berlin: Edition Sigma, pp.167-184.

Schumann, M., 1990: Breite Diffusion der neuen Produktionskonzepte - zögerlicher Wandel der Arbeitsstrukturen *(Broad Diffusion of New Production Concepts - Reluctant Change of Work Structures)*, in: Soziale Welt, Vol. 41, pp. 47-69.

Schumann et al. 1994 (M. Schumann, V. Baethge-Kinsky, M. Kuhlmann, C. Kurz and U. Neumann): Trendreport Rationalisierung. Automobilindustrie,

Werkzeugmaschinenbau, chemische Industrie *(Trend Report on Rationalization. Automobile Industry, Mechanical Engineering, Chemical Industry)*, Berlin: Edition Sigma.

Seelye, H. N., and J. A. Sween 1982: *Quality Circles in U. S. Industry: Survey Results,* in: Quality Circle Journal, Vol. 5, No. 4, pp. 26-29.

Shea, G. P., 1986: *Quality Circles: The Danger of Bottled Change*, in: Sloan Management Review, Vo. 27, No. 3, pp. 33-46.

Shi, S., 1991: Sagyo-soshiki to Gijytutsu-kakushin Katei *(Work Organization and the Process of Technological Innovation)*, in: Eiji, Ogawa (ed.): Gijyutsu-kakushin no manejimento *(Management of Technological Innovation)*, Chuoukeizaisha.

Shimada, T., 1990: Jouhou-gijyutsu ga keiei-soshiki ni ataeru eikyo *(The Influence of Information Technology an Business Organization)*, in: Soshiki-kagaku, Vol. 23, No. 4.

Signorelli, A., 1993: Il caso della Honda di Atessa *(The Honda Case in Atessa)*, Paper presented at the International Workshop, Pontignano (Siena), Italia, May 26-28.

Sisson, K., 1994: *Participation and Involvement in the UK: From Collectivism to Individualism*, in: M. Ambrosini and L. Saba (eds.): *Participation and Involvement in Great Britain,* Milano: Franco Anglei.

Sorge, A., and M. Warner 1986: Comparative Factory Organisation: An Anglo-German Comparison of Manufaturing, Management, and Manpower, Aldershot: Gower.

Spyropoulos, G., 1995: *Overview of Regulation of Direct Participation in Europe.* First European Round Table on Direct Participation and Organizational Change, Dublin, Feb. 14-15, 1995, Workshop I: The Process of Direct Participation.

Stavroulakis, D., 1989: *Worker's Participation in Decision-making. A Study of Organizational Structures in Greek Industry* (in Greek). Ph. D. Thesis, Polythechnic School of the University of Patras, Department of Mechanical Engineeing (unpublished).

Steen, R., 1991: ABB Distribution, in: Arbeitsorganisation och produktivitet - Expertrapport nr. 5 till Produktivitetsdelegationen *(Work Organization and Productivity. Expert Report No. 5 to the Productivity Delegation)*, Stockholm: Allmänna Förlaget, pp. 45-62.

Takaki, K., F. Kondo and S. Fujii 1987: Me-ka ni Okeru Kiban-gijyutsu to Syokuba-soshiki no Henyo: A sya B kojyo no Jirei *(The Transformation of Basic Technology and Work Organization under Microelectronics: A Case Study of 'B Factory in A Company')*.

Tang, T. L., P. S. Tollison and H. D. Whiteside 1987: *The Effect of Quality Circle Initiation on Motivation to Attendance, Circle Initiation, and Collar Color*, in: Journal of Management, Vol. 15, pp. 101-113.

Taylor, F.W., 1911: *The Principles of Scientific Management*, New York: Harper & Row.

Tchobanian, R., 1995: *France: Has Direct Participation Disappeared From the Political Agenda?* Working Paper No. WP/95/68/EN of the European Foundation, Dublin.

Teikari, V., and A. Väyrinen 1992: Miten työyhteisön toiminnan voi muttaa - tapausesimerkkinä¨ Kansa-Yhtymä'n Porin toimisto *(How the Operation of a Work Community Can be Altered - the Kansa-Yhtymä'n Porin Office as an Example)*, Otaniemi: Institute of Technology, Industrial Economy and Labour Psychology, Report No. 139.

Teixeira, C., 1984: Du contenu du travail vers la gestion. Analyze critique d'un processus de changement organizationnel dans une entreprise industrielle portugaise *(From Work Content to Management. A Critical Analysis of an Organizational Change Process in a Portuguese Industrial Enterprise)*, Université de Lyon.

Thomas, R. J., 1989: *Participation and Control: A Shopfloor Perspective on Employee Participation*, in: Research in the Sociology of Organizations, Vol. 7, pp. 117-144.

Touraine, A., 1955: L'évolution du travail ouvrier aux usines Renault *(The Development of Industrial Work at Renault)*, Paris.

226

Trist, E. L., and K.W. Bamforth 1951: *Some Social and Pychological Consequences of the Long Wall Method of Goal Getting,* in: Human Relations, Vol.4, pp. 3-38.

Trist et al. 1963 (E. L. Trist, G.W. Higgin, H. Murray and A.B. Pollock): *Organizational Choice.* London: Tavistock.

Türk, K., 1989: Neuere Entwicklungen in der Organisationsforschung *(Recent Developments in Organizational Research),* Stuttgart: Enke.

Turnbull, P.J., 1986: *The 'Japanisation' of Production and Industrial Relations at Lucas Electrical,* in: Industrial Relations Journal, Vol. 17, No. 3, pp. 193-206.

Turner, L., and P. Auer 1994: *A Diversity of New Work Organization,* in: Industrielle Beziehungen, Vol. 1, No. 1, pp. 39-61.

U.S. Merit Systems Protection Board 1986: *Getting Involved: Improving Federal Management with Employee Involvement.* Washington, D.C., U.S. Merit Systems Protection Board.

van der Meché et al. 1995 (P. van der Meché, B. van Beers, M. van der Veen and W. Buitelaar): *The Netherlands: Management-initiated Direct Participation,* in: I. Regalia and C. Gill (eds.) 1995, pp. 175-201.

van Fleet, D. D., and R. W. Griffin 1989: *Quality Circles: A Review and Suggested Future Directions,* in: C. L. Cooper and I. Robertson (eds.): *International Review of Industrial and Organizational Psychology,* Chichester, UK: John Wiley, pp. 213-233.

van de Water, H., E.H.M. Goessens and J. de Vries 1988: Kwaliteitskringen, kwaliteit van de arbeid en produktiestructuur *(Quality Circles, Quality of Working Life, and Production Structure),* The Hague: Ministry of Social Affairs and Employment.

Vanbuylen, J., 1993: De ronde van Belgie: Arbeidsorganisatorische veranderingen in de automobielnijverheid *(The 'Tour de Belgique': Changes in the Labour Organization in the Car Industry),* in: CMB Inform (Belgium), No. 134, pp. 25-55.

Varela, M., and M. Sener 1988: Una decisión estratégica. Los Círculos de Calidad *(A Strategic Decision: The Quality Circles)*, in: Dirección y Progreso, No. 100 bis, pp. 20-26.

Veiga, J., and J. Yanouzas 1991: *Differences Between American and Greek Managers in Giving Up Control*, in: Organization Studies, Vol. 12, pp. 95-108.

Vermeulen, D., and P. Gevers 1989: Kwaliteitskringen. Toetsstenen voor een modern kwaliteitsbeleid? *(Quality Cicles. Touch-Stones for a Modern Quality Policy?)*, in: Economisch en Sociaal Tijdschrift (Belgium), Vol. 43, pp. 721-742.

Vieveen, C., 1994: Kwaliteit én arbeid meer dan certificeren; Case studie naar de kwaliteit van de arbeid als onderdeel van kwaliteitszorg in zes elektrotechnische bedrijven *(Quality and Labour Needs More Than Certifying; a Case Study Investigationg the Quality of Working Life as Part of Quality Care in Six Electrotechnical Companies)*, Nieuwegein, Industrie- en Voedingsbond CNV.

Volst, A., and I. Wagner 1990: Kontrollierte Dezentralisierung. Computer-gestützte Verwaltungsautomation in Dienstleistungs- und Industrie-unternehmen *(Controlled Decentralization. Computer Supported Automation of Administration in Service and Production Firms)*, Bonn: Edition Sigma.

Wall et al. 1986 (T. D. Wall, N. J Kemp, P. R. Jackson and C. W. Clegg): *Outcomes of Autonomous Work Groups: A Long-Term Field Experiment,* in: Academy of Management Journal, Vol. 29, No. 2, pp. 280-304.

Walton R. E., 1977: *Work Innovations at Topika: After Six Years,* in: Journal of Applied Behavioral Science, Vo. 13, pp. 422-433.

Walton, R. E., and J. R. Hackman 1986: *Groups Under Contrasting Management Strategies,* in: P. S. Goodman et al. (eds.): Designing Effective Work Groups, San Francisco: Jossey-Bass, pp. 168-201.

Wehner et al. 1992 (T. Wehner, N. Richter, K. P. Rauch, E. Endres, K. Dirks, E. Kohn, M. Waibel and R. Bromme): "Von der Linie zur Box und zurück" *("From the Line to the Box and Back")*, Bremer Beiträge zur Psychologie, Nr. 102, 5/92.

228

Weibler, J., 1989: Rationalisierung im Wandel. Chancen und Risiken einer technologischen Entwicklung für das Individuum in der betrieblichen Organization *(Change of Rationalization. Chances and Risks of Technology De-velopment for the Individual in the Organization)*, Frankfurt/Main et. al.

Westerberg, L., 1992: Föreställningar på arenan - ett utvecklingsarbete kring eget budgetansvar på kommunala barnstugor *(Different Conceptions - an Organizational Development Project Concerning Economic Decentralization at Day Care Centres)*, Stockholms Universitet: Ph. D. Thesis.

Western, B., 1993: *Postwar Unionization in Eighteen Advanced Capitalist Countries,* in: American Sociological Review, Vol. 58, April, pp. 266-282.

Wilkinson, A., et al. 1992: *Total Quality Management and Employee Involvement,* in: Human Resource Management Journal, Vol. 2, No. 4, 1-20.

Willeke, S., 1995: Spezialisten graben den Teams das Wasser ab. *(Specialists Dominate the Teams)*, in: VDI-Mitteilungen, No. 8, 1995.

Womack, J. P., D. T. Jones and D. Roos 1990: *The Machine That Changed The World,* New York: Rawson Associates.

Work in America 1973 (Report of a Special Task Force to the Secretary of Health, Education and Welfare), Cambridge, Mass., and London: The MIT Press.

Xirotiri-Koufidou, S., and F. Vouzas 1993: *Human Resource Utilization and Quality Assurance: The Case of Three Industrial Enterprises* (in Greek) Unpublished paper.

Zoccatelli, M., and M. Umberto 1992: La partecipazione nel settore alimentare *(Participation in the Food Industry)*, in: M. Ambrosini, M. Colasanto and L. Saba (eds.): Partecipazione e coivolgimento nell'impresa degli anni '90, Milano: F. Angeli, pp. 230-257.

Zöller, W., and A. Ziegler 1992: Total Quality Management. Stellenwert von TQM in Deutschland *(Total Quality Management. The Rating of TQM in Germany)*, Frankfurt/Main: PA Consulting Group.

European Foundation for the Improvement of Living and Working Conditions

**Direct Participation and Organisational Change – Fashionable but Misunderstood?
An Analysis of Recent Research in Europe, Japan, and the USA**

Luxembourg: Office for Official Publications of the European Communities

1996 – 244 pp. – 16 x 23,4 cm

ISBN 92-827-6673-X

Price (excluding VAT) in Luxembourg: ECU 25